*A Wine Journey along
the Russian River*

The publisher gratefully acknowledges the generous contribution to this book provided by the General Endowment Fund of the University of California Press Associates.

A Wine Journey along the Russian River

STEVE HEIMOFF

UNIVERSITY OF CALIFORNIA PRESS

Berkeley   Los Angeles   London

Unless otherwise noted, all photographs are by the author.
Map art © 2005 by David Cain.

University of California Press
Berkeley and Los Angeles, California

University of California Press, Ltd.
London, England

Library of Congress Cataloging-in-Publication Data
Heimoff, Steve, 1946–
A wine journey along the Russian river / Steve Heimoff.
p.   cm.
Includes bibliographical references and index.
ISBN 0-520-23985-7 (cloth : alk. paper)
1. Wine and wine making—California—Russian River
Valley.   2. Tourism—California—Russian River Valley.   I. Title.
TP557.H44   2005
641.2'2'0979418—dc22   2004024163

Manufactured in the United States of America

14   13   12   11   10   09   08   07   06   05

10   9   8   7   6   5   4   3   2   1

The paper used in this publication meets the minimum requirements
of ANSI/NISO Z39.48–1992 (R 1997) (Permanence of Paper).♾

Dedicated to God

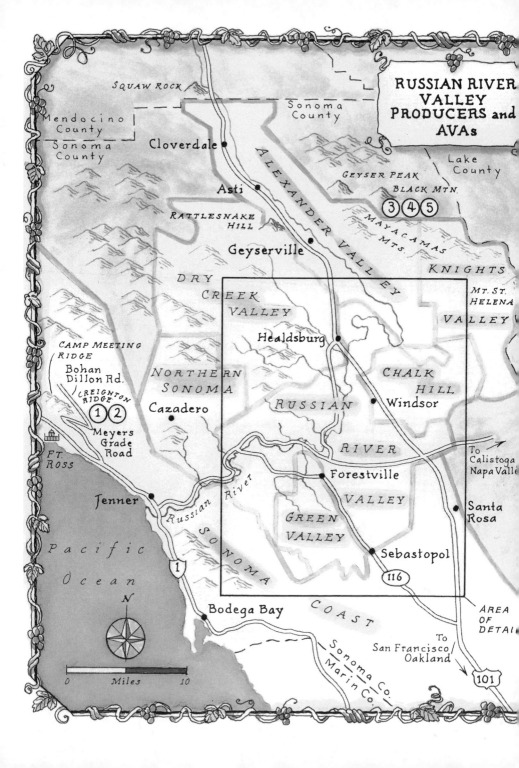

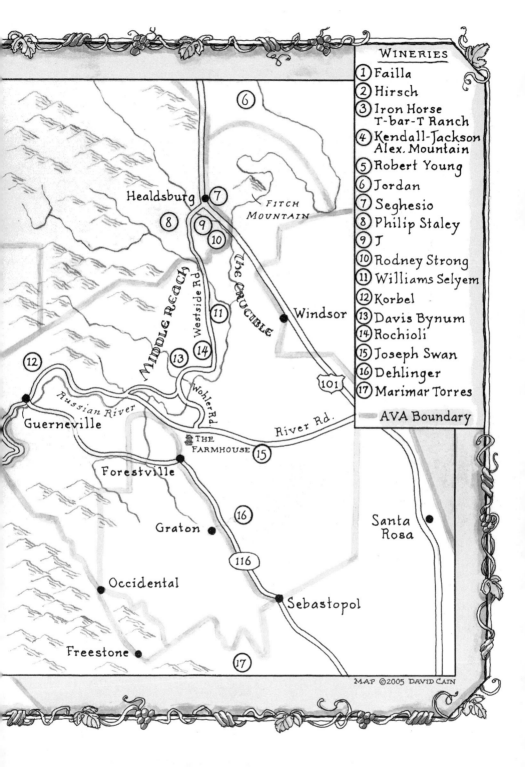

CONTENTS

ILLUSTRATIONS

Introduction

The world possesses many great wine rivers that have writ their legends large in the epochal story of wine and the vine: the Loire, the Rhine and Mosel, the Rhône, the Dordogne and Garonne, the Saône, the Douro.

Among this exalted company, the Russian River deserves a place.

Though its known history is briefer than that of the ancient waterways of old Europe, it has now begun to write its own wine saga—and the wines are great. Just a mention of the varied appellations through which the river flows and the great wineries, vineyards, and winemakers to be found along its banks and in the hills above evokes memories of bottle after bottle of succulent wine.

Someone—I'm not sure who—reportedly once remarked, "There are no common wines in Vôsnes," the Burgundy town that is home to the Domaine de la Romanée-Conti and other prestigious properties. While it is not true that Sonoma County has never produced a common wine, most impartial observers would agree that few wine regions in the world enjoy as high an overall reputation.

To be sure, there is no objective way of measuring the inherent quality of the wines of any given region or of fairly comparing one region to another. Such things are, by their very nature, subjective. But I have reviewed more than twelve thousand wines in my career, and I find that Sonoma wines are consistently at or near the top of the list in almost every variety and type, including sparkling. Individual Sonoma wines and vine-yards do get the credit they deserve. But all too often lost in the glare is the role of the Russian River in linking most of Sonoma County under a single umbrella of quality.

The river, together with its associated tributaries, is the central nervous system of Sonoma County viticulture, with the exception of the Sonoma Valley proper, where the river has no geophysical impact. It drains 1,485 square miles in Mendocino and Sonoma counties and a few additional square miles in Lake County. More than two hundred named creeks and streams feed into its watershed, as well as numberless unnamed ones, many of which appear only in the rainy winter months. By summer's drought, they become *arroyos secos,* dusty dry washes choked with poison oak and wild blackberry.

Sonoma County now includes thirteen American Viticultural Areas, or AVAs, totaling nearly 60,000 acres of vineyards, whose fruit is made into wine by close to 200 wineries. To put these numbers in context, Napa Valley, just across the Mayacamas Mountains to the east, contains about 45,000 acres of vines and about 270 wineries.

Sonoma's greater acreage of vines also includes a much broader range of varietals than Napa or, for that matter, any other county in California. In the monoculture of Napa, three out of every four grapes is red, with Cabernet Sauvignon dominating. In the crush season of 2002, more than 80 percent of all red grapes processed in Napa were of Bordeaux varieties. In Sonoma, only a little more than half the planted acreage is to red grapes, 36 percent of them Cabernet Sauvignon in 2002. At least sixty varietals of the species *Vitis vinifera* are grown within the county's borders. In the breadth and depth of its grape types, Sonoma is California's winiest, most cosmopolitan, and most experimental county—and much of the reason for that has to do with the Russian River.

Not only vineyards mark the region. Nearly every sort of geologic feature found in California makes an appearance within the Russian River's watershed: almost-mile-high mountains, their escarpments piled deep with snow in winter; broad, windswept upland plains, where sheep and cattle graze on grassy highlands; estuarial lagoons and reedy swamps and marshes, particularly in the cool south; temperate rain forests of giant ferns and magnificent, long-lived coast redwood and Douglas fir; rocky coastlands and wide, sandy beaches lapped by pounding breakers; gentle valleys and fertile, rolling farmland; and arid inland savannahs where little but drought-resistant scrub can grow.

Within this watershed, too, are cities and rapidly urbanizing suburbs. Everyone wants to live in a place that is beautiful, that is not too far removed from the allures of San Francisco, and that possesses a benign Mediterranean climate. This book reflects a little of the tension that is created when people by the millions invade pristine nature.

Today, we have a Russian River Valley AVA, or appellation (I will use the terms interchangeably, although, legally, they have slightly different meanings). But the *real* Russian River Valley is the one created by Mother Nature, not the artificial designation approved by the U.S. Bureau of Alcohol, Tobacco, and Firearms in 1983. In the perceived world of wine, however, this real valley has become obscured in a welter of appellations, which were designed to promote clarity but in actuality have accomplished just the opposite.

The federal government established the system of AVAs in the United States over a period of a few years spanning the late 1970s and early 1980s. Napa Valley was the first AVA to be officially approved in California, in March 1981. (It was not the first in the country—Augusta, Missouri, beat Napa by nine months.)

But the Sonomans bested the Napans on at least one score in those early years: the sheer number of appellations they churned out. In retrospect, Sonomans were far more astute in apprehending the need, or desire, on the part of the public for ever-smaller appellations as more precise indices of wine origin. In 1982, Sonoma Valley was approved; before the decade was out, in a whirlwind of activity, Sonoma had launched twelve more AVAs. Sonoma's most frenzied year was 1983, the *annus mirabilis* when Green Valley, Dry Creek Valley, Chalk Hill, Knights Valley, and the Russian River Valley arrived on the scene—not to mention Carneros, an appellation Sonoma shares with Napa. In contrast, Napa County for years seemed content to sit back and digest the big fat cow of Napa Valley, although it, too, eventually succumbed to appellation mania; the county now has fifteen AVAs.

Precisely because of the eagerness with which Sonomans carved up their county so early in the game, people have missed the importance of the Russian River as a wine river; with all those interesting trees, they lost sight of the forest. The Sonomans' intentions were good, but the sense of wineland unity the river could have provided vanished. As a result, Sonoma became a vinously fractured place, like a rare vase that falls to the ground and shatters. All those AVAs can indeed seem confusing, even to the initiated.

Happily, that is now changing, albeit slowly. Appellation boundaries are being redrawn to more closely conform to physical realities, and some of the newer AVAs, such as Rockpile, as well as those yet to come (the Russian River Valley and Carneros both are likely to be further appellated), make a great deal of sense. But through the chaos, one element winds its way consistently and reassuringly, like the familiar theme in a fugue: the Russian River.

It is not a wild California river, like the Eel or Trinity, although in a rainy winter and spring, its white waters tumble and occasionally take a human life. Nor is it a particularly long river, like the Sacramento, whose 377 miles drain the Central Valley of California. The Russian is not even the longest river of the California Coast Ranges; that would be the Klamath, at 250 miles. At a mere 110 miles in length, the Russian River is very much junior to its longer, more powerful sisters.

Yet it is unique in several respects. Climatologically, it passes (during summer and early autumn) through five distinct weather zones, from places too cold to ripen grapes to areas as bakingly hot as anywhere in Sicily or southern Spain. On any given day between June and October, 60 degrees of temperature may separate Jenner from Cloverdale—which are less than thirty miles apart, as the red-tailed hawk flies. Between these two extremes, the jumble of what scientists call landscape and geologic provinces is more varied than anywhere else in California.

That vast discrepancy in weather is, of course, what makes Sonoma's wines so diverse and interesting. One way of looking at the Russian River Valley (the real one, not the AVA) is thus as a journey from Bordeaux—the warm, Cabernet- and Merlot-dominated Alexander Valley—to Burgundy—

the cool stretches of the Russian River Valley, Green Valley, and Sonoma Coast appellations, where Pinot Noir (and Chardonnay) rule. All journeys have midway points; on this one, we stop, however briefly, in a putative Rhône zone. I once read that Mount Kilimanjaro passes, vertically, through every kind of climate on earth, from desert to alpine. The wine lands of the Russian River are a sort of horizontal Kilimanjaro.

The Russian is also unique among California's fifty major rivers for the highly unusual turn it takes midstream, near Healdsburg. There, it abruptly ceases its southerly flow and then, after a series of random meanderings, turns radically to the west. Chapter 5 offers an intriguing theory that might explain the river's behavior.

Before we begin, I should clarify the focus and nature of this book. First, I have written only about the Russian River in Sonoma County. The part of Mendocino County through which the river runs does not seem as interesting to me. Many fine and intelligent growers and vintners are working in central Mendocino, and the area might well find itself squarely on the fine-wine map someday, but the region is not yet producing, on any consistent or widespread basis, wine of the quality found south of the county line.

Second, this book is not an encyclopedic compendium of the vineyards and wines of Sonoma County. There are wineries located in Sonoma whose names you will not find in this little volume. What I instead try to do is to describe things, places, and people, as well as history, through the eyes of one who is both an affectionate traveler and a professional reporter. If on occasion a streak of sentimentality creeps in, I hope the reader will forgive me for it.

And now, on to the Russian River. Without it, there would be no Sonoma County viticulture as we know it. Like Plato's Prime Mover or cosmology's Big Bang, the river started it all, creating and shaping the possibilities, forming the template. The Russian River in so many ways *is* Sonoma viticulture. But how, when, and why did it start?

I

Out of the Pangaean Mists
a River Is Born

When I set out to write this book, I decided that a part of it had to be devoted to an account of how the Russian River was born.

It proved to be no easy task. I searched for some account that would describe the geologic processes that led up to the great moment (or so I imagined it) when the first few droplets of water gathered into a trickle, the trickle into a brook, the brook into a mighty stream. . . .

But there was no such book. So instead I set out in search of scientists who could help me understand not only the river's genesis but also why it takes its weird turn west. As it turns out, however, little agreement exists among geologists, except in an overall sense, about the Russian River's origins and behavior. Even long-cherished theories about Northern California's plate tectonics, forces central to the region's formation, are rapidly being revised and debated.

When I asked winemakers to suggest a geologist to consult, the first name to surface was that of Terry Wright, a geology professor, since retired, at Sonoma State University in Santa Rosa. "He's the man," people said. "Nobody's done more to understand Sonoma's geology and its effect on wine than Terry Wright."

His full name, I discovered, was William H. Wright; he had a geology Web site. I emailed him to request a meeting. The reply came back promptly.

Terry Wright: "Have some rocks!"

"You can interview me," it read, "if you buy me lunch."

The professor chose Sassafras, one of the most expensive restaurants in Santa Rosa. I drove up from Oakland and, on a sunny autumn day in 2002, made the acquaintance of this boisterous, friendly, and larger-than-life academic.

I recognized him the moment he walked in from the parking lot. He looked like an aging Indiana Jones, from the rumpled khakis to the big brown safari hat. His face sprouted a full, bushy white beard and a flaring walrus mustache. Terry Wright is a great bear of a man, somewhere in his sixties, tall and well fed, a rock hound who can identify any pebble you show him. Moreover, he possesses a passion for fine wine.

Later, when I got to know Terry better and visited his house, I was hardly surprised, for it seemed well suited to such a character—a funky, ramshackle hobbit's hut spilling down the side of a mountain in Forestville, on a tortuously crooked road, deep in a conifer forest above the Russian River. In the front yard lay piles of stones, brought home from his excursions. In the house, every shelf and level surface was covered with rocks, fossils, lava, little plastic Baggies filled with dirt. It was as if he had brought the earth inside.

Over lunch (three glasses of red wine for him, none for me), Terry described, in increasingly rapturous tones, his adventures rock climbing, his whitewater rafting trips on the Colorado River through the Grand Canyon, his nights of carousing and partying and living always on the edge, sometimes risking his very life for excitement. I began to feel that I had lived a very safe and timorous existence, I told him, and to wonder whether I had missed out on some elemental, manly rite of passage. "Maybe you'll find out someday," Terry replied.

He was a swashbuckler and a charmer.

I also got to know Daniel Roberts, then director of winegrowing research at Jackson Family Farms, an upscale branch of the empire created by Jess Jackson, of Kendall-Jackson. Roberts is as famous as Wright among winemakers and grape growers. Julie Martinelli, whose family owns the well-known Russian River Valley winery that bears their name, calls him "Dr. Dirt." He is the Apollonian opposite of Terry Wright's Dionysian sensuality: intellectual and precise, well-organized to a fault, orderly in his habits, a man who does not suffer fools gladly. Roberts is a sort of Colonel Pickering to Wright's Henry Higgins.

I soon realized that there was little love lost between Drs. Wright and Roberts. But then, Wright studies geology—the deep-down structure of rocks—and Roberts focuses strictly on surface soils. And plenty of tension exists between these two sciences when it comes to viticulture.

Their rivalry (if that's the word) underscores the deep ambiguity that surrounds the topic of the influence of rocks and soil on grapevines and wine—a topic generally referred to by a word I will use only sparingly in this book: *terroir.* Although much is made of the nuances of silt over clay, or clay over silt, or sand over pebbles, or hardpan below clay, or limestone soils and volcanic soils, et cetera ad infinitum, the truth is that no one fully understands the precise mechanisms by which soil and rocks influence viticulture and wine; indeed, it may be impossible to understand and calculate such impact, especially when the geology is as complex as Sonoma's. Then, too, much depends on the talent of the viticulturalist, who can undermine a potentially great piece of land so that it produces only mediocre grapes.

The third scientist to whom I turned was Dr. Deborah Elliott-Fisk, a professor in the Department of Wildlife, Fish, and Conservation Biology at the University of California at Davis. You'd never guess it from her title, but Elliott-Fisk has developed something of a cottage industry analyzing the geology of wine country in Napa and Sonoma counties. Like Wright

Dan Roberts, also known as Dr. Dirt.

and Roberts, she consults for wineries. Her theory about the Russian River, described in chapter 5, turns out to be a real stunner—although it is rather at odds with the current understanding of Northern California's geology.

All three of these scientists offered patience, knowledge, and additional resources. But none of them could tell me the complete story of how and when the Russian River began. For that, I had to create my own account. Thus, caveat lector, for I am not an expert in this field. I absolve the three good scientists of responsibility for any errors that may appear and give them credit for all that is correct in my account.

It is not necessary to recapitulate here the history of Pangaea—"all lands" in Greek—the last (but not the first) great supercontinent, on whose vestiges all land life currently resides. Suffice it to say that Pangaea arose from the watery depths toward the end of the Paleozoic era, about 250 million years ago. By the time of the Cretaceous period, about 110 million years ago, it was already splitting apart, in the never-ending process of continent formation, destruction, and recycling.

Eastern North America was part of Pangaea. But 100 million years ago, the California coastline was located about where the present-day foothills of the Sierra Nevada lie. Everything to the west, including modern Sonoma, was underwater, part of the ancient sea floor.

Most of the county's foundation is built of bedrock that was formed beneath that sea between 150 million and 40 million years ago. Yet there are remnants of rocks in Sonoma whose paleomagnetic properties suggest that they are far more ancient. They exist in isolated outcroppings of granite that can be seen at Bodega Head, on the coast near Bodega Bay, and are as exogamous to Sonoma as that monolith in *2001: A Space Odyssey* was to the moon. These rocks are identical to granites found far to the south, in the Big Sur, Santa Lucia, and Gavilan ranges of Monterey County; in the Tehachapi Mountains of Southern California; and even in Baja California. This suggests that, once upon a time, rocks now separated by hundreds of miles were in physical proximity.

Understanding how those southern rocks got up to Bodega Head is the key to understanding Sonoma's geology, and it involves the theories of plate tectonics and continental drift. For hundreds of millions of years, across the world, undersea volcanoes have belched forth molten igneous material that hardens on exposure to cold water, forming sea floor, which then congeals into large formations called plates. Plates are separated by fault lines, which are where earthquakes happen, as the gigantic slabs of land crunch and grind against each other.

Sonar, which was developed during World War II and originally used to locate German submarines, has subsequently been employed by scientists eager to map the ocean floor, an area even less well understood than parts of outer space. They discovered undersea mountain ranges separated by valleys riven with fissures. Geologists attempting to explain this pattern theorized that the sea floor was spreading very slowly away from the fissures as lava oozed out from them, driven by fierce convection currents in the earth's molten mantle—a conjecture now supported by evidence from underwater photography.

The earth's mantle is a deep well of hot liquid and semiliquid rock, or magma, located many miles below the hard outer crust. It is heated to the melting point by the decay of radioactive elements such as uranium and thorium and by residual heat that remains from the planet's fiery creation. Off the California coast, the lava-oozing fissures run in a more or less north-south orientation. As the magma spilled out and spread, the new ocean floor pushed relentlessly to the east and west, like a part in thick, wavy hair, until it came into contact with something that impeded it.

Where the sea floor flowed east, it met the ultimate obstacle: the gigantic wedge of the North American continent, which itself was lurching westward, the result of the continuing breakup of Pangaea. Finding its way blocked, the eastward-flowing sea floor had only three options: it could switch direction and flow north or south; it could rise up and over the continent, swamping it; or it could dive down below the continent, in a process geologists call *subduction.*

The new ocean floor—let us now call it by its proper name, the Farallon plate—dove down below the North American plate, in a subductive motion. When it was entirely subsumed beneath the North American plate, the Farallon disappeared from geologic history. The plate that replaced it—created by the same undersea forces that had created the Farallon plate—now began to grind sideways against the North American plate, rather than subducting beneath it. Geologists call this new slab of bedrock the Pacific plate.

The Coast Ranges are the mountains that run for 550 miles along the California coast, in parallel ridges located close to the ocean and about thirty miles inland. Geologists further differentiate the Southern Coast Ranges and the Northern Coast Ranges, with the dividing point at San Francisco Bay. Although they are considered part of a single great mountain chain that also includes the Klamath and Siskiyou mountains and the Sierra Nevada, the two Coast Ranges are built of different rock.

The northern mountains are composed of a type of bedrock geologists refer to as the Franciscan Complex, or Franciscan Formation. Formations are mappable, large-scale rock units that possess common characteristics, such as origin, age, or physical and chemical composition. They are usually named after a locality; the Franciscan honors San Francisco. Many of the big rock outcrops you see in San Francisco and Marin counties, such as the soaring cliffs on the northwest side of the Golden Gate Bridge, are made of Franciscan material. They are the visible parts of the western continent's undergirdings. All of Sonoma County east of the San Andreas fault and most of it west of the fault—which is to say about 98 percent of the county—is built of Franciscan rock.

The Southern Coast Ranges, by contrast, are built of Salinian rock, named after the city of Salinas, a hundred miles south of San Francisco. And that brings us back to those outcroppings at Bodega Head. They are made of Salinian rock. How did they find their way into Northern California?

The Farallon plate was subducted beneath the North American plate for tens of millions of years, until a milestone date in coastal California's geologic march through time. That milestone occurred about 29 million years ago. Mention that time frame to any geologist in California, and you'll see a flash of recognition.

At that time, the Farallon plate had been entirely subducted beneath the North American plate; subduction along the Central California coast had come to an end. Following the Farallon, the Pacific plate began (for reasons no one has ever successfully explained) to grind against the North American plate, the former inching slowly toward the northwest, the latter inching equally slowly toward the southeast. In geologic parlance, the two plates were in strike-slip, or horizontal fault, motion relative to each other. It was this strike-slip creeping that brought those old Salinian granites up from the south to Bodega Head. Like the latch on a zipper, they hitchhiked a slow ride north, at the rate of a couple of inches a year, on the migrating Pacific plate. With the arrival of strike-slip, this new line separating the two plates became the San Andreas fault.

The formation of the Coast Ranges resulted, initially, from subduction. Under a subduction regime, the top plate is thrust upward; the bottom plate becomes the recycled material for more land-building. Terry Wright, in a homely metaphor, refers to this subductive crunching of land as "mooshing two piles of Cheerios together."

When strike-slip took over, according to past theory, the Coast Ranges continued to rise ever higher, as earthquakes buckled the land—much as the 1989 Loma Prieta earthquake raised the height of that peak by a few inches. This is true, as far as it goes, but this strictly mechanical model fails to take full account of the heat of the Earth's magma.

A new theory arose in the 1990s, based on what was called the Mendocino Triple Junction model. It argued that the Southern Coast Ranges had indeed been built by subduction and, later, by strike-slip horizontal motion caused by earthquakes. But the Northern Coast Ranges were more problematic and more complicated. To understand them, we must take into account the Gorda plate.

The Gorda runs off the Pacific Northwest; it is being subducted beneath the North American plate, just as the Farallon plate was, in what is known as the Cascadia subduction zone. That subduction is responsible for creating the Cascade Mountains and may someday also cause the huge earthquake geologists are concerned may wreak havoc on Seattle.

The Pacific, North American, and Gorda plates currently come together off the Mendocino coast, at the so-called Mendocino Triple Junction. The junction has been migrating northward since it formed (it was south of San Francisco 16 million years ago, and off the coast of Sonoma County 10 million years ago). Where the three plates intersect, their edges don't fit perfectly together; imagine three irregularly shaped pieces of slate, with various gaps. Through this slab window, the mantle's hot magma wells up. At some 2,000 degrees Fahrenheit, the magma blisters the crust, just as a flame blisters the varnish on a table. Writ on a large scale, the "blisters" are mountains; as the slab window drifted from south to north, so did the blisters we call the Northern Coast Ranges.

It took a Pennsylvania State University scientist, Dr. Kevin Furlong, and his colleagues to refine the Mendocino Triple Junction theory into the current model. They were alerted by troubling findings uncovered by other geologists who studied how earthquake waves are propagated in Northern California. These geologists discovered that the crust is substantially thicker at the Mendocino Triple Junction, where it averages thirty miles in depth, compared to only about twelve miles thick north and south of it. This disconcerting fact discouraged the slab window theory of mountain building, because a thirty-mile-thick wedge of crust would effectively insulate the "varnish" from the underlying heat, like asbestos wrapped around a hot water heater. A new twist was needed to explain the Northern Coast Ranges.

Furlong's theory, still controversial, is called the Mendocino Crustal Conveyor, or MCC, model. According to MCC, as magma welled up through the slab window at the Mendocino Triple Junction, it cooled and became viscous, forming a sticky glue that welded the bottom edges of the Pacific, Gorda, and North American plates together. This did not prevent strike-slip from occurring, however. As the northwest-trending Pacific plate continued to grind against the southeast-flowing North American plate, to whose western edge it was now partially "glued," the Pacific plate dragged the North American plate along with it, creating enormous geophysical stress and forcing the North American plate to buckle and substantially thicken near the Mendocino Triple Junction but to thin out south of it. In the wake of the Mendocino Triple Junction's northerly migration, this pattern of thicker and thinner crust has resulted in two great mountain-building "humps" that continually are conveyed northward along the San Andreas fault; hence the use of the term "conveyor." The recycled material for the thickening comes from south of the Mendocino Triple Junction, where the crust had earlier been thickened. The result has been the steady uplifting and lengthening of the Northern Coast Ranges.

Furlong's theory also provided a rather unexpected explanation of why some of Northern California's rivers abruptly change direction. According to the MCC model, rivers north and south of the Mendocino Triple Junction tend to flow north-south (or northwest-southeast), following the orientation of the Northern Coast Ranges. But between the two humps, where all that tortured pulling and tugging is occurring, they meander, taking hairpin turns and turning back on themselves. As the land over which they flow is distorted and distended, their courses slowly, but violently and ineluctably, shift. This is one possible explanation of why the Russian River twists westward below Healdsburg. Whether it is in conflict with Elliott-Fisk's explanation or complements it, however, remains to be seen.

THE SONOMA VOLCANICS

About 10 million years ago, when the Mendocino Triple Junction had drifted west of Sonoma, another milestone in that county's geologic history occurred. The Coast Ranges (including the present-day Mayacamas and Vaca mountains, on Napa Valley's western and eastern sides, respectively) began to erupt, in a period of intense volcanism that ended about 2.4 million years ago.

If you had been in the Russian River Valley looking east at any point during that epoch, says Terry Wright, "your attention would have been dominated by erupting volcanoes." I'd been told—and it's a fairly common belief among some Napa and Sonoma winemakers—that there had been huge blasts in the Mayacamas, and indeed that Mount St. Helena, which looks so Fujiesque from certain perspectives, itself had erupted in a gigantic explosion, which turns out not to be the case. In reality, these Coast Range eruptions weren't big, explosive events, like the eruption of Mount St. Helens in the Oregon Cascades, which blew its top in 1980. "The 'booms!,' the Big Ones, are the kinds of volcanoes you see existing over subduction zones," Terry Wright says, and subduction had halted millions of years before the era of the Sonoma Volcanics.

The Coast Range volcanoes over the strike-slip zone of the San Andreas were relatively piddling affairs. Some localized blowouts may have caused the kinds of ashfall that buried the Petrified Forest, in Calistoga. But mainly these were small-scale debris and fluid eruptions, in which fissures belched forth bombs, ash, and other ejecta or oozed lava that flowed for miles, solidifying into iron-rich compounds. They were smallish events, but since they occurred over a period of 8 million years, their cumulative effects were great. So much litter was deposited, over so long a time, that these debris piles can be a thousand feet deep. Geologists call these igneous materials and the processes that created them the *Sonoma Volcanics;* the term refers both to those long-ago geologic events and to the volcanic solids that even today are scattered throughout Napa and Sonoma counties.

These ejecta littered a huge area. "Look at a map," Terry suggests. "The Sonoma Volcanics stretch from the east side of Napa Valley, at Stags Leap, across the Mayacamas Mountains and Sonoma Mountain, and north to Mount St. Helena. Then they slop over Highway 101 a little bit." Terry knows of one volcanic area as far to the west as Peterson Road, south of Sebastopol. "But," he adds, "it's fair to say that the Sonoma Volcanics were concentrated east of Highway 101."

Not all scientists are united on the origin of the volcanic debris that litters Sonoma County. Daniel Roberts believes that some of the material "could have come from the Sierras in a big blowout." When I mentioned this to Terry, he arched a dubious eyebrow and snorted. But he was concerned enough to refer the matter to a colleague, the tephrochronologist (volcanic ash specialist) André M. Sarna-Wojcicki, who works at the U.S. Geological Survey in Menlo Park. Sarna-Wojcicki dodged the issue, replying (Terry copied me on the email), "I think that there may be pre–Sonoma Volcanics tephra [volcanic dust and ash] layers in sediments that underlie the SV [Sonoma Volcanics], and that some of these may be 'exotic'—derived from sources outside the Bay Area." But, Sarna-Wojcicki added, the only way to confirm this hunch would be to conduct extensive, and expensive, geochemical tests. "So," he concluded, "to answer your question, I would suspect local sources first."

Wherever they came from, the importance of the Sonoma Volcanics is in the debris the eruptions deposited. It has eroded into the volcanic soils in which the grapevines grow, which tend to be on peaks and upper slopes or washed down as alluvium onto benchlands. These soils can often be easily identified by their red color, the result, in part, of oxidized iron.

Since at least Roman times, red dirt has been considered beneficial for wines, and today that belief is still widespread throughout wine country. Forrest Tancer, the proprietor of Iron Horse Vineyards and a modern pioneer in the Russian River Valley, describes red soil as "richer for growing grapes in." The winery consultant Jack Larsen, who works with Davis Bynum at that winery and is something of a legend in western Sonoma County for his expertise in the arcane practices of biodynamic grape growing, believes that the iron in volcanic soil "changes the terroir, the feeling of the mouth," by giving wine a minerally tang. Ehren Jordan, who is the winemaker at Napa Valley's Turley Wine Cellars and also has his own small label, Failla, on the Sonoma coast, speaks of a special property of red dirt: "It's a much cooler soil, so the vines come out later and are further behind." The dates of flowering, veraison, and, especially, harvest are critical to a wine's character.

I have seldom found an instantly identifiable "volcanic" quality in wine, although it is a very romantic notion. When you are drinking a wine you know comes from volcanic soils (Louis M. Martini's Monte Rosso red wines are a good example), it's not hard to conjecture something contributed by the earth, what the French call a *goût de terroir*. The situation has been well summed up by a Sonoma County vineyard manager named John Pina, who used to oversee Jess Jackson's vineyards high up on the slopes of the Mayacamas above the Alexander Valley, where there are heavy concentrations of Sonoma Volcanics. "I don't know if there's a tie-in between red soils and vine quality," Pina says, "but when you look at all the places with red soils, they're my favorites for drinking red wine."

So recent in geologic time were the Sonoma Volcanics that it can seem like they were created only yesterday. One day I was in a vineyard called Endeavor, which is on the west side of Highway 101, near Healdsburg, and whose grapes are used by the Dry Creek Winery for a good, but rather tannic, Cabernet Sauvignon. I was looking down at a grapevine when I noticed, lying on the surface of the soil, two small stones, both of which now sit on my kitchen counter. One was jet black, hard, mirror smooth, and shiny, with sharp, bladelike edges, like an Indian arrowhead: obsidian. The other was white, weathered with yellow stains, grainy and rough to the touch, and when I scraped it with my fingernail, hard particles of white dust flaked off: tuff, or ash that had been compressed into stone. Both rocks had their origins deep inside volcanoes. I looked up; across from the Endeavor vine-yard, seemingly near enough to touch on such a clear day, were the Maya-camas Mountains. They looked peaceful enough, their peaks dappled gold with sunlight, their forested flanks stippled in purple shade. But it was not hard to imagine them boiling and churning, spewing out volcanic debris that worked its way over to Sonoma, where, millions of years later, these stones had found their way back up to the surface. They were true geologic time travelers, mute souvenirs of a fiery, cataclysmic past. And, yes, the soil in Endeavor was streaked with red.

But what of the Russian River?

To the north of Sonoma, some 5 or 6 million years ago, the Mendo-cino plateau began to appear, part of the same process of drag and stretch along the San Andreas fault that created the Coast Ranges. This plateau was a high shelf, rather like the flat bottom of a bowl turned upside down. The Mendocino plateau not only rose vertically; it also warped and tilted southward. It was from this plateau that the first waters of the Russian River may have gathered and spilled to the south.

At a point roughly 1.6 million years ago, the water that had inundated western Sonoma for millions of years had drained away, as the land con-tinued to rise. From Healdsburg and Santa Rosa down to Petaluma, and to the west including most of the Russian River Valley, the land finally was high and dry. By 1 million years ago or even less, the topography of the North Bay was firmly etched in place. What remains today of this inland waterway is embayed to the south, in the great San Pablo and San Fran-cisco bays. Much of the rock in this area of western Sonoma was originally formed underwater; referred to as the Wilson Grove Formation, it overlies the Franciscan Formation. Wilson Grove rock is soft and claylike, classified by the U.S. Geological Survey (USGS) as "erodable" to "highly erodable" because it consists primarily of a fine-grained sandstone. As we'll see in chapter 5, the nature of this rock may have been critical in determining the eventual flow of the Russian River.

We must now switch our attention to present-day Lake County, east of Mendocino, where we find Clear Lake. With an elevation of 1,300 feet, Clear Lake is dominated by 3,280-foot Mount Konocti, which last erupted one hundred fifty thousand years ago and thus is considered extinct. Volcanic debris in this neck of the woods is known as the Clear Lake Volcanics.

Clear Lake is one of the oldest lakes in North America, judging from core samples that date its existence to at least a half million years ago. At one time, it drained both to the west and to the east. The westward flow was blocked, perhaps as recently as a few centuries ago, by a massive landslide so that today Clear Lake drains only to the east, into the Sacramento River. But when it drained to the west, in all likelihood it did so through creeks and streams that flowed down onto the Mendocino plateau. Once there, the waters would have sought (if this is not too anthropomorphic a description) an outlet to the sea.

The main valley south of the Mendocino plateau is the Ukiah Valley, which runs down through the heart of Mendocino's inland wine country to the Sonoma line. There, a chain of hills closes in, choking off the river's flow, which becomes narrower and more turbulent. Terry Wright calls this passage the Cloverdale Gorge. Just south of it, the hills once again part, opening up into the Alexander Valley. We can imagine the waters of Clear Lake draining westward onto the Mendocino plateau and then, because the plateau tilted south, flowing through the Cloverdale Gorge into the Alexander Valley. Compressed by the gorge, the flowing water increased in velocity, deepening its channel and increasing its power. At some point, the Russian River was born.

For the first part of its life, because of the Mendocino plateau's tilt, the river flowed to the south, emptying—although we do not know precisely where—into San Pablo Bay. Today, however, the Russian River does not flow into San Pablo Bay. Instead, near Healdsburg, it makes its crucial turn west and flows to the sea at Jenner. In chapter 5, we will look at Deborah Elliott-Fisk's theory of why it does so. For the time being, though, we can begin by visiting the gentle valley where the Russian River first touches down in Sonoma, the valley called Alexander.

2

Cyrus Alexander Finds a Valley

In southern Mendocino and northern Sonoma counties, they still tell an old tale concerning the massive stone plinth, hundreds of feet high, called Squaw Rock, a towering mound of basalt that hulks over Highway 101 beside the Russian River like the shattered ruins of some medieval battlement.

Everyone has a different version of how Squaw Rock got its name. Here's the one I heard from Pete Seghesio Sr., patriarch of Sonoma's Seghesio wine clan. "There was an Indian squaw, and, supposedly, she lost her lover to another woman," he says, his eighty-four-year-old eyes twinkling brightly. "So, despondent and lonely, she climbed up to the top, clutched the biggest rock she could find to her breast, and jumped.

"I never could figure out," he chuckles, "why she needed that rock!"

Why she needed it was explained in a volume that Sonoma County officials published in 1880—a book to which I often refer in these pages. The *History of Sonoma County*, written by J. P. Munro-Fraser, tells of the Sanel, a local Native American tribe, and the incident it describes is one of the oldest surviving tales (in English) of these indigenous people. It is set in the early 1800s, just before the first white settlers arrived in Sonoma County.

A young chief named Cachow was "a fine looking fellow of faultless physique, a mighty hunter." One day, at a feast, he met a Sanel princess, Satuka, the beautiful daughter of a neighboring chief. She took one look at Cachow, "with all his fame and manly beauty," and fell head over heels in love with him.

A marriage was arranged, but Cachow said he had to return home on business before the wedding. He made a promise to Satuka's father that he would "come back in two moons . . . and make the lovely daughter his bride." Unfortunately, Cachow was a cad. He "was unfaithful to his promise, and before two moons had wedded another."

Satuka found out, and this woman scorned took her revenge. "Cachow and his new love, in making their bridal tour, built their camp fire at the base of the great rock, underneath the precipice." That night, Satuka ascended the peak "and looked down where, by the light of the little camp fire, she saw her faithless lover and his bride fast asleep. With the merciless vengeance of 'love turned to hatred' and the desperation of unrequited affection, she clasped in her arms a stone as large as she could lift, and sprang off the fearful height upon her sleeping victims."

Satuka must have had pretty good aim, or maybe she was just lucky, for we learn in the *History* that a search party the next day found three dead bodies, entwined in a grisly *ménage à mort.* A funeral, in the Sanel style, was quickly arranged. "To the music of a solemn dirge . . . and the roaring of the flames, the spirits of the departed, as the Indians say, rode upon a chariot to the happy hunting grounds."

Squaw Rock is just north of the Sonoma County line. For me, it represents the symbolic gateway to the northern portal of the Alexander Valley, much as the Statue of Liberty is the icon for those arriving in New York City. When I am driving back to Oakland from some distant destination in the north, the familiar sight of its soaring east wall means home is near.

A few miles below Squaw Rock, there is a little clearing in a wood just off the highway, across an old iron foot bridge with a "No Trespassing" sign. This is where the Russian River splashes across the Mendocino-Sonoma county line and, after a short sprint through Terry Wright's Cloverdale Gorge, enters Sonoma's Bordeaux, the Alexander Valley.

The valley is marked by three small cities or largish towns: Cloverdale in the north, Healdsburg in the south, and, in the middle, Geyserville. Between and around them is the monoculture of Alexander Valley viticulture, dominated by five varietals: Chardonnay, Sauvignon Blanc, Cabernet Sauvignon, Merlot, and Zinfandel. Slowly but steadily, vineyards also are spreading from their base on the valley floor and benchlands up into the foothills and even, in some cases, onto the high peaks of the east and west mountains.

The flatlands on either side of the Russian River, as a century and a half of farmers have happily discovered, are blessed with rich silts and bottom soils, deposited over the millennia by the river's repeated flooding or washed down in voluminous quantities from the mountains, forming broad and deep alluvial fans. The author of the *History* wrote of the "tract of rare fertility on either bank" of the river and of its "picturesque scenery." It is both fertile and picturesque today.

The valley is also blessed with an almost preternaturally benign climate. It is said that Cloverdale is the northernmost place in coastal California where oranges will dependably ripen. Certainly there are palm trees aplenty, and from late spring until the onset of winter the Alexander Valley becomes a fantastically prolific garden. You can grow almost any crop, from figs and plums to corn and tomatoes, and whatever you plant will almost always thrive, including grapes.

Through the center of the valley flows the Russian River, hidden down in its embankment by thick entanglements of stalky bamboo, wild berry bushes, willow, shrubby dogwood, reeds, and gnarly ground plants that keep anything much larger than a rabbit or a wild goat from easily passing. Except at bridge crossings or certain vantage points in the vineyards that line it, the river is not usually visible. But every local knows a footpath that winds down through the thicket to a beach or fishing hole, and the kids like to bring their all-terrain vehicles down to the gravel bars during the dry season and tear things up.

The valley has an air of languid contentment about it, that quality of prosperous, conservative, well-fed country life that Germans (many of whom settled in the south valley during the late nineteenth century) call *gemütlichkeit.* You see it and feel it especially along the little country lanes— Lytton Station Road; Alexander Valley Road; Geyserville Avenue; twisting Route 128, which leads over the Mayacamas Mountains to Calistoga; River Road—with their neat, two-story farmhouses that are always brightly painted and seldom without a flower garden, a few rows of old vines in the backyard, and a child's tire-swing hanging by a rope from the low bowers of an olive or oak tree. A lot of money poured into the Alexander Valley during the wine boom of the 1990s, as it did everywhere in California wine country, but the modest nature of the locals prohibits them from flaunting it—so unlike Napa!—except for the occasional McMansion built in the hills by an outsider.

Cloverdale has long dominated the north county; it was a way-station on the stage route to Mendocino and Humboldt counties from San Francisco and points south. Some kind of settlement has existed there at least since Gold Rush times—and far earlier, considering Native American residents. In 1856, it is said, the site was dubbed Cloverdale, for the wild grasses, by a Mrs. Markle, the wife of one of the original town settlers; the name was "a happy departure from the peculiar mining names or Indian appellations then in vogue," says the *History.* One can only imagine what its author would have thought about the names that housing developers give to the many local subdivisions that flourish here today.

Timber and sheep made Cloverdale's fortunes, especially after the railroad came chugging into town in 1872 and a toll road was built beside the Russian River three years later. "Beginning with the year 1880," recalled J. S. O'Neal, an early settler, in his 1923 book *Early Days of Cloverdale,* "Mendocino county had over four million sheep, and Southern Humboldt County half as many more, [and] nearly all product had to find a market through Cloverdale."

There aren't many sheep left in Cloverdale today, but it's still very much a timber town, the southern terminus of the vast logging industry that wiped out the old-growth forests of the North Coast. Sawmills remain on the edge of town, and on hot summer days the smoky-sharp scent of hewn wood perfumes the air, while the dull drone of the saws creates a pleasant, beelike buzz in the shimmering heat. Flatbed trucks laden with piles of logs rumble through the streets, slowing traffic and leaving flakes of sawdust in their wake. In the town newspaper, the *Cloverdale Reveille* ("Published weekly since 1879"), the police log suggests a backwater drowsiness:

11:54 P.M. N. Franklin St.
    Man reports that a dog belonging to his son was lost. The dog is a black and white fox terrier named Zip.

But Cloverdale also has fancy new boutique shops, an Internet café, and other amenities that cater to well-to-do residents and tourists. Bed-and-breakfasts are filled during the season and charge a hefty price. Rented limousines convey parties of wine-tasting tourists up from San Francisco, who are amused to explore this curious and rather exotic outer limit of the Bay Area's wine country.

Today, the town of 6,800 is trying, just a little too self-consciously, to stay old-fashioned, but forces beyond its control are sweeping in, and Cloverdale is struggling to come to terms with them. One hot afternoon, with North Cloverdale Boulevard all torn up in an orgy of dust, planks, and construction, I wandered into the fancy new Wine and Visitors Center and asked the woman behind the counter what was going on outside.

"Oh," she shrugged, "that's going to be our new pedestrian mall."

"Cloverdale's getting pretty upscale," I suggested.

"Yes," she replied. Then, after a suitable pause: "Unfortunately."

A dozen or so miles to the south is Geyserville. Cloverdale and Healdsburg may be the Alexander Valley's biggest towns, but Geyserville, population 2,100, represents its heart and soul.

The town was named for the nearby geothermal geysers, another gift of the San Andreas fault. These geysers feed the warm waters and hot springs whose healing properties were famous among the Native Americans for thousands of years. Reportedly, the steam spouts were first seen by a white settler in the spring of 1847, when a certain William Elliott, who was hunting bears 1,700 feet up in the Mayacamas (bears were plentiful in those days, and the occasional black bear still sometimes takes out a succulent grapevine), came across smoke arising in such volume that he thought it was coming from an Indian encampment. It wasn't—it was simply the steam from the hot springs.

The hot springs seemed to be (the *History* reports) "a means of attracting many visitors to the spot," an enticing proposition to the kind of ambitious entrepreneur the Alexander Valley has long attracted. A town was established beside the river on the flatlands, by a doctor, in the post—Gold Rush year of 1851, when discouraged miners who had failed to find riches in the mountains were striking out for the coast, scrambling for something, anything, to try their hands at. Within a few years, a general store, a post office, a hotel, a blacksmith shop, and, of course, a saloon had appeared; but even by the time the *History* was published, in 1880, Geyserville was "not so much a place as it [was] these establishments."

It's still, with all due respect, not so much of a place. There's a Mayberry-like lethargy to "downtown." You can stand at the main intersection and see just about all there is to see of the village. Farmers and vineyard workers in their pickup trucks, out doing errands on an early morning, will pause at the stop sign, roll down their windows, and call smilingly to a stranger, "How ya doin'?" Anglos and Mexicans mix easily, down beer at the same bars, and buy their blue jeans and work boots at George Bosworth & Sons Western Wear, as they have since 1909. Change has rolled over California wine country in recent years and always threatens, like the sword of Damocles, to invade Geyserville; every once in a while, somebody opens a fancy new restaurant, and the critics rush up from San Francisco, eat, and drive home again. But so far, little Geyserville has remained unspoiled and stubbornly attached to the old ways.

One blazingly hot summer day, I was talking with the late Julia Child, who was leaning back in a little wooden chair and fanning herself with a piece of paper. We were drinking Chardonnay in the wilting heat. Suddenly she sliced her big, flat hand through the air as if she were karate-chopping a melon and, apropos of something or other, declared in that singsong voice of hers, "What this country needs is a good three-dollar red and a good three-dollar white!"

We were sitting on a redwood deck by the Russian River, just north of Cloverdale. I am often reminded of the famous chef's comment whenever the subject of the Alexander Valley comes up, because for well more than a century this lush valley has been the source of great quantities of good, sound, and inexpensive red and white wine for Americans.

Because it is so large, flat, and easy to farm, the Alexander Valley contains by far the greatest volume of vineyards in Sonoma, 13,600 acres in 2001, nearly one-third the county's total. Of that, more than 9,000 acres are planted to the red varietals—predominantly Cabernet Sauvignon and Merlot, followed by Zinfandel—that have given the valley its modern reputation for Bordeaux varietals.

On the east is the imposing wall of the Mayacamas, beyond which are Lake County, Knights Valley, and Napa Valley. The Alexander Valley AVA line there runs high, rising to the top of 1,750-foot Black Mountain and skirting the flanks of the mountains north of it—Geyser Peak and Pocket Peak. On the west, the boundary is lower, in general remaining below the 900-foot level of the rugged coastal hills—Big Ridge, Red Mountain, Bradford Mountain—that roll in waves to the Pacific. The western appellation line roughly parallels Highway 101, which is where the Native Americans put in a foot trail millennia ago.

The valley's growing season is long, dry, and warm to the point of hot, a Region III on the scale developed by the University of California at Davis, although people who live in the valley, sensitive to its reputation as a furnace, will tell you almost apologetically, "Oh, it's not *that* hot." Then they will say, "Besides, you get used to the heat." The temperature rises the farther north or northwest you go, as it usually does in Northern California's inland valleys, so that on any given summer day, Cloverdale will be a few degrees hotter than Geyserville, which itself is a little warmer than Healdsburg.

Because it is well shielded from the Pacific by parallel chains of the Coast Ranges, the northern Alexander Valley is the hottest part of Sonoma County, except perhaps for the "banana belt" in mid–Sonoma Valley or the floor of Knights Valley, even farther inland. Cloverdale in fact possesses the dubious distinction of having the highest mean maximum temperature of any of Sonoma County's main measuring stations. Temperatures above 100 degrees have been recorded there in every month between May and October, with readings over 90 in the months between April and November, and over 80 between December and March. The average high in July is 92.2 degrees, the all-time high a baking 113. It is a dry, desert heat.

But the Alexander Valley is no Mohave Desert, and it can be as doggedly fogged in as any other place in the Bay Area. There have been summer mornings when I left Oakland (where it should have been foggy) under sunny skies, with the temperature already well into the 70s, only to find Geyserville socked in and miserably dank and cold when I arrived ninety minutes later. When conditions are just right—or, depending on your point of view, wrong—a wispy finger of fog will snake up along the Russian River in the early morning hours or flow in from Bodega Bay or San Pablo Bay and pour through gaps in the hills, reaching and inundating the flatlands. That is the only reason why the Alexander Valley is not the Central Valley; it is, at least on occasion, air-conditioned. Nonetheless, compared with other coastal areas, the Alexander Valley is a hot spot.

ZINFANDEL AND CLARET

Cabernet and Merlot may rule the roost today, but Zinfandel was the grape that made the Alexander Valley famous. It was not, however, the first variety to be planted there. That would likely have been the Mission grape, the favorite of the old Spanish monks who used it for their sacramental wine.

The Mission was a plentiful producer, but it made "a rude wine," the author of the *History* wrote, not mincing words. As soon as people started drinking wine for their own enjoyment and not only for religious purposes, they tore out the Mission vineyards (with zeal, one imagines) and replanted them. To what? Often, to Zinfandel. The origins of Zinfandel have been well documented elsewhere; suffice it to say that the grape laboriously made its way west to California and was certainly established in the state by the 1850s.

By the post–Civil War 1880s, America was enjoying an economic boom that spread from coast to coast. The good times did not bypass Sonoma County. San Francisco, the Queen City of the West, was churning along, and the hotels, drinking establishments, and fine restaurants of the Barbary Coast needed liquid refreshment in the form of wine—and they needed it fast and in copious quantities.

In the Alexander Valley, there was a viticultural explosion to supply this need. In the quick-growing economy, people saw grapes and wine as a way to make a profit. Not all of the new wineries succeeded, of course, but some of today's famous names date from that era. Geyser Peak and Italian Swiss Colony began life in 1880, and Simi in 1881. Scores of other ventures remain only in dusty old records and in the ivy-covered rock piles of unnamed ghost wineries.

What kinds of grapes did these enterprising viticulturalists grow? The Mission was out, Zinfandel in. But few growers felt secure planting all their vineyards to a single variety. In those days before insecticides, fungicides, and herbicides, planting a single type risked total crop failure. So the growers hedged their bets and put in more than one type. Next to their Zinfandel they planted some varietals that would be familiar to us today—

Riesling, Carignane, Alicante Bouschet—and some that would not: Burer, Crabb's Burgundy, Grosseblau, Rousseau. They blended them, in various combinations, to see what tasted most pleasant and what would fetch the highest price from the buyers to the south.

They quickly found out. By 1887, the *San Francisco Examiner*—which had just been taken over by the young William Randolph Hearst—was able to quote "authorities" who claimed that "the Zinfandels of Alexander Valley and other grape regions around Healdsburg make a claret worth at wholesale 10 cents a gallon more than any other claret made in the State."

Zinfandel and "claret"—the old word for the red wines of Bordeaux. Already, more than a hundred years ago, the Alexander Valley had begun to achieve a good reputation for these kinds of wines. Not only that, people were willing to pay more money for them.

Of course, the "claret" back then was not made with Cabernet Sauvignon, Merlot, Cabernet Franc, and the other varietals we associate today with red Bordeaux. Claret was a *style* of wine—red, dry, and full-bodied—not a specific varietal or blend. And of all the grapes from which it was or could be made, as far as "authorities" were concerned, Zinfandel emerged as the best. "We have not fairly tried the quality of Zinfandel," wrote Munro-Fraser, author of the *History*—keep in mind, this was in 1880—"but there is a shrewd belief among the initiated that the rival of the Chateau wines of the Gironde does exist [and] that Zinfandel . . . will be the equal, perhaps more than the equal, of Chateau Lafite."

With that kind of recommendation, no wonder people planted it! The suitability of the Alexander Valley for Zinfandel, for a claret-style wine, was a given by the turn of the twentieth century. Today, "claret"—now in the form of authentic Cabernet Sauvignon, Merlot, and the other Bordeaux varietals—is the Alexander Valley's greatest, or certainly its most expensive, wine. But it was Zinfandel that put the Alexander Valley on stage and kept it famous for a hundred years, until Cabernet made an unexpected appearance, barely a generation ago, and caused a ruckus.

CYRUS'S VALLEY

The valley is named after a remarkable pioneer, the kind of heroic character the filmmaker Ken Burns might celebrate in a documentary. We actually know quite a lot about Cyrus Alexander, who died in 1872 at the age of sixty-seven, because his son, Charles, authored a hagiography four years after his father's death, "hoping," he wrote, "that it will furnish a history . . . and that many may be profited by watching the energy, integrity and perseverance of Cyrus Alexander."

His father's favorite books, Charles tells us, were "of travel, Lives of Pioneers, Explorers, Discoverers, Adventurers [and] Hunters, etc." Cyrus, an original Horatio Alger type, trekked endlessly westward, looking for something to do that would nurture his spirit of freedom and not tie him down. "Solitary in his ways," this true Western pioneer tried his hand at leather tanning, shoemaking, grinding flour, and lead mining, "watching every opportunity for a chance of bettering his condition." He eventually discovered the fur trade and became part of the marauding army of men who struck out for Indian territory in the Rocky Mountains and even as far west as the Oregon Territory, living off the land and hunting beaver, buffalo, pronghorns, and sea otters for the fur that fashionable easterners demanded.

It was dangerous work. Cyrus's "friends tried to prevail on him to give up this hazardous undertaking . . . [warning him] of the horrible Indian massacres, scalping, the danger of wild animals, starvation, privation, of the many chances of freezing to death in the bitter cold." But Cyrus listened to no one and nothing except his inner urges. With only a horse, a mule, some traps, and a gun, he set off in the spring of 1831 for the wild unknown. "Everything must have an end," Charles wrote, "and so had the parting of Cyrus from his relatives and friends."

It was an end, but also a beginning. Cyrus's further adventures, as told by Charles, read like something out of Jack London. By 1840, he had landed in San Diego, then still Mexican territory, where he made the acquaintance of a certain Captain Henry Delano Fitch, who was in the livestock business.

Fitch himself deserves brief mention here. Born in 1767 in New Bedford, Massachusetts, he became, as did so many from that old whaling town, a seafaring man. By the late 1820s, he was captain of a Mexican fishing brig and had become a Mexican citizen, based in San Diego, where he was baptized into the Catholic Church in 1829. As ambitious as Cyrus Alexander, Fitch was apparently more industrious, or maybe just luckier, and rose rapidly. He became a successful businessman and politician and held the title of *juez de paz,* justice of the peace.

Captain Fitch found young Cyrus "frugal and industrious" and offered him a proposition that sounds Biblical in its injunction: "Go north of the [San Francisco] Bay, take a good look at the country, and if you can find enough unclaimed land suitable for a stock range, I will ask the [Mexican] Government, and if I can get it I will stock it, and you can run it." Cyrus took Fitch up on his offer, persuaded, no doubt, by the captain's promise to give him 10,000 acres for his efforts if he succeeded.

Fitch's offer sounded good to Cyrus, who, after a life of job-hopping and insecurity, was no longer such a young man. At the age of thirty-five, he was starting to think it was time to secure his future and perhaps time to marry and establish a family. Cyrus went north of the bay and found just what Fitch was looking for.

In 1841, the captain, true to his word, wangled a deal with the Mexican government for ownership of what became known as the Sotoyomi (sometimes spelled Sotoyome) Rancho, located at the rich and fertile junction of the present-day Dry Creek, Russian River, and Alexander valleys, in a bowl of land extending below Geyserville to Healdsburg. The nearly 1,000-foot-high Fitch Mountain, which plays a prominent role in the topography of the region, is named for the captain; but, ironically, the valley Fitch came to own ended up named for his chief tenant. Fitch died in 1849, wealthy and respected.

It's interesting to note that Fitch had married Josefina Carillo, the sister-in-law of General Mariano Vallejo, the last Mexican military governor of Northern California—an example of the small world of pioneer Northern California. In early 2001, reports surfaced in California newspapers that Josefina and Henry Delano Fitch had been the great-great-grandparents of Franklin Delano Roosevelt. That led me to contact the Franklin Delano Roosevelt Presidential Library and Museum, in Hyde Park, New York, where a kindly archivist did a little digging and discovered that Henry Delano Fitch indeed was a distant relative of FDR—not his great-great grandfather, but his grandfather's second cousin. Small world redux.

For his own home, Cyrus Alexander "selected a place on the east side of the [Russian] river" (Charles writes), "just opposite from where the flourishing town of Healdsburg now stands." At the time, however, there was no town at the site of the future Healdsburg; the nearest sizable municipality was Sonoma Town, thirty-five miles away.

Healdsburg was named after Harmon G. Heald, who had tried his hand at gold mining, and failed miserably, before squatting on the Sotoyomi Rancho. With other forty-niners swarming into the area, Heald opened a little general store in 1851. By this time, Captain Fitch was dead, and his widow,

Josefina, was having financial difficulties. In 1857, she was forced to auction off part of her land to pay taxes. Heald managed to scrape together two hundred dollars, enough to buy 100 acres, and a little community soon arose on his land. The settlement was called Stringtown by the early inhabitants, because it was one of several tiny hamlets "strung" along the Russian River northward.

As the population swelled, Heald laid out a town in typical Mexican fashion, with streets in a grid pattern around a large central square or plaza—today the center of Healdsburg's bustling downtown. The first buildings were his own residence, a blacksmith shop, and a saloon. Heald sold individual lots for fifteen dollars each. (Wouldn't it be nice to have a time machine to go back and buy some of them!) As houses went up, the locals abandoned the name Stringtown in favor of Heald's Store. U.S. postal authorities established a Healdsburgh (sic) post office in 1857. The town itself was incorporated ten years later.

Meanwhile, Cyrus Alexander was doing well, running Captain Fitch's livestock and remaining "frugal," although he seems to have made astute, careful investments. But Cyrus had always wanted to be his own boss. He left Fitch's employ, on more or less friendly terms, in the summer of 1845, four years before the captain's death and a year before ownership of California passed from Spain to the United States. (As a replacement for Cyrus, Fitch hired Moses Carson, a half-brother of the famous trapper, scout, Indian agent, and soldier Kit Carson.) Cyrus went on to become (so Charles writes) "a Cigar-maker," a new line of business that was "quite profitable."

From the front page of the July 29, 1880, *Cloverdale Reveille:* "Mrs. Sarah M. Moore, dealer in fresh fruits, confectionery, and a full line of canned goods, fruits, salmon, jellies, et cetera, also a full line of the choicest brands of tobacco, cigars and cigarettes." It's tempting to think that Mrs. Moore was selling Cyrus's brand of cigars.

When Cyrus Alexander died, in 1872, he left behind a large estate and a big family. He had raised beans and wheat, run cattle and oxen, and sold horses and wool, not to mention the cigars. He was probably one of the richest men in the county.

His father's years on the rancho, Charles concludes, "found [him] peacefully living under his own vine and fig tree." What the "vine" was, Charles does not specify, nor does he tell us where Cyrus obtained his vine cuttings, although we do know, from the *History*, that the orchard he planted was started from "sprouts from the Russian settlement at Fort Ross," which had been abandoned in the 1830s. As for Cyrus's grapes, a good many were, in all likelihood, Zinfandel.

ITALIAN SWISS COLONY

Following Cyrus Alexander's death, many wineries sprang into existence north of Healdsburg, but none was to have a greater or more long-lasting impact on the Alexander Valley's viticultural destiny than Italian Swiss Colony.

This winery was established in 1880 by Andrea Sbarbaro, a Genoan immigrant who, like so many others, failed to strike it rich in the Gold Rush. By the 1870s, however, he had moved on to San Francisco, where he finally found success as a banker.

The Italian Swiss Colony was his idealistic conception of a social experiment in communal living and farming. The idea was to give Swiss and Italian immigrants, who were swarming into Northern California, a dignified place to dwell and raise their families. In exchange for their labor in Sbarbaro's vineyard and winery, they would receive room, board, and wine as well as a monthly salary of thirty-five dollars. Sbarbaro also offered to deduct five dollars a month from their wages and invest it in the colony's stock, giving workers an ownership stake in the company.

Not all the workers liked the idea of the five-dollar deduction. "When they told my great-grandfather he could get less pay in exchange for shares in the company, he refused," says Steve Domenichelli, the young vineyard manager for Ferrari-Carano's vineyard operations. "He just didn't trust anybody. He'd come over from working the marble mines of Italy, and he wanted the money up front."

Sbarbaro named the region Asti because it reminded him of the Piedmont countryside, with its pretty valleys, rolling hills, and warm Mediterranean climate. His idea in starting the Italian Swiss Colony may have been philanthropic, but Sbarbaro himself had no qualms about living the high life, to judge from the stately white-pillared mansion he built. With its bizarre outbuildings, their walls made of tens of thousands of little rounded river pebbles and stones, the mansion still stands at the end of an avenue of royal palms on the old Italian Swiss Colony estate, now owned by Beringer Blass and operated as a production facility for that company's local brands. (It is sad that this interesting old property is not open to the public.)

Italian Swiss Colony went on to become a great success for the better part of a century. After World War II, it was the nation's third largest wine company. Some will remember its TV commercials from the 1960s, in which a twinkly-eyed little old man dressed in an Alpine hat and lederhosen closed each ad with the catchy phrase "That little old winemaker . . . Me!"

But changing consumer tastes sent Italian Swiss Colony into decline. Its jug-style wines, bottled not just under the ISC label but also under a slew of old-fashioned brand names such as Mello-Red, La Paloma, and Early Colonist, increasingly were relegated to the bottom shelf in liquor stores. As a new generation of consumers switched over to cork-finished varietal wines, ISC began a long, steady decline. It was eventually purchased by Heublein (a huge company that never could figure out how to successfully manage a winery) and in the 1970s went out of business.

But what Italian Swiss Colony accomplished in laying the foundations of the Alexander Valley wine industry was awe-inspiring. It brought the sleepy old region its first modern acclaim—although the heralded name was Asti, not Alexander Valley. (The latter was a name little used beyond Sonoma County—and not even by everyone there.) After the repeal of the Volstead Act, which ended Prohibition in 1933, books aiming to educate a public who knew little about wine began to roll off the nation's printing presses, and they gushed about the wines of Asti, which meant, almost exclusively, those of Italian Swiss Colony. One of the first American women to write about wine, Mary Frost Mabon, in her charming 1942 volume *ABC of America's Wines,* noted that ISC's red and white Tipo Chiantis were "on the wine list at San Francisco's famous Bohemian Club," whose members included business tycoons and former U.S. presidents. ISC's wines had "real character and charm," she wrote. This, coming from the gracious and well-connected wine and food editor of *Town & Country* magazine, was a distinguished seal of approval.

Italian Swiss Colony also left its mark in other ways. It established a viable economic basis for Alexander Valley wines, not only through cultivating its vast vineyard plantings but also by building its facility right next to the old San Francisco and North Pacific Railroad tracks. The tracks had originally been constructed in 1869 in order to compensate for the shallow Russian River's lack of navigability, but by the 1880s they were owned by the Southern Pacific Railroad. Those rails rolled right down to the great cities of the Bay Area, meaning that ISC's huge quantities of grapes and wine could be transported quickly and efficiently to the buyers who wanted them.

Italian Swiss Colony also trained generations of vineyardists and wine-makers, much as Gallo later did in Modesto. Many of these individuals, such as Eduardo Seghesio, then fanned out to establish their own wineries; and many of their descendants, such as Steve Domenichelli, remain in the top tier of Sonoma's grape and wine industry today.

In addition, probably before 1900, ISC planted the first Sangiovese vines in California, in a vineyard now called Chianti Station, owned by the Seghesio family. But ISC's greatest and most long-lasting success was with Zinfandel. That grape and wine proved the excellence of the Asti/Chianti part of the valley for this varietal, a success it continues to enjoy today. If Americans have reawakened to the glories of Zinfandel, it is in no small part thanks to Italian Swiss Colony.

The Zinfandels of Asti were thoroughly famous by the 1930s and 1940s, especially among the new, post-Prohibition cognoscenti—bulk wine producers and shippers in San Francisco and home winemakers everywhere—who treasured Zinfandel for the deeply colored, aromatic, richly mellow wine it made. Some of the old-timers still regard Zinfandel as the region's greatest treasure and eternal legacy. To them, Cabernet Sauvignon is an upstart, an *arriviste* without credentials.

One day I drove up to the Seghesio winery to spend the day with Pete Seghesio Jr., a handsome and friendly man in his thirties, with a square-cut jaw, sky-blue eyes, and an earnest manner. We met in the little winery office, on the outskirts of Healdsburg, where Pete introduced me to his father. Pete Sr. liked to hang out there in the morning, sitting quietly as the staff went about their business. The elder Mr. Seghesio was not in the best of health, but he was eager to share memories. He'd been through all the changing styles of wine, he said, and while he could appreciate that many of these changes had been for the good—and had brought, finally, after so many hard years of labor, an improved financial situation for his family—he was still firmly and forever a Zinfandel man.

"It's just hard to beat, is all. Cabernet, Pinot, what have you— Zinfandel is still a better wine."

His son laughed. "All the old Italians," Pete Jr. said, "used to call it the Boss Grape."

I wanted to visit Seghesio's Chianti Station and Home Ranch vineyards at Asti, so we hopped into Pete Jr.'s SUV and headed north on Highway 101. It was high summer, hot and dry, and the valley was a Cézannesque canvas of pastels: the beige and burnished gold of the tinder-dry hillsides, the turquoise sky, the purple folds of the mountains, the green vineyards, the roadsides dappled with blue larkspur and pink lupine. On the drive up, we talked about Sonoma's rich Italian American history and how quickly the old-timers were dying off, taking with them the old tales and ways. Pete grew passionate as he emphasized how important it was to preserve these local stories.

Suddenly we came to a small barn and a modest one-story farmhouse, set in the middle of an expansive old vineyard on the outskirts of Geyserville. Pete slowed down.

"Do you want to meet old man Pastori?" he asked.

"Who?"

He laughed. "He's this crotchety guy who does a thousand cases of jugs out here, and it's all second-crop Zin." Grape growers sell the first, main crop to buyers; usually, the vines will sprout a few more grapes after the first crop has come out, but the second crop is never considered all that good. "Jugs," of course, meant jug wine.

"He's got all the old stories in his head," Pete continued. "You'll love

Generations: Frank Pastori and Pete Seghesio Jr.

him. He's probably the last person alive who knew my dad's mom." That would have been Rachele, Eduardo Seghesio's wife.

Pete pulled into the driveway and cruised slowly through the dusty yard toward the barn, where we spotted seventy-five-year-old Frank Pastori tinkering under the hood of a truck, hatless in the bright afternoon sun. He waved, and I could see the strength in his shoulders and thighs as he strode toward us.

We all shook hands, and I asked Pastori to tell me what he was growing in his vineyard.

"Why, Zinfandel!" he exclaimed, as if the answer should have been obvious.

"Oh, it's the Cadillac of wine!" he sang out, his sunburnt face creased and good-looking. For him, only one variety was suitable for planting in the Asti/Chianti area, and that was the Boss Grape. "No one can compete with it up here, is all. It's the quality of the land."

During the Depression, he recalled, when home winemakers back east wanted to buy grapes to make into wine, "all they ever asked for was Zinfandel from Asti/Chianti," because that was the best, far better than anything grown south of Geyserville, which was (and here he practically spat out the words with contempt) "prune country."

"Where in the world could you get a better wine than he gets at his Home Ranch?" Pastori asked, indicating Pete Jr. with an outstretched chin.

Pastori remembered when Geyserville had been a hard-drinking town with six hotel bars, back in the thirties. It was a difficult time, what with the Depression and the worsening situation in Europe, and politics were getting mixed up with local issues and rivalries. After a night of heavy drinking, the Italian Americans, down from Asti/Chianti, would get into scraps with the German Americans, who dominated Geyserville and points south. Fistfights would break out in the bars and spread to the streets. Pastori talked also about "pettaserra"—Petite Sirah—and what a heavy, dull wine it made, although some people liked it. He complained that the Internal Revenue Service or some such branch of the government wouldn't let him put the word "Chianti" on the front label of his wines anymore, even though "that's where we are—Chianti Station!" For some obscure reason, he said, shaking his head, the Italian government objected.

As Pastori spun his yarns, Pete watched and listened with an affectionate smile and respect in his eyes. He'd been taught by his parents to revere the old-timers. (On our drive back, we visited the old local cemetery, where Pete somberly pointed out the elaborately carved tombs and grand mausoleums where so many of them are interred.) Just before we left, I asked whether Pastori was entirely sure that Zinfandel, and not Cabernet Sauvignon, was really the best grape to grow in the Alexander Valley. He looked at me as if I were an idiot child who hadn't understood a word he had said.

"I told you," he declared, "this is *not* Alexander Valley. We're in Asti/Chianti here!"

"So the only thing you grow," I asked, "is Zinfandel?"

There was a little moment of silence. I thought I saw Pete glance at Pastori. Then the old man said, "Well, my *main* crop is Zinfandel. But I do have a little Cabernet."

Pete, who was sitting in the SUV, doubled over in laughter, leaning his forehead on the steering wheel. Even Pastori grinned.

As we drove back, Pete was still chuckling. "That's the thing about Frank," he said. "He just regards Asti/Chianti as the King of Zinfandel, and I think he's right. This is Zinfandel country."

A few minutes later, we reached the Seghesios' property. The oldest Zinfandel blocks are in the Home Vineyard, just across the street from Chianti Station, in the east-central part of the Alexander Valley, on flatlands hard by the Russian River. They were planted in 1895 by Italian Swiss Colony, but Eduardo Seghesio eventually acquired the property.

There is no question that these old vines produce exquisitely beautiful Zinfandel. In the summer of 2003, my colleagues at the *Wine Enthusiast* magazine and I blind-tasted more than three hundred California Zinfandels in a three-day marathon, and Seghesio's easily stood out, along with the always dependable Ridge and a couple of others. Yet for all the quality of its wines, Seghesio's Home Vineyard is not much to see. The vines are head-pruned, stubby old things, low to the ground, scraggly and wild. They are not grandly trained along wires and trellises as vines in a modern vineyard would be. These feral-looking bushes make you think that they were there when pterodactyls flew overhead.

The dirt in which they grow is dry and sparse in summer, a desert ochre in color, scattered here and there with little rounded river pebbles. If you stoop down and gather a handful of dirt and sniff it, you will detect a faint scent of mothballs and candle wax, courtesy of some elemental substances that seem to work their way into the wine's complex aroma, alongside the grapier scents of cherries and blackberries. Even though these are valley-floor flatlands, the soil is so poor in plant-sustaining nutrients and water that the vines have to be irrigated, or else they will fail to thrive.

Still, the vines are extremely low-yielding, a function, no doubt, not only of the meager, well-drained soil but also of their great age and of stubborn old viruses that affect the vines' productivity, though not their quality. Under the hot sun, the grapes ripen evenly and well, developing the rich, intense flavors that make a perfect glass of Zinfandel so good.

So it was that for the remainder of the nineteenth century, and for a good part of the twentieth, King Zinfandel reigned supreme in this stretch of the Alexander Valley (or Asti/Chianti). But in the southern part of the valley, below Geyserville, in Frank Pastori's "prune country," a pretender to the throne was hovering in the wings. Cabernet Sauvignon's grab for power, as the boutique winery era began, would soon cause a civil war.

3

Alexander Valley Cabernet Sauvignon

Dueling cultures still pervade the upper and lower valleys today. The northern culture, at Geyserville and Cloverdale and points in between, is, much as we saw with Frank Pastori, stubbornly old-fashioned.

The southern culture is both centered around and symbolized by Healdsburg. This gentrified town has become Sonoma County's most chichi destination, its version of glitzy St. Helena. "No one goes to [the town of] Sonoma anymore. It's all about Healdsburg," sniffs Iron Horse's Forrest Tancer, whose family long owned the T-bar-T ranch and vineyard in the mountains high above the Alexander Valley, property they sold only in early 2003.

Old Stringtown is today a thriving upscale community of boutique clothing emporiums, expensive souvenir shops, gourmet food stores, fancy restaurants, art galleries, bookstores, tastefully renovated Victorian homes, and, of course, sleek, air-conditioned tasting bars, where you can sample a pour of the local wines in crystal glasses. Downtown is still centered around the old square, but Harmon Heald would rub his eyes in disbelief if he returned, Rip van Winkle–style, especially if he saw the large, modernish Hotel Healdsburg, which commands the western side of the square.

These two cultures, north and south, reflect the disparity between the way of life among the old Italian Americans, with their grape, Zinfandel, and that of the newer crowd, whose members hold Cabernet Sauvignon as their heraldic grape and wine. It may be true that a little Cabernet Sauvignon and a few of its allied varietals were growing here and there in the Alexander Valley in the old days. Edward Seghesio Jr., Pete Seghesio Sr.'s brother, recalls some Cabernet at Italian Swiss Colony's vineyards in Asti. But, he adds, "the yield wasn't there"—a powerful indictment against a grape back then, when crop levels meant cold cash to hardscrabble growers. Moreover, remembers Pete Jr., relying on his boyhood memories, "nobody liked how Cabernet tasted." It could be harsh and astringent in youth, and rather olivaceous and herbal, so unlike a rich, fruity Zinfandel. "I remember being told as a kid," Pete says, "that Cabernet wasn't a grape you could drink early on. So it fell out of favor."

It must have fallen out early, because by the 1930s, Frank Pastori claims—if his memory is correct—no more of it could be found in Asti/ Chianti. "There just wasn't any Cabernet," he insists, pronouncing it with a hard "t," as if it were "cabernett." "They never knew what it was."

Nor did they know much about it in the south valley. Robert Young, who founded his eponymous winery and whose forebears had settled on Black Mountain back in 1858, just below what later became Forrest Tancer's T-bar-T Ranch, planted some Cabernet on the lower slopes in 1963. But it was only an experiment, and his reasons for putting it in seem accidental to the point of triviality. "It was a grape he could grow that would ripen after the prune harvest," recalled his son, Jim Young, meaning that the late-ripening Cabernet would provide an additional crop after the tree fruits had been picked. At any rate, the Youngs sold off their Cabernet grapes to others for decades before establishing their winery and releasing their first wine in 1997, so they cannot really be regarded as Alexander Valley Cabernet pioneers.

When the Wetzel family put in their first grapes, in 1966 at what later became their Alexander Valley Vineyards & Winery, on the benches below Black Mountain, they included a little Cabernet and the far rarer Merlot, in addition to Chenin Blanc, Johannisberg Riesling, Gewurztraminer, Chardonnay, Pinot Noir, and Zinfandel. But this very promiscuity of varietals indicates the total uncertainty of the times. "Who knew what varietal would grow well?" Katie Wetzel Murphy asks. Who indeed? Three years later, Tancer, who earlier had worked for the Wetzels, put in a little patch of Cabernet at T-bar-T. But even as late as 1970, when so much hoopla was coming out of Cabernet-centric Napa Valley, on the other side of the Mayacamas, Alexander Valley's acreage of Cabernet and other Bordeaux varietals remained negligible.

The valley was still agricultural country. From Geyserville south, past the Jimtown Store and down to Healdsburg, the land was almost exclusively planted to pears, prunes, and apples, while cattle grazed as they had for a century in the rolling fields along Route 128 and up into the foothills. The Alexander Valley was still such a backwater, such a pastoral place, that when a certain gentleman by the name of Tom Jordan arrived in the south valley in 1972, "there might have been a patch of grapes here and there, but basically it was all plum trees," he later recalled.

Things were about to change, however, although it would take someone forceful and imaginative enough to tip the balance and carry the valley into modernity. That someone was Tom Jordan. The valley's modern era, and its connection to Cabernet Sauvignon, has a definite beginning: the launch of Jordan Vineyard and Winery in 1976.

Jordan, a Denver oilman, was the first outsider to come into the Alexander Valley with an aggressive vision and a boldly ambitious plan concerning

Tom Jordan and cigar in his Healdsburg engineering office.

wine. He represented a type of entrepreneurial spirit the valley had not seen since the days of Cyrus Alexander—determined to achieve success and leaving as little as possible to chance. (Of course, unlike Cyrus, Jordan already had money when he arrived.)

His vision, to create a world-renowned Cabernet Sauvignon modeled after First Growth Bordeaux, played out; and, in the process, Jordan single-handedly launched the Alexander Valley's modern reputation for Cabernet Sauvignon. He carried out his project with great care, despite the huge risk he took in choosing his location. Napa Valley would have been the logical choice for a Cabernet visionary, and it was where all the other Cabernet-dreaming millionaires were going. Instead, Jordan chose the Alexander Valley, a place known almost exclusively during the previous eighty years for Italian Swiss Colony's Chianti and for Zinfandel—not exactly chateau-bottled Bordeaux.

I talked with Jordan one day in his offices in downtown Healdsburg. The walls were covered with large, colorful, computer-generated geologic maps for his latest oil-drilling project. I asked why he had decided to try his hand at Cabernet Sauvignon in so unknown a place as the Alexander Valley. Was Napa land even then too expensive?

"Absolutely I could have gone to Napa," he grunted, chomping on the big old cigar that is his trademark. His large, expressive eyes looked a little sad, like a basset hound's, and his raspy voice was just above a whisper.

A self-described "city kid," Jordan in the early 1970s was looking for "someplace bucolic," a country retreat to spend part of his time. He'd earlier been hugely taken with a 1958 Beaulieu Private Reserve Cabernet Sauvignon and subsequently decided to live the life of a gentleman farmer and grow Cabernet grapes. At first, he did indeed go to the obvious place, Napa Valley, but he was less than impressed by what he saw. As anyone knows who drives up from the south, as you approach the city of Napa along Highway 29 through Vallejo and American Canyon, the landscape, then as now, is a flat, dreary, commercial stretch of warehouses, bars, roadside restaurants, and billboards that is anything but bucolic.

"I had the sense going through there," Jordan recalled, choosing his words, "that this is all very nice, but ..."

He took a drag on the cigar, being careful to blow the blue smoke out of the corner of his mouth, away from me, and let the sentence hang unfinished. Through friends, he learned that there was a place called the Alexander Valley, just over the Mayacamas Mountains, that fit the bill. It was beautiful and unspoiled, "and," Jordan grinned, "they said you could throw a rock from there and hit Calistoga."

As an oilman, Tom Jordan was used to taking risks, but he didn't strike me as the sort of man who would sink a few million dollars into an entirely unproved scheme. I asked whether he had had any solid reason to suspect that he could grow a good Cabernet Sauvignon in the Alexander Valley, beyond being able to hit Calistoga with a rock.

"Well," he replied, "we did extensive geochemical testing, which is an area I'm comfortable with, and we looked carefully at temperature studies. And there were no discernible differences between the southern Alexander Valley and most of northern Napa Valley."

Jordan's decision to focus on Cabernet Sauvignon was solidly in keeping with the temper of the times. From the late 1960s to the mid-1970s, California's reputation for Cabernet was soaring. It was the era of the "boutique winery," when the likes of Cuvaison, Chappellet, Caymus, Robert Mondavi, Joseph Heitz, Stag's Leap, Diamond Creek, Clos du Val, and Chateau Montelena—all in Napa Valley—were causing consternation among wine aficionados for the quality of their Cabernets.

But this was the Alexander Valley, not Napa, and Jordan knew that, no matter how good his wine turned out to be, he had his work cut out for him. He would have to convince people that a Cabernet Sauvignon from a winery named Jordan, from a place called Alexander Valley, was worth not only their attention but also the money he planned to ask them to fork over.

He convinced them the old-fashioned way, by dropping a bundle on

PR. For starters, he built a chateau on his estate on Lytton Springs Road, a mansion that is one of the most glamorous in all of California. (It's set well back from the road and is not open to the public, so unless you've been invited, you won't see it.) With its eighteenth-century French Empire styling, ivy-covered cream walls, red-clay tiled mansard roofs, flower-filled formal gardens, and winding driveways hedged with poplars and sycamores, it was as elegant as anything in Bordeaux itself. It was designed to impress. And impress it did—and still does.

"Early on, I realized the challenge was, How are you going to get recognized?" Jordan said. The answer was to bring tastemakers—restauranteurs, sommeliers, wine merchants, liquor distributors, and the odd food and wine writer—out to the chateau and then wine and dine the pants off them. And here Jordan spared no expense.

"We had guest suites and guest houses and a superb kitchen operation, and we brought chefs in from France to cook," he related. "I knew the wine was never going to taste better than it would in that nice setting, with good food. So by the time it was released, in the spring of 1980, many hundreds of people in the trade had come to stay, have dinner, have fun, and so were already exposed to the product."

"The product." It was a sophisticated, well-oiled publicity machine, and it raised eyebrows among some longtime valley residents who had watched this wealthy businessman come in and spend more money on his buildings and roads than many of them would earn in a lifetime. "Tom Jordan spent three years flying people out here and taking them out to dinner and telling them how great his Cabernet was," recalls Katie Wetzel Murphy, entirely without resentment. "They built up a press identity before they even released their first wine. It was something we hadn't seen much of in Alexander Valley," she acknowledges, giving Jordan ample credit for boosting the valley's reputation.

"The product" was a huge success. The '76 was even served to Queen Elizabeth II and President Ronald Reagan when they had dinner together in San Francisco in 1983. I remember the hoo-hah that '76 Jordan Cabernet caused in the wine community when it was released in 1980. It temporarily stole the spotlight even from Napa. Critics oozed praise from every pore. One referred to its "lofty eminence," while another called it "the quintessential Cabernet in its region." These lavish encomiums were soon repeated by every wine, food, and travel writer in the country, including, one suspects, some who had never tasted the wine. In becoming famous, Jordan's wine also served notice that the Alexander Valley and its Cabernet Sauvignon had to be taken seriously by the newly emerging class of wine mavens. "Before Jordan, there weren't any superpremium wines in Alexander Valley," Forrest Tancer remembers. "Jordan was the first."

THE BATTLE OF ALEXANDER VALLEY:
THE APPELLATION WARS

With Jordan's success, Cabernet's tempo picked up. Others came into the south valley and planted, hoping that some of the Jordan limelight would shine on them. Below Jimtown, on the stretches and benchlands along Route 128, out came the plum trees, away went the cows, and in went that prestigious new cash crop, Cabernet Sauvignon. Jordan "started to influence small farmers like my dad," says Steve Domenichelli. "He said, 'Maybe we need some Cabernet, too.' We didn't know anything about it, but it was supposed to be the new varietal."

By the 1980s, the split between north and south, between Zinfandel and Cabernet, between an old Italian ethos and a more modern California one, had become a chasm. The proof of this, I think, lies in how long it took for the Alexander Valley to become an AVA and how contentious the process proved to be. The county's other appellations—Sonoma Valley, Dry Creek Valley, Russian River Valley, Green Valley, even Knights Valley, which for all practical purposes didn't even have any vineyards until the 1970s—all had easily achieved AVA status by 1983. It took the Alexander Valley another year to do it.

As it turned out, a furious struggle ensued over where the appellation's northern boundary ought to be. The tug-of-war was between the two cultures. The majority of growers and vintners in the south wanted the northern line to stop at the Geyserville Bridge, where modernism itself seemed to cease. The north valley, they suggested, was some kind of viticultural Podunk, dominated by old-time jug-wine producers like Frank Pastori and hardly worth an honored position on the premium wine map. The south valley, by contrast, was the historic heart of Cyrus Alexander's Sotoyomi Rancho; it alone, they contended, deserved the prestige of the appellation named for him. For a century, when southerners had used the term "Alexander Valley," what they really meant was "Cyrus Alexander's valley"—the bowl of land below Geyserville.

The strength of the southerners' feelings, and some residual bitterness, can still be sensed even today, long after they fought their losing battle. "To me, historically, Alexander Valley ended at the Geyserville Bridge," Forrest Tancer says. Jim Young agrees: "When I was a kid, Alexander Valley only went up to Geyserville Bridge." Even as late as 1962, when her parents bought what became Alexander Valley Vineyards, "Alexander Valley was regarded as south of the Geyserville Bridge," notes Katie Wetzel Murphy. Everything north of that, recalls Tancer, was "Asti." It might as well have been Mars.

But shrewd wine and real estate interests were moving into the areas up around Asti and Cloverdale. These ambitious people had bought their land on the cheap, and they were putting in vineyards, or thinking about it—thinking, also, that a prestigious new appellation would boost land values. "Alexander Valley was kind of becoming famous, and that was creating demand on those grapes," Jim Young remembers. "Everybody up there wanted to be included." These newer interests understood that the smaller an appellation is—and certainly an Alexander Valley appellation would be smaller than the Sonoma County appellation to which they were currently entitled—the more prestigious its wines will seem to consumers, who in turn will be willing to spend more money on its wines. (Among these grower interests, the well-known Sonoma vintner Richard Arrowood told me, was the late comedian, vintner, presidential candidate, and, for a time, self-proclaimed "mayor of Asti" Pat Paulsen, who was growing Chardonnay, Cabernet, and Sauvignon Blanc in Cloverdale.)

As we now know, the northern interests won, and the AVA wound up extending from southeast of Healdsburg all the way up to the Mendocino County line, a distance of about twenty-five miles. So much for Cyrus Alexander's old valley.

The southerners were shocked when the Bureau of Alcohol, Tobacco, and Firearms handed down its ruling. "We were all thinking, 'You've got to be kidding!'" Arrowood recalls. His family had lived in the south valley for more than a century. When he jokingly told his elderly grandmother that the Alexander Valley now went up to Mendocino, she could hardly believe her ears.

I asked Tancer why the BATF, in its wisdom, approved the extended boundary. "There's an interesting story about that," he replied. "On the old U.S. Geological Survey map, the words 'Alexander Valley' sort of went up to Cloverdale, so the BATF figured that if it said that on the map, it must all be Alexander Valley." Such are the vagaries by which appellations sometimes are drawn.

"Why we lost," sums up Tom Jordan, "is because [the northerners] had more political pull." Jordan had once done a stint in the Colorado state legislature and considered himself something of an operator. "I thought we had a slam-dunk case, and so I didn't get in and politick. And I regret that."

However it came about, there was a certain geographic, if not historic or cultural, logic in extending the Alexander Valley's northern terminus to Cloverdale. Nothing at the Geyserville Bridge indicates a change of terrain. Throughout its length, the Alexander Valley—unlike, say, the Russian River Valley AVA—is a single valley of fairly uniform topographic construction, albeit with differences here and there in soil, elevation, and climate. If you drive Highway 101 from one end of the appellation to the other, things look and feel pretty much the same. The hills close in near the Mendocino line, where both the valley and the appellation snap to an abrupt end at the Cloverdale Gorge, but they otherwise bear a unified sense of place.

In fact, the physical differences between north and south pale when compared to the differences between the flatlands and the hills. The higher you go, the more complex both the mini-climates and the soils become. But that's getting ahead of the story.

That '76 Jordan Cabernet did more than just make a name for itself and for the Alexander Valley. It created, or at least bolstered, the paradigmatic notion that Alexander Valley Cabernets—and the valley's reds in general—are softer and simpler than those of neighboring Napa Valley, which is inevitably (for better or for worse) the point of comparison.

By the 1980s, it had become a journalistic truism that a Napa Valley

Cabernet had to be aged in order to be drinkable—such were its tannins—
while a gentle Alexander Valley Cabernet could be enjoyed instantly. This
impression continues, to some extent, today. Arrowood calls Alexander Valley "the St. Julien of the North Coast," the implication being that Napa
Valley is Pauillac. I asked Tom Jordan what he thought about this "softness" theory.

He leaned back, holding his cigar like a conductor's baton between
long, elegantly tapered fingers, and told a story. "I remember, it must have
been in '77—I had André Tchelistcheff out, and we were tasting the '76—
and André said, 'You know what your vineyards are going to do? This is
going to be a feminine wine.'" Tchelistcheff was the longtime winemaker
at Beaulieu and California's first modern Cabernet master, the man his
many generations of disciples called the Maestro.

Jordan's face winced at the memory of the pain that long-ago remark,
obviously still fresh in his mind, had caused. "'Feminine wine'?" he exclaimed. "My heart almost sank!" He perceived the term "feminine" as a
criticism, indicating a wimpy wine without substance, not a glorious one
that would age like the '58 Beaulieu, much less like a First Growth Bordeaux. He confided this fear to Tchelistcheff. "But André said, 'Look, there's
nothing wrong with a feminine wine. Latour's a tannic monster, and Margaux's feminine. So don't get defensive!'"

I asked Jordan why Tchelistcheff had made that comment.

"Well, he could taste it. He knew what the style of wine was going
to be."

"No, I mean, did he say why it was a feminine wine?"

"He just said it was the terroir."

"What did he mean by 'terroir'? Did he explain? Was it the weather?
The soil?"

Jordan shook his head; Tchelistcheff hadn't elaborated, or perhaps

Jordan hadn't asked. "But as a generality," he continued, "I think that's right. Alexander Valley Cabernets *are* soft. Sometimes I'll taste some of the new cult wines in Napa, whether it's high-volume Mondavi Reserve or a Harlan or somebody like that, and I'll taste my own, and my first reaction is, 'My God, all I'm doing is making Beaujolais!'"

It certainly wasn't Beaujolais, but the Jordan Cabernet was gentle and smooth. It went down easy, and lots of people liked it. "Americans," Jordan theorizes in explaining his wine's early and amazing success, "were not looking for heavy-duty tannins. So along comes Jordan, and all kinds of people, especially women, who thought they didn't like Cabernet, all of a sudden could say, 'This Cabernet isn't so bad!'"

Not so bad, indeed. To this day, Jordan's is the most requested Cabernet Sauvignon served in America's best restaurants.

Lost, however, in the din of praise pouring down on that historic Jordan Cabernet Sauvignon were darker rumblings, whispers that, for all its popularity and fame, the wine was not without its shortcomings. As it turned out, Americans—or, at least, some American wine critics—were looking for more concentration, structure, and fruity complexity than Tom Jordan's Cabernet seemed able to provide.

There could, twenty years ago, indeed be a thinness not only to Jordan's but to other Alexander Valley Cabernets. Mary Ann Graf, the winemaker at Simi in the 1970s, once referred to "the earthiness of Alexander Valley wines" and then added, significantly, "Whether that is complimentary or not remains to be seen." It turns out that it wasn't. "We used to refer to the 'Alexander Valley veggies'" when it came to Cabernet, remembers Rick Sayre, the winemaker at Rodney Strong. Strong, a former dancer, had been a Cabernet pioneer in the south valley with his Alexander's Crown vineyard, which he planted in 1971.

"Veggies" is a harsh epithet to apply to a wine—any wine. The word once was used with almost savage reference to the Cabernet Sauvignons of the Salinas Valley, in Monterey, which could taste like canned asparagus because they utterly failed to ripen in the region's windy, cold summers. But "veggies" had a different meaning in those early Alexander Valley Cabernets. Under the hot sun, they failed to ripen in a different way; for some reason, they weren't developing the lush fruit and sweet, ripe tannins that Napa Cabernets almost invariably did.

When I turn to my own experiences, I find that the earliest Alexander Valley Cabernets I had *were* problematic. I see in my old tasting diary a Simi 1978, a 1978 Clos du Bois Marlstone, an '81 Woltner, that '76 Jordan, and a few others; and I notice that the same words occur over and over: "soft tannins," "mellow and soft," "could be fruitier," "lean," "short finish," "not much stuffing," "not a lot of stuffing," "simple." I didn't use Rick Sayre's word, "veggies," because I wasn't familiar with it at the time, but the meaning of my own descriptions was pretty much the same.

But when you think about it, the herbaceousness and softness of those early Alexander Valley Cabernets are puzzling. Why should the wines have been so different from those of Napa Valley? The temperature in the southern Alexander Valley, as Tom Jordan's research showed, is pretty much the same as in Napa Valley. The average temperatures and the average daily high temperatures between June and September at St. Helena and Healdsburg are within one-half to one degree of each other, despite the commonly held belief that the Alexander Valley is cooler. True, the Alexander Valley is rainier than Napa during the winter months, because the Mayacamas Mountains wring water out of the storms that arrive from the west, creating a slight rain-shadow effect to the east. But by the time summer comes, the Alexander Valley is as dry and drought-stricken as anywhere in Napa Valley.

The soils are not all that different, either. They are deeper in the Alexander Valley's bottomlands than in Napa Valley's flats because the Russian River is a lot bigger than the Napa River, but the soils are made from pretty much the same stuff, and with similar physical properties. Nor did the Cabernet clones, rootstocks, or general viticultural practices vary all that much from one side of the Mayacamas to the other.

So why had the "softer" paradigm arisen? More important, was it still true?

The answer lies in where the vines were located: on the flatlands. "I don't think planting by the river has ever been the best growing conditions in Alexander Valley, actually," Tancer observed one day. Yet "by the river" was where most of the Cabernet, and everything else, was planted, as it had been since grapes first went into the valley. But if planting Cabernet in the river-bordering flats was not the best approach, the growers of the 1970s and 1980s could be forgiven for having done so, for that's exactly what the viticultural experts at the University of California at Davis told them to do.

"U.C.'s advice was to plant Cabernet for miles everywhere, with no distinctions about river floor or valley floor or hillside," recalls Marie Gewirz, a longtime valley resident who does public relations for area wineries. Dan Roberts, "Dr. Dirt," remembers arriving in Sonoma as a young soil scientist and being shocked by people's resistance to putting Cabernet above the valley floor. "According to U.C. Davis, you couldn't plant in the hills because it was too cold!" he says, in mock horror. "That's when I realized that, even though Davis was the hottest school in the book, they didn't know squat."

Domenichelli recalls the situation from a grower's point of view. "In the late 1970s, there was a big movement to put Cabernet on riverbottom, so we had all our Cabernet down there. All these buyers who represented Gallo, Sebastiani, and so on, the big wineries, would come and tell us, 'We need you to plant Cabernet along the river in deep soils. It'll give you great flavors.'"

Tchelistcheff himself earlier had declared, "As soon as we touch deeper soils, the [wine] quality goes down." But, aside from the handful of wineries where he was consulting in Sonoma, the Maestro did not possess the influence in the Alexander Valley that he enjoyed in Napa Valley. And, at the time, it made sense for the big wineries to encourage riverside plantings. They had inherited the same old Italian American ethos that worshipped at the shrine of Yield. Riverbottom grapevines would be vigorous vines that would reliably produce tons and tons of commodity Cabernet Sauvignon to the acre—grapes that the marketing and sales wizards at the big wineries knew could be manufactured into (and this is key) *varietally labeled* wine. They knew also that valley-floor Cabernet would be relatively inexpensive wine that could slug it out in the perennial wine wars occurring on the shelves of the nation's supermarkets.

Did they know that the deep soils by the river would *not* give "great flavors"? Did they misrepresent conditions to growers such as the Domenichellis, who, after all, assumed that if Gallo and Sebastiani said so, it must ipso facto be true? Who can say? Whether or not they believed it, the big wineries were wrong when they promised that riverbottom Cabernet would give great flavors. Instead, it gave thin, herbal wines that were slenderized versions of the best of Napa Valley.

Domenichelli ticks off the bill of particulars that prevented flatland Alexander Valley Cabernet from rising to the heights. "The wine was very veggie, very herbaceous. The fruit wasn't dark; the color was really light. It's really [better for] pears and prunes down there by the river."

All kinds of problems arise in growing Cabernet on the valley floor. First, during the summer, it's hotter there than up in the hills, where the temperature can drop a degree or so with every hundred feet of elevation, and where the occasional downdraft, as well as high winds coming in off the coast, can help to cool things off. Heat and sun, beating down on grapes, can lower their acidity, making the wines unfresh and unvital on the palate and overly soft. In the worst of cases, the sun will burn some of the grapes, leading to raisiny, cooked flavors. And the heat does something else: it causes grape sugars to soar to very high levels, while other measures of ripeness, such as the development of fruitiness, lag behind.

"Think about what happens to your own biochemistry when it gets that hot," Dan Roberts suggested one day, with the demanding eyes of a university professor grilling a student defending a thesis.

"I sweat."

"Exactly so," Dr. Dirt replied. "But plants don't have a way to sweat. Instead, you get a huge accumulation of sugar without actually getting any phenolics [aroma and flavor compounds that make wine smell and taste good]. Now, some varietals, like Grenache, Mourvèdre, and Tempranillo, and possibly Syrah, are adapted to that. But the majority of the French varietals—Cabernet, Merlot, and Pinot Noir—are not."

When you get high sugars with low phenolics, you risk producing the Alexander Valley veggies. The grapes have to be picked before they shrivel into raisins but, unfortunately, also before they have had a chance to develop fruity flavors. Not a great recipe for world-class Cabernet Sauvignon.

But the greatest problem with planting vines in bottomlands is that the soil is usually much too fertile. Although some land adjacent to the river, such as that at Chianti Station, is sparse in nutrients and well drained, thanks to its sandy structure, most of the Alexander Valley's flatland soils are just the opposite. Enriched by repeated flooding of the Russian River and by thousands of years of nutrient-carrying runoff from the hills, they are, precisely as Domenichelli suggests, heaven for farm crops. Grapes, too, will fatten up with flavor-diluting water; it's like fertilizing them every day with Miracle-Gro. But the wine they make will be pale and wan.

Growers can employ a few tactics to counter both the heat and the plants' vigor. The most brutal effects of the sun can be averted by proper trellising—by training the vines to grow on overhead wires that shade the grape bunches, creating leafy canopies that prevent sunburn, particularly on the rows' western side, which receives the hottest portion of the afternoon sun. There are many different forms of canopy management, and every grower has his or her favorites; a particularly popular one for Cabernet is vertical shoot positioning.

Growers can also use drip irrigation or overhead sprinklers to cool the plants and give them a little drink on a hot day. But Dan Roberts, for one, argues that the cooling effects of water only minimally mitigate the damaging effects of heat.

"I don't care what anyone says, you cannot irrigate away . . . the damage the sun does to [grape] clusters," he states. "Every day it's over ninety-five degrees, a cluster will hit fifteen, twenty degrees above that [internally]. So that cluster is one hundred ten, one hundred fifteen degrees, and irrigation doesn't do squat. And even if you use overhead sprinklers, you'd have to run them every day, all day," which could have the unintended consequence of further stimulating the vines to rampant, uncontrolled growth.

The invigorating effects of valley-floor soil can additionally be countered by inducing stress, which reduces crop loads. This can be done in different ways. Growers who use irrigation can control yields by shutting off the water at crucial times, thus limiting the vine's ability to grow, although this is far less effective after a wet winter, when the soil holds more moisture. Growers also can select devigorating rootstocks that naturally limit the plant's nutrient and water uptake. Then, too, some varietal clones and selections (about which more in chapter 8) limit crop yields better than others. It can be tricky, and it invariably takes a long time, for a grower to figure out exactly the right combination of rootstocks and clones for any particular site. This is why the North Coast phylloxera epidemic of the 1990s was a disguised blessing: it gave growers the opportunity to re-plant their vineyards with new and possibly more effective selections.

The classic way to reduce grape crop is also the simplest: cutting it off. This means sending workers out into the vineyard to relentlessly trim the vines, hacking off unwanted shoots and clusters in order to lower yields by as much as 50 percent. Jim Murphy, at Murphy-Goode (and Katie Wet-zel Murphy's brother-in-law), calls this "banzai-ing the grapes."

It took growers a long time to understand, much less to take, the eco-nomically drastic step of dropping fruit and limiting yields. "My dad, if he'd been alive today and seen us pulling leaves and thinning grapes—boy, you better have good legs!" jokes Frank Pastori. Dropping fruit certainly helps to concentrate flavors in the remaining grape bunches, but it has its limits. Domenichelli says, "You can take your pruning shears and cut Cabernet back, but you cut and cut, and the vine responds by putting out more and more growth," which makes it sound rather like that prolific broomstick in *The Sorcerer's Apprentice.* Valley-floor Cabernet "is like a colt that's gone crazy," he adds. "You want to calm it down and train it, and you just can't."

Which is where the mountains come in. Lacking water and nutrients, mountain soil is naturally devigorating. It is so meager that Mother Na-ture herself doesn't grow much there, except weeds such as poison oak, gnarly wild grasses, and drought-resistant trees such as eucalyptus, Cali-fornia oak, and madrone. Under such conditions, the grapevine limits its own vigor—and most winemakers are convinced that it's far better to have a vine's yield curtailed naturally than through human intervention. Mountain berries are smaller, contain less water, have thicker skins, and are more concentrated and muscular in every way.

"We'll never get a vigorous vineyard up here," Tancer says of his T-bar-T vines.

"For Cabernet, I'd much rather be in the benchlands and hills, not the valley floor," says Nick Goldschmidt, the Aussie who was Simi's longtime winemaker. (He moved over to Allied Domecq in the summer of 2003.) For decades, Simi has staked a large part of its reputation on Alexander Valley Cabernet Sauvignon, and its best wines are still benchmarks.

But Simi, no less than Alexander Valley growers in general, was slow to head for the hills. Tom Jordan himself kept his grapevines in the valley-floor part of his extensive real estate holdings until 1996, when he finally decided, or was persuaded, to install Cabernet on the slopes. Many other Alexander Valley growers held off doing the same until around that time. In that decade, it was as if a lightning bolt exploded in the skies above them, and people suddenly saw the light.

Ferrari-Carano, which put in their first Alexander Valley vines on the valley floor in 1978, developed their Tre Monte mountain vineyard only in the 1990s. So did Alexander Valley Vineyards, which, after relying exclusively on valley-floor grapes for many years, installed mountain vineyards during the final decade of the twentieth century. "Not that long ago," Jim Murphy recalls, "you would drive through this valley and think, 'There should be grapes along these hillsides.' But, no, there weren't."

Why were Alexander Valley growers so slow to plant in the hills? It was odd. Tchelistcheff certainly valued mountain fruit. Even when J. P.

Munro-Fraser, author of the 1880 *History of Sonoma County,* praised Alexander Valley Zinfandel as being potentially better than Chateau Lafite, he added this telling caveat: provided that it is "planted on the most precipitous slopes [in] our enormous stretches of foothills."

Yet few people cared to place a vineyard in the hills. Growers were interested in ease of cultivation and in high yields—two ends that were fostered by planting in the fertile flatlands. The author of the *History,* probably intending a compliment, went so far as to compare valley-floor grape growers to "wheat cultivators" in their zealous pursuit of profit through a mass crop.

Then, too, even if growers had wanted to plant in the mountains, most instinctively realized how cost-prohibitive it would be. Mountain growing costs money—a lot of money. You often have to fell trees and clear roads and then must farm slopes so rugged that only a fraction of the acreage is plantable. You usually have to fence the vineyard to protect it from deer and also figure out a way to practice erosion control. On top of all that, those low yields mean a smaller cash crop for the grower.

Alex Hogstrom manages Alden Vineyards, a privately held growing operation located below Geyser Peak, whose Cabernet Sauvignon grapes, grown at altitudes between 1,200 and 1,400 feet, go exclusively to Rodney Strong for a vineyard-designated bottling. Until the late 1980s, the area was virtually inaccessible, reachable only by traveling down five miles of a dirt trail originally cleared for mule trains. "It was awfully hard getting equipment up here," Hogstrom says, understating the case.

Beyond the difficulties of transport, another major challenge in the mountains is water—or, rather, the lack of it. Like any plant, vines need water to survive, which means that irrigation is usually required. But it's not so easy finding water high up in these parched hills.

"Down on [the] valley floor," Hogstrom says, "wells are shallow, and there's plenty of water. But in these mountains, water is difficult to access, and the lack of it prevented people from planting up here." Only with technological breakthroughs in well construction, such as horizontal drilling using rotary air drills, and with improved roads—not to mention an influx of money from the wine boom—did mountain viticulture become possible on a larger scale during the 1990s.

The initial reluctance to invest in hillside vineyards lasted well into modern times. Domenichelli remembers that, even into the late 1980s, grape growers—including those producing Cabernet Sauvignon in the south valley—still possessed antiquated ideas concerning farming.

"It was that old orchard mentality that was still here, and it was just so hard to get out of it," Domenichelli says. "It was follow-the-leader viticulture, and it just made me sick. They weren't exploring. They were too busy farming in their own little worlds."

Napa Valley, in contrast, attracted wealthy investor-vintners who hadn't been raised as farmers. Rather, they were doctors, industrialists, real estate developers, CEOs, airline pilots, investment bankers, or simply born to old money. They were university educated, entrepreneurially aggressive, open to new ideas, and willing to take risks, while too many in the Alexander Valley were coasting.

Even with all those luscious slopes practically begging to be planted, Alexander Valley growers preferred the devil they knew to the one they didn't—places near roads, where their grandparents had planted, which their vehicles and field crews could easily reach, where wells were easy to sink, or where inexpensive water for irrigation could be sucked up in unlimited quantities through plastic pipes that ran straight through the vineyard down to pumps on the Russian River.

By the mid-1990s, however, as the Cabernet race in California heated up and wine prices rose enough to justify greater spending in both viticulture and enology, Alexander Valley growers began to reconsider their options. Slowly but surely, they rebudded their valley-floor Cabernet vines over to Sauvignon Blanc and Chardonnay—white varieties that were not as dependent on ripe fruitiness as Cabernet and that could make decent wine when grown by the river (although, as Tancer rightly observes, "even those are not considered the best of either of those varietals"). In a classic case of better late than never, growers headed for the hills, planted new vines, and made wines that had never been made before in the Alexander Valley. They found the intensity they sought in wines, but also found, in the super-sized tannins those wines contained, considerably more than they had bargained for.

4

Mountain Cabernet Sauvignon

From out of the blue one day, Terry Wright emailed, asking me to join him for a canoe trip south from Cloverdale.

We'd paddled the river before, but never along that particular stretch. I was eager for the opportunity to leisurely study the terrain of the mountains from the vantage point of the river and to observe the pattern of the new hillside vineyards.

It was early June; summer had finally come, after the never-ending 2003 late winter and early spring rains that had lasted well into May. In the High Sierra, record snows had piled up, leading to huge melts that completely eradicated any fears of drought raised by our near-rainless January and February. (Snowmelt is the prime source of water for Northern California.)

We met up early in Geyserville, at the intersection of Geyserville Road and Route 128. The streets were quiet. I parked my car in front of Bosworth's and climbed into Terry's old van, as cluttered and creaky as his house. It choked and shuddered as we wheeled north up Highway 101. The long canoe was shakily lashed to the roof, and I could see its prow bobbing up and down, left and right. Near the Mendocino County line, in a state park, we launched. Terry had brought along the young son of a university professor friend. The boy would drive Terry's truck back down to the Geyserville Bridge, where it would be waiting for us at the conclusion of our one-way journey.

It was a gray day, foggy and chilly for June, with a needling northwest breeze that hinted of the cold North Pacific. The water was as still and glassy as a mirror. Crows cawed, unseen, in the trees, and wispy little tendrils of mist curled up from the river's calm surface and evaporated as they hit the warmer air.

With the onset of the dry season, the river's width was much reduced, and its level much lower than it had been the previous winter. Gravel bars and sandy little weed-fringed islands now rose up, causing the river to fork off to the left and right and forcing us, at each point, to decide which way the true current ran, which course to follow. Once or twice we disagreed, but Terry, being captain, had the final call. He was always right.

Huge, rounded, yellow-orange boulders that had been underwater all winter, the eroded skeletal bones of the old Franciscan bedrock, loomed above the surface like whales' humps. Along the banks, numerous strainers, or fallen trees, were sticking out like witches' fingers, threatening to snag anything that floated into their clutches, including people.

After five miles or so, we took a lunch break on a sloping gravelly shore. I told Terry about the winemakers who had claimed that Mount St. Helena had once been an erupting volcano and how I'd believed them without checking my facts.

"St. Helena never was a volcano," he said, between bites of meatloaf sandwich. "It looks like a volcano, but it's not. It has that shape due to erosion."

"Then how did it get covered with volcanic—what d'ya call it?"

"That's welded tuff, ash, breccia. But the answer is, nobody knows. It's a big mystery."

"It's not a mystery," I said. "It's Sonoma Volcanics."

"Yeah, but where was the volcano?"

I was left to contemplate that mystery. Deborah Elliott-Fisk earlier had said that the suspect volcano that plastered Mount St. Helena could have been somewhere along the eastern ridge of Napa Valley, in the range people call the Vaca Mountains, possibly even at Howell Mountain; and she had estimated that the eruption occurred about 2 million years ago. But she acknowledged that it could just as easily have been on the western ridge, in the Mayacamas. Perhaps more than one volcano had erupted. A big enough and long enough period of ejecta certainly could have encrusted St. Helena, no matter which side of the valley it came from.

After lunch, I explored the beach. In some places, the round little river pebbles were piled as high as snowdrifts.

A short but steep trail led up the bank through dense undergrowth. At the top, the valley floor was choked with vineyards—Chardonnay, it seemed to me—as far as the eye could see. After the spring rains, the vines had exploded into the riotous, uncontrolled growth vintners call, disparagingly, California sprawl. They looked like bursts of fireworks, arcing out in thick, symmetric sprays of leafy tendrils. This was not a great vineyard. Whoever had planted it was looking for quantity, not quality; no great wine would ever come from these grape factories. The Chardonnay would be drenched in oak barrels (or something smelling and tasting like barrels); possibly stretched with a little Colombard or Chenin Blanc or something else, just enough to keep it 75 percent Chardonnay so that it could legally be called a varietal; and end up passable to the public's taste. At least the owner had cared enough to plant a pretty border of pink, white, orange, and lavender oleander, interspersed with bright red geraniums, along the vineyard's edge.

Back on the water, we came to a marker sign attached to a bent metal pole that was screwed to an orange boulder rising out of the river: "Warning—Conditions Change!"

"What do you suppose that means?" I asked.

"Beats me," Terry replied.

What we did not know—I, at any rate, didn't—was that, while the Russian River is not particularly dangerous as far as rivers go, it has risky stretches. It last took the life of a boater in 1989, just below Squaw Rock, when a young man got caught in a strainer upside down in his kayak. Directly below Squaw Rock is the Graveyard Run, and a few miles below that is the Asti Run, into which we were now obliviously paddling.

There is a bend in the river below Asti where the outer edge of the turn, which is below a high, steep grade, is undercut by flowing water, creating a powerful, twisting current. Because of the high bank, there is no beach on which to seek shelter in the event of a washout. And, after the big, late storms of that season and the great snowmelt, a higher than usual volume of water was feeding the river, which increased the current's velocity.

But we did not know these things, and so we paddled on. In a few moments, we came across another canoeing party. They had capsized and made their way to a gravel bar. We would have stopped to see if they needed help, but they waved us on, laughing. I saw six-packs of beer on the beach, along with their gear.

"Tourists," Terry muttered.

A few minutes later, we saw an upended canoe caught in a strainer by the bank. Then an abandoned kayak, bobbing half-submerged, yoked to a tangle of branches.

Fifteen minutes later, I heard the roar. It sounded like the oncoming rumble of the old D-train on the New York City subway. Then you could see it: foamy, boiling water, churning and heaving up in waves that rolled against the orange boulders and exploded in clouds of white.

The current quickened, and the water grew choppy as the canoe began to bounce. "Hang on!" Terry yelled over his shoulder. "Do exactly what I tell you!"

We heaved and pitched. At first, paddling was instinctive. Right paddle in the water to steady; put your shoulder muscles into it; now quickly to the left. Terry and I seemed to be moving together in perfect, wordless synch.

Suddenly, we were shooting rapidly toward the bank, where the whitecaps rose up and fell off into gullies three feet deep.

"Why are we—" I was about to ask, "going toward the bank?" But before I could get the words out, I was upside down underwater, in what whitewater fans call the spin cycle of the washing machine, tumbling along head over heels, feeling the rough bottom gravel with the skin on my forehead.

Then the river spat me up, thanks, I suppose, to Terry's battered old life vest, which did its job despite missing two of its three clasps. Paddling doggie-style to stay afloat and coughing out the water I had swallowed, I looked for Terry but saw only his head, being carried swiftly away from me like a pink beachball.

The canoe was nearby, half filled with water, sinking even as it drifted away. My only thought, other than to save myself, was to secure it. My camera was in there, my tape recorder, and my notes, dry and secure (I hoped) inside a waterproof canvas pouch tied to a hand grip. I also knew that, even if we could save ourselves, without the canoe there was no way out, except on foot.

With one hand, I clutched the water-logged boat. The current was like a powerful vacuum, sucking it under and away. I found the branch of a strainer and grabbed it under my armpit. Steadying myself, I hung onto the canoe with my free hand. Terry, who luckily had been swept by the current onto a gravel bar on the opposite side of the rapids, called my name. I looked across. He was in shallow water, bent over with his hands on his knees, his hair and beard water-logged, looking as bedraggled as a wet cat. He had lost his eyeglasses.

"You all right?"

"Fine," I yelled. "What do we do now?"

"You have to get the canoe over to me." Behind me, the bank was 8 feet high, its mud crumbly with rocks and spiky roots. On top was a dark thicket of trees and bushes. Between Terry and me was rushing water.

Ropes and nylon cords were still in the canoe. I found my footing—the river was only about 4 feet deep where I was, although it was hard to keep steady because of the current. I maneuvered the canoe so that I could keep it in place with my hip. With both hands now free, I tied the cords together, lashed one end to the handgrip, wadded the rest into a ball, and threw it across. Terry waded out as far as he dared and caught it.

He pulled the boat over to his side.

"Now you have to get over here," he shouted.

"How?"

"Swim."

Swim? There was no way I was going to swim out into the middle of a raging river. I'd seen enough episodes of *Storm Stories* on the Weather Channel to know that you can drown even in shallow water if it's moving fast enough. And this was fast-moving water.

"No way!" I hollered.

Standoff.

I figured there must be a place upstream or downstream where the river was narrow enough to cross. "I'm climbing up the bank," I yelled. "You stay there. I'll try to get over."

After attempting three times to scale the bank, only to fall twice into the water on my backside, I managed to clamber to the top. The thicket was dense with sharp little branches and thorny bushes, and tangles of ground-hugging plants tripped up my feet. There were spiderwebs everywhere, especially, it seemed, at face level. It was impossible to see very far through that jungle.

I made my way a few hundred feet north, clawing through the branches and cobwebs with my hands, and then headed back down to the bank. No luck; the river there was even wider than where we had wiped out. I went twice as far to the south, but the situation was the same. I stopped to reconnoiter. My nose was bleeding from scratches. There were sticky spiderweb filaments on my fingers and face, in my eyelashes, in my hair, and on my lips; and already I could feel itchy spots on the back of my neck where the angry little insects were biting my flesh. I was sweating, even though it was a cool day; my clothes were drenched; my breathing was labored. I was thinking stupidly. With surprise, I realized I was panicking.

I took a few deep breaths and went back to the original place. I jumped down into the water.

"There's no way across," I shouted.

Terry looked very unhappy. "Look," he said, and now there was real exasperation in his voice. "I can't paddle out of here alone. I need you to help me."

I wondered why my life was not flashing before my eyes.

"Throw me the line," I said. It took a few tries; the rope kept plonking down short and drifting away. Finally it landed close enough for me to lunge and grab it. Terry held onto his end and then told me to go for it. I steadied myself, took a deep breath, said a little prayer, and hauled myself out on the line, hand over hand. In the middle, the force of the current was very great, and the river tried to steal my footing. Then I was over.

We laughed like two wild men, embracing and pounding each other on the back. I reminded Terry of the time at Sassafras when I'd wondered what it felt like to risk your life at something.

Terry said, "Be careful what you wish for, man!"

He might have said the same thing about mountain tannins, which is where the irony lies. For if Alexander Valley vintners got more of everything when they headed for the hills, that "more" included palate-numbing tannins.

Smaller mountain grapes have thicker skins, which means that they possess a greater skin-to-juice ratio—and skins (along with seeds) are where tannins come from, as the ever-increasing alcohol in the fermenting tanks leaches these bitter-tasting compounds out into the must and, eventually, into the wine. Mountain Cabernet, it turned out, could be imposingly tannic, so mouth-deadeningly astringent that it was almost undrinkable.

Rodney Strong's Alden Vineyard Cabernet Sauvignon is a good example of this problem and also of the learning curve that mountain winemakers face in learning how to make balanced wines. At home one summer night in 2003, I tasted the 1996, 1997, 1998, and 1999 Strong-Alden Cabernet. The '96 was still so mouth-puckering that, after a single sip, I poured the rest down the sink. That didn't mean it might not have come around someday, as, for example, the 1870 clarets did—after forty years. The '97, in keeping with that vintage's quality, was riper in fruit but still achingly tannic. The '98 once again was hard and tough as nails, and lean to boot.

"Man, we get those intense tannins," Alex Hogstrom, Alden's grape manager, exclaimed when I told him about the wines.

But good winemakers and vintners love a challenge, and they will tackle a problem such as overly strong tannins the way NASA engineers solve the mystery of what went wrong with the space shuttle. This was proven to me by the 1999 Strong-Alden. I have now tasted it three times over the course of a year, and each time it has blown me away. The last time, it was so good that I wrote, "Almost Harlan-like in voluptuousness." I had just tasted a range of Harlan Estate wines, the famous Napa Valley "cult" Cabernet from the rolling hills of Oakville, and the memory was fresh in my mind.

"Still, the tannins are tough, hard, edgy," I added in my notes. But it was a matter of degree. As edgy as they were, they were sweeter than in the older wines, so that they became not the wine's dominant theme but only one note integrated within it, a deep, throaty oboe in the sweep of the general orchestra. And the polished fruit from that fabulous vintage, so powerfully sweet in itself, also helped to balance the tannins. That '99 Strong-Alden was proof positive of just how far and fast things are changing up in that eastern wall of the Alexander Valley.

I experienced another example of how Alexander Valley Cabernets run the continuum from softer to harder tannins as they ascend a slope when I tasted through three wines, all from the 2002 vintage, made by Nick Goldschmidt before he left Simi for Allied Domecq. From a hilly vineyard that Simi had dubbed Landslide, in the southern part of the valley, Nick had produced wines from three altitudes, each of which he christened with a name representing its place on the hill: Lowlands, Midlands, and Uplands. These three bottlings provided a rare opportunity to compare how wines made in precisely the same manner differed merely with elevation.

It was November, soon after the harvest; whatever differences the wines displayed could be a result only of their respective origins. There was no question that they corresponded to what Nick called "Lowlands Elegant," "Midlands Powerful," and "Uplands Dense." (When you taste with winemakers, they will sometimes try to color your perceptions with their own descriptions. Writers learn to ignore these not-so-subtle promptings.) All three Simi wines held fine, ripe blackberry and blueberry flavors, but the tannins went from soft, easy, and Beaujolais-like in the Lowlands to firm in the Midlands to tough and hard in the Uplands. After we had tasted the three, I poured equal amounts of each into my glass, and it made for a round, complete Cabernet Sauvignon, with all the richness and depth you could ask for. The three levels of Landslide, Nick told me, would be the backbone of future Simi Reserve Cabernets. Two years later, after Simi released the 2000 Landslide, I tasted it at home at the same time I happened to be tasting the 2000 Dominus, from the Napa Valley property owned by the proprietor of the famous and expensive Bordeaux Chateau Petrus, and the Landslide blew it out of the water.

BLACK MOUNTAIN

Geyser Peak, Alexander's Crown, Alden Vineyard, Landslide, and the rest are interesting places for Alexander Valley Cabernet Sauvignon. But the most promising of all may be 1,750-foot Black Mountain, which rises over Cyrus Alexander's old Sotoyomi lands like a sheltering angel. Here are Robert Young and Iron Horse's T-bar-T, among others, and, almost at the top, on the site of the old Gauer Estate winery, Jess Jackson's Alexander Mountain Estate.

("Alexander Mountain," as Jackson calls his estate vineyards there, is not a historical place name, although it sounds like it should be. In the winter of 2003–2004, Jackson applied to the feds for an Alexander Mountain AVA and also announced that he would file for a Mount St. Helena appellation, but only for the side of the mountain in Sonoma County.)

Black/Alexander Mountain soils, like soils throughout the eastern wall of the valley, are enormously complex. My friend Bob Thompson, the dean of California wine writers, once called North Coast soils like these "a slagheap." "There is no uniformity at all," Forrest Tancer says of them. "You cannot go from this spot where we're standing to another spot and expect to find the same soil."

In some cases, such as swales where deposits of clay and other materials have gathered, Black Mountain soils, like those on other peaks, can be water- and nutrient-rich and as vigorous (or nearly so) as those down in the valley; these are not the best places to plant, and good growers avoid them. Growing is also ill advised in other areas: where serpentine rock is plentiful, for example, or where landslides are likely; or where a northern exposure would rob the vine of needed sunshine and heat; or where the slopes are too wooded. For such reasons, only a fraction of mountain property is even plantable. So variable are conditions in these hills that a grower will return to the same vineyard up to half a dozen times in a single season to pick the same varietal, because the grapes ripen at totally different paces.

Dan Roberts, who as a Jess Jackson employee studied Black Mountain extensively, points out the extreme complexity of its soils, as evidenced by soil profiles. A soil profile is an analysis of the soil's composition and structure—its micronutrients, water-holding capacity, depth, chemical composition, and other physical factors—as determined by digging deep trenches at regular intervals. These data are vital in determining which variety to plant, what type of rootstock to put it on, and even which clones to select. (Computer software technology, especially database capability, has made managing the storm of data points much easier.)

Whereas valley soil might have a single profile, the dirt in a mountain vineyard can have five or more, all within yards of each other. Dig a trench a few feet deep and a dozen feet long up in these hills, and the resulting soil profile chart looks like a map of the Balkans. But in general, it's true that, no matter what the specific composition of the soil is, Black Mountain dirt is poor, thin stuff, arid and lacking in nutrients. And this means that it's good for grapes, including Cabernet Sauvignon.

So what is Black Mountain Cabernet Sauvignon like?

In a word, extraordinary. If the vintner can control the tannins, that is, which is no small task. You have to consider Black Mountain Cabernet— and, by extension, Alexander Valley mountain Cabernet—a work in progress. It might be useful to consider the wines from the highest vineyards, Jackson's, down to the lower foothills, where Robert Young rules the roost.

Some of the most interesting developments have been with Jackson's wines, on the old Gauer Estate property. They are frankly experimental. Jackson continues to tinker with different brand names and vineyard designations up here, most notably producing a range of proprietarily named Bordeaux blends under the Verité label that cost as much as a hundred dollars a bottle and also bottling some single-vineyard wines under his Kendall-Jackson Highlands Estates program.

The original Gauer vineyard was one of the first ever installed on Black Mountain, although many, if not most, of the vines have since been replaced as a result of phylloxera. They were first planted in the mid-1960s by a now-deceased businessman, Ed Gauer, the owner of Roos-Atkins, a San Francisco clothing store chain that sold upscale menswear from the likes of Brooks Brothers. The man with perhaps the most extensive knowledge of the estate is its former vineyard manager, John Pina, who was hired in 1992 by the estate's then-owner, Chevron Corporation, to oversee the vineyards. Although Pina never met Ed Gauer, he told me what he knew.

"Mr. Gauer was trying to make it in cattle, sheep, and prunes, but nothing was paying its way," Pina remembers. "So he decided to get into the grape business." Gauer owned 6,000 acres on the mountain and luckily discovered a spring there that produced more than 700 gallons of water a minute. Gauer not only grew grapes but also made a little wine.

I dimly recall hearing about Gauer Estate wines in the 1980s, but I never tasted any, and none of the many wine books I have from that period even mentions them. The business seems to have been something of a cipher. Jackson says, "I think his wines were mainly to entertain his friends and for his own consumption."

When Gauer died, a division of Chevron Corporation bought the land, with the intention of developing fifty "ranchettes" on the mountain. Such plans were terribly popular with real estate developers in the prosperous 1990s. People were looking to buy themselves a, yes, bucolic lifestyle, and what better place than on some exquisitely beautiful wine country mountain, with a view and just minutes away from country clubs, golf courses, and fine restaurants?

But the oil company ran into unexpected problems. Local residents and environmentalists, fiercely protective of their own rural lifestyle, rebelled at the thought of earthmovers tearing their mountain apart for years, followed by hordes of nouveau-riche outsiders moving in. At about the same time, phylloxera struck the vineyards. And 1989's Exxon *Valdez* oil spill in Alaska was proving to be a huge embarrassment to oil companies.

"Chevron took a PR hit, and it was internally suggested that subdividing a mountain into home sites might not be considered environmentally sensitive," Jackson observes, wryly. Under the circumstances, Chevron did an abrupt volte-face and decided, since the vines already were there, to try its hand at the grape-growing business.

The company's executives realized that they needed a grape expert to run this new side of their business, and that's where Pina came in. "They hired me to replant a hundred acres a year for ten years of new mountain vineyards," he remembers. But Chevron soon became bored with its vine-yard plaything and bailed out in 1995. That's when Jackson, flush with Kendall-Jackson's success and determined to prove to the world that he could make boutique wine just as handily as the mass-produced fighting varietals K-J was known for, bought the vineyards, equipment, and land. He also retained Pina's services.

But Pina had little more success than Hogstrom in managing the fierce tannins. "I always commiserated with John Pina," Hogstrom says, "because we both had the same challenges in these mountain vineyards." Pina left Jackson's employ after five years and now runs his own vineyard consult-ing company.

Considering all the changes the Gauer-Jackson vineyards have experi-enced over the years and the discontinuity of ownership, it's not surpris-ing that no one has yet fully mastered these grapes. A related complica-tion is that Jackson, who is well known for his commitment to blending fruit from different regions, crafts Verité's wines with grapes from other parts of Sonoma County, and even from Napa Valley. As a result, it's im-possible to know just which specific qualities Black Mountain contributed, although I suspect it was the hard-edged tannins.

(In the spring of 2004, Jackson, with great fanfare, revealed a new range of Highlands Estates wines, including a really good single-vineyard Hawk-eye Mountain Cabernet entirely off Alexander Mountain. These clearly are wines to watch.)

In the spring of 2003, I tasted through four Verité blends, and all were quite tannic. The 1998 La Joie, which is 100 percent Cabernet Sauvignon, in particular was tough as nails. The 2000 Le Desir, a Cabernet Franc–Merlot blend, was also extremely tannic, and it seemed a gamble whether age would do anything for it. But 1998 and 2000 were in fact weaker vin-tages. The 1999 La Muse, based on Merlot, which came from a great vintage, was softer and richer in fruit. Later, I tried the 2001 Le Desir, again a Cabernet Franc–Merlot blend from a great vintage. It too was a work in progress and rather reminded me of an artist's study for a great masterwork: the outline was there, the brilliance, in sketchy form; it needed only to be realized.

Then I came to the 1999 La Joie Cabernet Sauvignon and began to understand what Jackson and Verité's Pierre Seillan, a Bordeaux-trained *vigneron* (winemaker), were aiming at. The wine still was tannic, with a hard-edged mouthfeel, a wine to stick away in a cool, dark place for a long time; but the fruit was rich, and the wine possessed a healthy balance that bodes well for the future. The critic Robert Parker, writing of this very wine, called it "not a wine for those looking for immediate gratification, as this will require 5–6 years of cellaring and keep for 25+ years." I never know whether these quarter-century prognostications are true, particularly for a wine with absolutely no track record; but the '99 La Joie obviously has much life ahead.

Eight months later, Jackson invited me back up to the mountain to retaste the Verités with him; his wife, Barbara Banke; and Seillan. It was a brilliantly clear day; the previous night, the first hard freeze of the 2003 winter had descended. Because the cold air is heavier and tends to "pool" in low points, the leaves on the valley-floor vines—but not those on the vines planted on the warmer mountain slopes—had been burnt brown.

We took an aerial tour of the mountain in Jackson's Boeing helicopter. What you can't see from the ground is how extensively Jackson and others have planted Black Mountain. Its interior subridges have been heavily carpeted with vines, although wild corridors, where black bears and cougars prowl, remain between the vineyards. It was easier to appreciate why, in that jungle of mini-climates and terroirs, Jackson is taking his time deciding things.

On this occasion, the Verité wines had mellowed. That '98 La Joie was considerably more elegant and feminine than I recalled from my earlier tasting, although I still found the '99 tough and tannic. The '00 and '01 Le Desirs were wonderful for their harmony and delicacy, opening my eyes to the possibilities of Cabernet Franc–Merlot blends. The '99 La Muse also had softened considerably and possessed Merlot's rounded, supple mouthfeel, although it still had reams of hard tannins.

Jackson, incidentally, had snuck several "ringers" into our blind tasting: Chateaux Cheval Blanc, Latour, and Petrus, all from the 1999 vintage. In each flight, I rated the French wines significantly lower than the Verités, fully conscious that my California palate prefers sweet, sunny fruit to the earthier subtleties of Bordeaux.

I asked Seillan, a friendly, rosy-cheeked man with twinkling eyes, to tell me about tannins in his mountain wines.

"It is a very important question," he replied, in French-accented English. "We do have difficult tannins here, but I say, okay, the tannin, I will manage it." And then he launched into Tannin Management 101. He described his approaches to canopy management and pruning on a vine-by-vine basis, to cold-soaking the grapes, to pumping the must over in the fermenting tanks, to adding sulfur dioxide, to shortening the maceration times—all designed to "privilege the fruit," to allow it to be the star of the show.

Then Jackson, who had been listening, jumped in. "What Pierre's explaining is that he's protecting the fruit and managing the tannins at the same time."

If there were lessons to be learned, among them was that tannin management on Black/Alexander Mountain is an ongoing effort, that it takes money, and that the same wine will taste different over time. This last consideration brings up the important question of ageability. Jackson and Seillan are intent on producing wines designed for the cellar, and Seillan may well be making a virtue out of necessity. But the truth is that, when it comes to the wines of Black/Alexander Mountain, no one can really know how or whether they will improve with age, although if Jackson's passion (and pocketbook) continues to guide the effort, these experimental wines some-day could be among California's greatest.

I did have one Jess Jackson wine that was made entirely from his Black/ Alexander Mountain vineyards: the 1999 Stonestreet Christopher's Caber-net Sauvignon, made from grapes grown at 2,400 feet. (Christopher is one of Jackson's kids, and Stonestreet is Jess's middle name.) Only a thousand cases were produced. The wine was aged in French oak barrels that were 80 percent new, and it sold for eighty dollars a bottle.

It was, as you might guess, a big wine. Like its Verité cousins, it was extraordinarily tannic, a tough, chewy wine that in its youth resembled the Rod Strong Alden 1997 Cabernet. I have now tried it three times over the course of a few years. The third time, when it was exactly five years old, it was still hard. But it had a wonderfully rich and succulent core of blackberry and cassis flavor, with that mocha, plum-sauce spiciness you sometimes find in a great Cabernet. It made me think that it too could become a standard—if the mercurial Jackson continues to produce and refine it.

Lower down on the mountain, Forrest Tancer grows his Cabernet Sauvignon–based wines at his T-bar-T vineyard. In conspicuous contrast to the situation with the Gauer/Jackson grapes, Tancer has had more than twenty years of consistent hands-on experience figuring out his grapes. Although he encountered significant early difficulties, his learning curve is obvious, as shown in the wines' qualitative improvement.

T-bar-T is the perfect perch from which to reconnoiter this southern part of the Alexander Valley. At nearly 1,000 feet, it's high enough to get

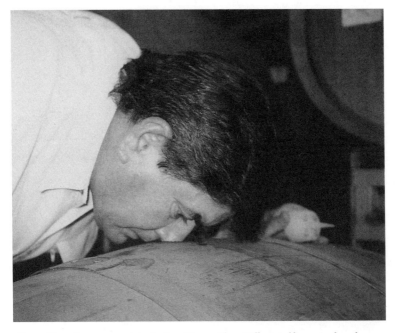

Forrest Tancer's nose at work in the Iron Horse–Green Valley sparkling wine barrel room.

a sense of the topography and to see and feel where the cooling breezes and marine intrusion come in. I visited there one brilliantly sunny October morning with Tancer. It was a day of high fire danger, as it often is at that time of year in the coastal hills of California; the state Department of Forestry had just issued a red flag alert. The infamous Diablos, Northern California's equivalent of Southern California's Santa Ana winds, were sweeping in at forty miles an hour from the northeast. A firefighter who had battled the Oakland Hills firestorm in October 1991 once told me that when the Diablos are howling, the tips of his fingers and his lips feel as rough and dry as sandpaper. I have not experienced that sensation, but the

Diablos do send a shiver along the spine. You can literally feel the hairs on the back of your neck bristle.

Tancer and I drove up near the top of his vineyard. From the edge of a vertiginous cliff, with the dry wind buffeting our backs, the view below was grand and inspiring—well-tended vineyards, their leaves just starting to turn a bright autumn red; trim little farmhouses with white wood-fire smoke curling up from their chimneys to ward off the early morning chill; and, running down the center of the valley, a dark, irregular line of trees and scrub, where the unseen Russian River flowed.

The hills were still the color of dried wheat, like the gold that gave California its nickname of Golden State; in a few weeks, the winter rains would turn the hills emerald green. The harvest was almost over, and there was a peaceful, in-the-barn feeling that, with the approach of the rainy season, another turn of the wheel had been completed.

To the west, across the valley, were the mountains separating the Alexander and Dry Creek valleys. In the southeast, you could see the squat, stolid nose of Mount St. Helena, while to our backs the wall of the Mayacamas rose up another 2,000 feet. Below us was the Robert Young vineyard, and spreading out across the flatlands to the river and beyond to the western hills were the great estates of the south valley: Estancia, Murphy-Goode, Clos du Bois, Alexander Valley Vineyards, Sausal, Simi, Chateau Souverain, Trentadue, Geyser Peak, deLorimier.

But there were no hills to the south, only a broad plain, extending virtually without interruption beyond Healdsburg down past the yawning Petaluma Gap to San Pablo Bay and Bodega Bay. It is from there, and coursing along the Russian River's twisting alleyway, that the fog and cool air sweep in.

I have followed Tancer's progress with Iron Horse Cabernet Sauvignon for many years. At first, he was no more able to figure it out than anyone else. Merely planting in the hills was no magic bullet. The wines were earthy, herbal, and tannic, the kind people used to predict would age, only to discover, to their chagrin, that this wasn't so. I used to wonder whether Tancer was overextending himself between his two properties. Iron Horse's prime efforts seemed to be lined up behind its Green Valley/Russian River Valley sparkling wines, Pinot Noir, and Chardonnay—all three of them glorious successes—and I wondered if he really had invested his heart and mind in T-bar-T.

He had—not only with Cabernet but also with Sangiovese, Sauvignon Blanc, and Viognier, which since the mid-1990s have been brilliant. Iron Horse's '99 T-bar-T Benchmark Cabernet was an extraordinary wine, as was his 2000 T-bar-T Benchmark Blend 1. The glorious 2001, easily one of the best Tancer has ever made, continued the tradition. Somehow, all three achieved the Holy Grail of Black Mountain, combining gentle but complex tannins with lush, rich fruit. But Tancer is the first to admit that, even after all these decades, he's still tinkering with Cabernet. When it comes to running in that particular marathon, "I'm not really ready," he says.

(In the winter of 2003, Tancer announced that he was selling T-bar-T to a wealthy Dallas businesswoman because his children did not wish to enter the wine business. Although Tancer is assured of getting the grapes for a few more years, Iron Horse's future as a Cabernet producer is in doubt. It is sad, after all the effort he has put in, but that's how things go in the wine business.)

I would have pressed Tancer for details of how he managed to control his mountain tannins, but I came across an even better—or perhaps more impressive—Black Mountain Cabernet. Two, in fact: the 1997 and 1999 Robert Young proprietarily named Scions. The Young's '97 Scion was not only the first Cabernet Sauvignon the family ever produced; it was also the first-ever wine under their own label. Quite a spectacular launch—and it took them only 139 years to get around to it.

As good as the 1997 Scion was, the 1999 impressed me even more. Although it was oaky—some critics accused it of being a toothpick—it was ripe and sweetly fruity and, I thought, easily able to stand up to all that new wood. But its prime quality was the luxuriously velvety texture, fat and plump as butter. It was a Marilyn Monroe of a wine, and I enjoyed it almost as much as any Napa Valley cult Cabernet I had from that vintage, and a great deal more than many—not to mention that, at fifty dollars, it was a lot cheaper. A wine like that forever shattered the myth of thin, featureless, herbal Alexander Valley Cabernet, while also demonstrating that mountain tannins can be controlled. And it's not just the Cabernet. Robert Young doesn't make a Merlot, but Murphy-Goode's 1999 Reserve, made from Robert Young grapes, was one of the best Merlots of the vintage. The 2000, sampled just as I finished editing this book, blew my mind.

I was determined to get to the bottom of what made that Scion wine so good. It raised the prospect—unthinkable just a few years ago, and controversial even today—of Alexander Valley Cabernet, in the best instances, rising to the level of Napa Valley's.

It's not necessary to detail the process that led the Young family to decide, in the mid-1990s, to become a winery rather than remaining growers, except to say that they got tired of seeing other people get famous off their grapes. Robert Young's Cabernet and Merlot are planted in the hills—the Chardonnay, Pinot Blanc, Riesling, Sauvignon Blanc, Viognier, and Melon are on the flats—although the Youngs' "hills," being lower than either Jackson's or T-bar-T's, are not quite as steep or rugged as those two areas.

Like so many others before and since, the Youngs had turned for crop advice in the early 1960s to the University of California's local county farm advisor, who suggested that they plant grapes wherever they had bare land. "They took a huge risk," recalls Steve Domenichelli, considering that, back then, there was no guarantee that any winery would buy grapes from the Alexander Valley.

Planting the reds in the hills was, as we saw in chapter 3, an act of serendipity. "But as it turned out," Young says, with considerable understatement, "we did a lot better with the grapes than with the prunes."

The Youngs have analyzed every square inch of their soils with the scientific precision of DNA experts mapping the human genome. Jim Young, the family's vineyardist, showed me a computer-generated colored map breaking down the estate's lands, and you could clearly see just where the flats ended and the hills started: at Red Winery Road. On its south side, the valley floor rolls flat as a carpet down to the Russian River. Across the street, the hills rise suddenly and inexorably. On the map, this was where the turquoise and yellow patches turned to hot pink, purple, and brown; it was also where the white grapes stopped and the reds started. The upland soils, as you would expect, are shallower, drier, more volcanic, and, in places, rockier; and they are tougher places to grow grapes. "To make the high-quality reds," Jim Young observed, "you need to stress those vines."

The best Cabernet comes from the soils colored hot pink on the map. They are of a form called Spreckels loam and are classic terrace and mountainous upland soils, well drained and with a clay subsoil underlain, at a depth of 22 to 60 inches, by uplifted river sediment and weathered, igneous rock. Young attributes the wine's quality to "the way the soil drains up there. It's a lighter soil and tends to slow the vines down, so they don't get overly vigorous."

Jim Young is one of the best vineyardists in Sonoma County, maybe one of the best anywhere, and he knows how to extract the most from his property, by adapting his spacing, trellising, irrigating, and pruning techniques almost down to the individual grapevine. Robert Young was the first in Alexander Valley to grow trellised vines—that was his Chardonnay—and also the first to put in vertically trellised Cabernet, which many vineyardists believe is the perfect way to grow it in California. Each grape gets the right amount of sunlight and shade during the growing season and is open enough to allow a swirl of refreshing air to circulate around it.

Nor is Jim Young afraid to drop fruit. In a way that would have shocked Frank Pastori's father, Jim prunes the vines that produce Scion down to a single bunch per shoot, a miserly quantity that is half that of most premium grapevines in California.

But I wanted to know more about why that Scion was so good, and so I pressed Young on the subject. "There's too many little things involved for me to speculate on what's causing that," he replied. "Dick Arrowood made it. Why don't you ask him?"

I put that in my back pocket. A few months later, when I was tasting with Ted Seghesio, who blends his own Cabernet Sauvignon with Sangiovese to make his very good super-Tuscan-style Omaggio wine, I asked him why Scion was so good.

"I haven't had it," he responded, good-naturedly. "But, hey, they have Dick Arrowood at the helm."

I figured, hey, I'd better ask the talented Mr. Arrowood what was up.

Richard Arrowood is one of the best and most famous winemakers in California. An outspoken conservative ("to the right of Attila the Hun," in his own slightly self-mocking words), he counts among his heroes and good friends the Gulf War commander General "Stormin'" Norman Schwarzkopf, with whom he shoots skeet and, presumably, shares politics. (But after a long talk we had while tasting through four vintages of Scion, I ended up telling Arrowood that he is not nearly as conservative as he likes to think he is.)

He may be famous, but he recognizes the ephemeral nature of this status and modestly dismisses it. "You're only as good as your last wine," he says. Far more important to him than mere worldly fame is the respect he has earned from his winemaker peers as a master of his art and craft. He is the man who put Chateau St. Jean on the map in the 1970s with a series of brilliantly crafted single-vineyard Chardonnays (including one from Robert Young, which also put the Youngs on the map). In 1990, he began his own eponymous Sonoma Valley winery, Arrowood, which leapfrogged over the competition to the forefront of wine making. (He sold it to Robert Mondavi a few years ago, but he still runs the place and makes the wine.) More to the point for the purposes of this tale, Arrowood is the consulting winemaker to whom the Youngs turned in the mid-1990s, when they decided to start their own label, beginning with a Cabernet Sauvignon.

I asked Arrowood what marching orders the Youngs had given him concerning Scion.

"They said they wanted to make the best Alexander Valley Cabernet they could, something worth the money, and that people would talk about."

Well, of course, they wanted buzz; to aim for anything less would have been pointless. But when it came to his role in Scion's success, Arrowood demurred to the point of shyness, insisting that the quality of Scion is almost solely a result of the Youngs' viticultural prowess.

"People say what great things I did at Robert Young. Well, I had a lot of nice fruit to work with! It wasn't as if I pulled a rabbit out of a hat."

Once the grapes are in, a winemaker can turn to certain tricks in the winery to minimize harsh and astringent tannins, or at least to de-emphasize

Dick Arrowood pausing during a busy harvest day.

the palate's perception of them. The fermenting must can be pumped over the grapes fewer times each day, which reduces the extraction of tannins from skins and seeds, although this technique can also reduce the fruity concentration. Likewise, the bubbling wine can be run off the grape skins before fermentation is entirely finished, since alcohol leaches additional tannins from the skins. But this practice also runs the risk of minimizing color and decreasing fruity extraction.

Conversely—it depends on the situation—a winemaker can extend the maceration period past its normal duration. It's counterintuitive, but this technique chemically alters the structure of the tannins, making them join into longer chains of molecules, which feel softer in the mouth than short ones. (Care is needed here, however, for extended maceration can decrease a wine's fruitiness.) This process of extended maceration has become very popular in California for Cabernet Sauvignon. I remember once seeing side-by-side electron microphotographs of an old-style "short"-maceration tannin molecule and a new extended-maceration one. The former looked like a cartoon lightning bolt, jagged and angular. The latter was as gently rounded as an amoeba. The palate feels the textural difference.

Deacidification techniques can also make tannins less apparent to the palate. Acids make tannins stick out like a sore thumb; reduce the acids, and even if the tannins remain unchanged, the wine feels rounder. Even a little residual sugar has sometimes been left in a red wine in order to make it feel softer and smoother. There is nothing wrong with any of these techniques, "but by and large," Arrowood says, "I don't do those things" with Scion. "When Mother Nature gives you grapes that good, all you can do is not stub your toe and screw up."

Arrowood credits the Youngs' willingness to limit yields as the basic reason why Scion is so good. "As a winemaker, they gave me all the colors, all the brushes, so all I had to do was apply my talent," he argues.

Yet Arrowood concedes that there's more to Scion than simply limiting the yield to a single bunch per shoot. Something about the terroir makes the wine so rich and balanced. Not even he can define it, despite the Youngs' exquisitely detailed soil samples. Arrowood is not a mystic; he's too determinedly realistic for that. You get the feeling he is not entirely comfortable with a fancy word like "terroir." But when he refers to "Mother Nature," it's the same thing.

"You're almost saying," I observed, "that you are irrelevant to the process."

He poured us another glass of Scion, grinned, and said, "I'll have to be more careful before I talk myself out of a job!"

TASTING THE 1997, 1998, 1999,
AND 2000 ROBERT YOUNG SCIONS

One day in 2003, Arrowood and I set out to taste the 1997, 1998, 1999, and 2000 Robert Young Scions. Arrowood himself had not tasted the four Scions he'd made for Robert Young for several years. (He left the Youngs after the 2000 vintage.) He is an easy and affable tasting partner, not one who feels he has to hammer away at his ideas or implant thoughts in someone else's head. At the same time, he is a good listener.

And so we began.

The 1997 wine didn't impress me at first. It did not seem as exuberant as it had three years earlier, in 2000. Some good Cabernets, after they've been in the bottle for a couple of years, enter into a brooding middle period in which they seem dull and uninspired (Chateau Montelena's winemaker, Bo Barrett, calls this "the blind spot"), only to reemerge at seven years or so better than ever. It's as if they'd crawled, as caterpillars, into cocoons and reemerged as butterflies. On this occasion, at six years of age, the '97 was closed, with little going on in the aroma, not particularly concentrated or intense.

But twenty minutes later, when we returned to the '97, it had developed considerably in the glass, as a wine often does under the steady assault of oxygen. (This is why it's a good idea to decant a young red wine.) Sometimes a wine needs to breathe a little. Like an athlete who must warm up before the big event, it's not at its best until it has limbered up the muscles and gotten the blood flowing, the heart pumping.

A delicate bouquet of dried autumn leaves had developed, mingled with a wood-forest scent and the sweet perfume of wild blackberries and cherries. It was heady stuff. Arrowood and I both found a floral smell and decided that it was violets. It was a fine wine, delicate as a pressed flower, with a shimmering, pastel quality.

I made no initial comment on the '98, because I went directly from the '97 to the celebrated '99, and, after those two monuments, the '98 seemed like a lightweight.

Arrowood sensed my reticence and knew the reason for it. The vintage had been suspect from the start, hammered by the wine press since the first releases had come out. He sniffed, frowned, and put his glass back down on the table.

"We had to do a lot of work with the Youngs that year to really pull crop, and we declassified a lot," he explained. Declassification is when a winery refuses to release wine under its primary label because it's not up to snuff. It will sell off the product as bulk grapes or wine to another winery or broker or put it out as a secondary brand, at a lower price. Either way, the winery takes an economic hit but preserves something far more valuable than temporary profits: its reputation.

The Youngs and Arrowood, however, eventually decided to release a small amount of 1998 Scion. "We took the best of the best from a very tough vintage," he said, "and I think it turned out successful, all things considered, because '98 was such a sonofabitch to deal with." The operative words being "all things considered." It was like saying that a hobbled runner, competing in a foot race, at the very least deserves credit for trying.

Twenty minutes later, though, that maligned '98 had also benefited from the air. It remained on the light side and was not what the French call a *vin de garde;* rather, it was a wine to drink young, while the bigger wines age.

Arrowood sniffed, tasted, and broke out into a broad grin. "This is what I'm always saying. When we wrote this damned vintage off—and a lot of people are writing the 2000 off, too—I think they're making a mistake, because there are some nice wines!"

From the get-go, the '99 vintage was heralded. The spring and summer that year had been so cold that the vines were far behind their normal growing schedule. The Cabernet was still weeks away from being picked when, in the third week of September, the remnants of Hurricane Hilary drifted up from west of Baja—just when you don't want rain. Precipitation was heavy throughout the state, especially in the south, but by September 24, Hilary was gone, the sun came out again, and Californians exulted in one of the most glorious Indian summers in memory. (It was very similar to 1978, a vintage Bob Thompson once described with a neat phrase: "Dancing in the cellars over this one.") The '99 Cabs are still dribbling out, one by one, and drinking them over the last several years has been an almost unalloyed joy.

I recalled the '99 Scion as being soft and mellow—"so good it makes you want to shout," I had previously noted, in a hyperbolic burst of enthusiasm. But on this occasion, its youthful tannins leapt out much more forcefully than before, which only emphasizes how the same wine will vary at different times and under different circumstances. As Arrowood and I ate lunch, though, the wine got better and better. By the time we were finished, it was as lush and intricate as ever, although it was a wine that demanded big, rich food.

It's one thing to form a judgment about a wine based on a single taste. It's quite another to return to it over and over, for a second, a third, a fourth sip—which, unfortunately, wine critics rarely have the chance to do. It's the trade's dirty little secret: so many wines, so little time. I would love (I thought to myself) to directly compare this '99 Scion to a really good Napa Valley Cabernet. Little did I know that, barely two months later, I would have exactly that opportunity.

After the heights of the '97 and '99, it was anticlimactic to deal with the 2000 Scion. "It's a nice wine," I said to my host, "but kind of, well, *dumb.*" This term has been in use for centuries to describe a young wine, usually red, that is not smelling or tasting particularly good at the moment, because its properties are shrouded under youthful tannins and acids. The implication is that a dumb wine will smarten up someday. It doesn't always happen.

Arrowood demurred. "Well, it's only been in the bottle for a month, so it's all beat up." The concept of "bottle shock" is widespread; vintners mean to imply that something akin to jet lag hits a wine after it's been manhandled on the bottling line and continues to adversely affect it until it sufficiently recovers. (For this reason, Bob Cabral, at Williams Selyem, urges people not to drink his new wines for at least two months after purchase.)

"Give it some time," Arrowood said. "I think it could eventually eclipse the '99." I didn't think it would, but asking winemakers to decide between their wines is like asking parents which of their children they prefer, an awkward question.

After lunch, I complimented Arrowood on his Scions—this was after a rather heated debate on George W. Bush, the religious right, and the war in Iraq—and he said, "The Youngs may be getting the best of both worlds with this wine: the softness and suppleness that Alexander Valley's always been known for, but at the same time more tannic concentration and flavor by reducing crop load."

Then I asked whether he thought Alexander Valley Cabernet Sauvignon would ever possess the cachet of Napa Valley.

"It's going in the right direction, for sure. I think you'll see them coming of age more and more. A lot of these comparative tastings are—"

He interrupted himself. "Say, did you hear about this *Santa Rosa Press Democrat* tasting?" He was referring to the local newspaper. "They did a ten-year retrospective—I just found out, the reporter called me—of the '93 Cabernets. Arrowood took first place."

Dick Arrowood is not the sort to bask in self-anointed glory. But there was no hiding the gleam of pride in his eyes.

It turned out that in a blind tasting of 1993 Cabernet Sauvignons conducted by the newspaper with some pretty good tasters, Arrowood's had beat out a clutch of superstar Napans: Shafer Hillside Select, Phelps Insignia, Dunn Howell Mountain, Beringer Private Reserve, Heitz Trailside Vineyard, Freemark Abbey Bosché, and other stellar luminaries. One of the tasters had made the intriguing observation that "the Mayacamas are an accident of politics," meaning, I think, that wines made on one side of the mountain or the other are not necessarily all that different.

These sorts of tasting "shootouts" have now become so commonplace, with one held nearly every week someplace, that I'm not sure they have the value they once did. The granddaddy of them all, the famous "Judgment of Paris" tasting of 1976, when Napa Valley wines topped the best of the French, really stirred things up and had lasting impact. But with each new shootout, the novelty began to wear off. Yet they have their place, if for no other reason than that they slowly, slowly (water on rock) chip away at stereotypes.

Alexander Valley Cabernet Sauvignon got a shot in the arm in 2001, when Franciscan Estates, the Napa Valley winery now owned by Constellation Brands, a New York company, held a "Battle of the AVAs." They invited dozens of members of the Court of Master Sommeliers—among the royalty of the winetasting world—to a blind tasting of Cabernet Sauvignons from Alexander Valley and Napa Valley. The master sommeliers were to rank-order the wines and try to identify each wine's origin.

The Alexander Valley wines were the pick of the litter: Simi Reserve, Jordan, Stonestreet, Iron Horse, Lancaster Estate, and a few others, although not Scion. The Napa Valley entries weren't too shabby either: Franciscan Magnificat, Quintessa, Phelps Insignia, Merryvale Profile, Silver Oak, Mount Veeder.

The upshot was that these expert palates could not tell, on any consistent basis, where the wines came from. As for the tasters' top-ranked wine, it turned out, by a show of hands, to be an Iron Horse T-bar-T Cabernet Sauvignon. David Fischer, Jordan's director of sales and marketing, who was there, later told me how reticent the master sommeliers had been when the moderator asked them to stand, one by one, and identify each wine's origin. "You couldn't get them to venture an opinion," Fischer said, "because they didn't want to look bad in front of their peers."

Who does? During my talk with Tom Jordan, the subject of these shootouts had come up. I'd told him that I'd tasted through enough great Alexander Valley Cabernet to make me wonder about the truism that Napa Cabernets were better, and would always be better. I speculated that it might be a self-fulfilling proposition: we expect a Napa Cabernet to be better, and that is what we find.

"Well, you're right to challenge the proposition technically," Jordan ruminated, stroking his chin, "and that makes one wonder, are we conditioned to believe these wines are feminine, and these are masculine?"

I was about to venture my own opinion when he thumped his fist down on the table and rumbled, "And the only answer to that is, I'm going to ask [Jordan winemaker] Rob Davis to set up an eight-bottle blind tasting, four Alexander and four over the hill," over the hill being Napa Valley. (It never ceases to amaze me how loath Sonomans can be to even utter Napa's name. Along the same lines, Mendocino residents refer dismissively to the two counties to their south as "Sonapanoma.")

I knew I wanted Scion to be included, and I asked Jordan whether he'd ever tasted it. He hadn't but said he would make sure Davis got a bottle.

HIGH NOON AT JORDAN:
ALEXANDER VERSUS NAPA

I drove up for the tasting in early August. At that point of the peculiar 2003 vintage, no one quite knew where it was headed. January and February had been so warm and dry that the vines had begun one of their earliest budbreaks in living memory. Then the rains came, and they lasted, on and off but mostly on, for months. It got so bad that growers wondered whether there would be any crop at all. When the rains finally stopped, in mid-May, the heat came on with a vengeance: day after day, week after week of relentless, brutal, pounding sun, punctuated here and there by cold snaps. With August, an almost unheard-of spell of monsoonal moisture and humidity wafted into Northern California, raising the dreaded prospect of rot. First came the remnants of a Gulf of Mexico hurricane, then a tropical storm that wandered off course and made its way up the Central Valley, then yet another hurricane. People murmured about global warming and climate change. The unnatural weather brought rain and humidity to a state unused to either in high summer. Winemakers, faced with Mother Nature's curveballs, could only scratch their heads and wonder what on earth was going on.

At Healdsburg on the day of the tasting, one of those tropical systems had blown in. The air was weirdly damp; under cloudy skies, the plaza was thronged with Hispanic men, laborers waiting to be picked up for a day's work. They scanned the face of each passerby with an eagerness so expectant that I averted my eyes, having nothing to offer.

At the Jordan chateau, the trees, hedges, fountains, and gravel lanes were as beautiful as ever, and all the flowers were in cheerful bloom in their beds. The tasting was held in an elegant little wood-paneled room on the second floor, past well-appointed offices where accountants and secretaries labored. We had expected Tom Jordan to attend, but he canceled at the last minute. That left Rob Davis, me, and David Fischer, who, in addition to being Jordan's sales and marketing director, also had once been a sommelier at a Ritz-Carlton hotel back east and prided himself on his palate.

Fischer had rounded up the wines, all 1999s: Jordan, Simi Reserve, Silver Oak (a Napa winery that bottles a highly regarded Alexander Valley Cabernet Sauvignon), and Robert Young Scion from the Alexander Valley; and Phelps Insignia, Chateau Montelena, Quintessa, and Far Niente from Napa. All of the wines, in other words, represented the highest quality of their respective appellations. I had brought along two additional wines: Alexander Valley Vineyards Cyrus and Stonestreet Christopher's Cabernet Sauvignon, also both from 1999. Of all the wines, the Jordan, at forty-five dollars, was the least expensive; Montelena, at one hundred twenty-five dollars, and Quintessa, at one hundred dollars, were the most expensive.

The wines were opened and brown-bagged by Davis's staff so that none

Rob Davis and assistant setting up for the Battle of the AVAs at Jordan.

of us knew which was which. We tasted through them all, sniffing and slurp-
ing with the usual guttural sounds, mumbling to ourselves, and making
notes. When we were finished, we stated, in turn, which appellation we
thought each wine was from, and why. After each round, Fischer withdrew
the bottle from its papery shroud, revealing its identity—there should have
been a drumroll and fanfare.

All three of us agreed on a few wines. One was wine "B." Both Davis
and Fischer instantly, and correctly, recognized it not only as Alexander
Valley but as Jordan. After twenty-seven consecutive vintages, Davis, of
course, might have been expected to recognize his own creation (although
I've been to blind tastings where winemakers couldn't), and so, perhaps,
might Fischer. I did not know that it was Jordan, but I did know that it
was an Alexander Valley wine: herbal and soft, with a cigarette ash and
cherry smell. A cheer went up around the table when Fischer unveiled it.

"We keep our day jobs!" he cracked.

We also all nailed the Cyrus as Alexander Valley because of its softness. Davis and Fischer thought it was too oaky, which, on this occasion,
it did seem to be, although it was still a lovely wine. In the end, I got only
five of the ten origins correct—fewer, as Fischer pointed out, than if I'd
simply guessed them all as Alexander Valley. Fischer himself correctly identified six. Davis identified nine of the wines, although he admitted that
he'd had to guess about several.

The result was troubling, and not just because I did so poorly. I'd been
hoping and half-expecting that no one would be able to distinguish the
two appellations. That would have been a neat, tidy ending to the Alexander Valley versus Napa Valley tale. Case closed; verdict reached.

But this ending was messy. Fischer and I, with our essentially random
results, had seemingly proved the case that the differences between the wines
were so negligible that most people, including industry professionals, could

not consistently tell them apart, except in those increasingly isolated cases, such as Jordan, where the wines were dead giveaways. But then came Davis to throw a monkey wrench into the process. I asked him how he had managed to get a .900 batting average.

"It's still the tannins," he said. He could tell Napa because the tannins were richer, thicker, sweeter, riper, more ageworthy.

Still the tannins? Was that proof that the old paradigm remained true?

Davis frowned. "No. I don't think the paradigm of early drinkability and softness in Alexander Valley is useful anymore," he replied, carefully choosing his words.

But if it wasn't, then how to account for his success in the tasting? "I can't get you to say it," I said, "but it sounds like you're saying the paradigm lives."

"Well," he replied, "I would say the gap is very, very tiny."

Fair enough. "Is it continuing to narrow," I asked, "or are we down to some irreducible terroir factor that will never go away?"

"No, I think it's continuing to narrow."

"So a few years from now, if we do this with the 2001 vintage, will you still be able to get nine out of ten?"

He laughed. "If I did this same tasting again tomorrow, I might not get five out of ten! I was just a little more fortunate in my guessing."

(In the summer of 2004, I was on a panel at the Society of Wine Educators' annual meeting, where we had a similar blind tasting of Alexander Valley and Napa Valley Cabernets and blends. Once again, these professionals were evenly divided on which was which.)

The Jordan tasting may not have ended according to the tidy little plot outline I had scripted in my head, but the result seemed to point in an obvious direction. A couple of professional amateurs, Fischer and I (not to mention the two dozen master sommeliers at the Battle of the AVAs shootout), had been unable to consistently distinguish Alexander Valley Cabernet from Napa Valley Cabernet without seeing the labels. True, Rob Davis had been able to do so—but that was either because his palate, in contrast to that of 99 percent of ordinary mortals, is exquisitely sensitive or because he had been lucky.

I remembered that Davis had been mentored by André Tchelistcheff, and I asked him what the Maestro would have made of the tasting.

"I think he would have said"—and here Davis imitated Tchelistcheff's throaty Russian accent—"'Drink both wines!'"

On the long drive home down Highway 101, I had a lot of time to mull things over. I recalled something Steve Domenichelli had said. "Napa's farming style is about eight years ahead of us. They're very hip and into quality. They know how to tweak things to make the best they can."

Alexander Valley is getting hip, too, I thought, as traffic ground to a halt at downtown Santa Rosa. The old farming mentality Domenichelli hated is evaporating faster than fog on a summer morning, and the valley's winemakers are starting to tweak things right along with their friends "over the hill." Suddenly, I had a vision of Frank Pastori, grudgingly tending his new-fangled Cabernet vines up at Asti, and I just had to smile.

5

Healdsburg

The Crucial Turn West

One day in Sonoma County, a few hundred thousand years ago, it began to rain. The sky darkened, the clouds thickened, and the first drops pelted the ground, staining the soil. Then it poured.

It was a good-sized storm, not necessarily a century event, but it might have dumped three or four inches of rain before it blew eastward into the Central Valley. Its after-effects, however, were extraordinary. For that storm, according to one theory, triggered a mudslide that changed the course of the Russian River, blocking it off from the southerly course it had followed to San Pablo Bay for millennia and sending it careening westward, to the Pacific.

It would have been a signal event in Sonoma's geologic timetable. But we might never have suspected such an occurrence had it not been for a series of fortuitous discoveries made by an earth scientist—discoveries that piqued her curiosity and led her to investigate their cause.

Deborah L. Elliott-Fisk is a professor in the University of California at Davis's Department of Wildlife, Fish, and Conservation Biology. She earned her PhD in 1979 at the University of Colorado at Boulder's Institute of Arctic and Alpine Research, and she continued her interest in mountain geology at Davis. Along those lines, she has worked to understand glaciation in the Sierra Nevada, shoreline development at Mono Lake, and the ecosystem of the giant sequoias of the east slope of the Sierra.

*Debbie Elliott-Fisk inspects a trench in wine country
(photo courtesy of Deborah Elliott-Fisk).*

But what Elliott-Fisk's official curriculum vitae does not show is her abiding passion for investigating the link between wine and the earth. A self-described "viticultural geographer," in the mid-1980s she consulted for the group of Napa Valley vintners, including Tim Mondavi and Warren Winiarski, who were drawing up their application to the BATF for approval of the Stags Leap District AVA. Word of Elliott-Fisk's work filtered over to Sonoma County, where she was invited by Zelma Long, then Simi's winemaker, to investigate the soils and structure of a hilly vineyard Simi was developing in the southern Alexander Valley, the one now called Landslide.

Elliott-Fisk was not looking to explain why the Russian River turns so abruptly at Healdsburg. Early in the twentieth century, a geologist had postulated that the river had always flowed west from there, since its beginning. Later, conventional theory argued that the river might have flowed south through Sonoma into San Pablo Bay at one time, but that tectonic uplifting had created a highland that warped and tilted to the west, sending the river seaward instead of bayward.

But what Elliott-Fisk found suggested otherwise and also yielded tantalizing clues that the Russian River might once have flowed not south through Santa Rosa and past Petaluma but through Napa Valley.

As part of her work, Elliott-Fisk was doing research in Knights Valley, the AVA in east-central Sonoma that forms a bridge through the Mayacamas to Napa Valley around Mount St. Helena. She was digging trenches on benchlands 1,500 feet above sea level when she found huge amounts of what she describes as "rounded river pebbles and rocks." They were smooth and polished and could have been formed and deposited only by the tumbling action of a great river. But there is no river 1,500 feet up in the mountains of Knights Valley.

(Dan Roberts told me that he, too, in his own research in the Knights Valley highlands, had found "hundred-pound rocks that are totally round that couldn't have been moved by that little stream that goes through there. They had to have been moved by something big." But Dr. Dirt did not pursue that particular line of inquiry.)

Elliott-Fisk previously had discovered exactly the same kind of rocks and pebbles in the Mayacamas foothills of Napa Valley, and even down in Calistoga. She now deduced that whatever river had formed and deposited them there must also have been the one that brought them up into Knights Valley. Aside from the numerous little creeks, some of which dry up completely during summer, there were only two possible suspects in the neighborhood, the Napa River and the Russian River. But which was the culprit?

Elliott-Fisk worked by process of elimination. "The Napa River just isn't big enough," she reasoned. It's too small and too short and was never powerful enough to have created, let alone carried and deposited, hundred-pound boulders and vast mounds of river gravel and stone. But the Russian River is a different beast. It is one of the great gravel-makers of California, fueling a mining industry that continues, controversially, to this day. So, Elliott-Fisk deduced, the Russian River not only must have flowed up into Knights Valley at one time; it must also have tumbled across the Mayacamas into Napa Valley.

Well and good. Back at Simi's vineyard, another clue came to light. Elliott-Fisk was in the vineyard's highest part, Nick Goldschmidt's Uplands, investigating the soil profiles. When she dug her trenches, she discovered a melange of ash, cinders, igneous bombs, and other volcanic debris, tossed together into a geologic stew, lathered in an ancient hardened muck that was peppered with—surprise!—rounded river stones. All of this stuff "was obviously associated with a volcanic eruption and mudflow," she concluded.

The eruption would have been an episode of the Sonoma Volcanics, although where precisely it occurred is anyone's guess. Wherever it was, the volcanic debris it unleashed settled into loose, unconsolidated piles on the tops and along the slopes of nearby hills, including Simi's.

Then came that rainstorm. The word scientists use for what happened next is "mobilize," which means "to put into motion." The martial connotation is perfect, for it suggests the violence of the subsequent catastrophe.

"The rainstorm event mobilized the volcanic debris," Elliott-Fisk theorizes. "In my hypothesis, a mudflow washed most of it downhill, forming a plug and damming the Russian River." Under the circumstances, the river, now blocked in the south, was forced to find another outlet, and west is where it went. The eruption and the storm, Elliott-Fisk guesses, occurred within "a couple weeks" of each other.

Following Elliott-Fisk's discovery, the Simi people named their hilly vineyard Landslide.

It may have occurred to the reader to wonder why Napa Valley does not have huge deposits of gravel, the way the Alexander and Russian River valleys do. It certainly occurred to me, and I asked Elliott-Fisk about it.

"Good question!" she replied. "Napa does have gravel, but it's buried." It turns out that there is a great deal of gravel on the Napa Valley floor, but it's been covered up by tens of feet of silt and mud deposited by repeated flooding of the Napa River or by dirt washed down in alluvial fans from the side canyons of the Mayacamas and Vaca ranges. Once the Russian River abandoned Napa Valley, there was nothing to continue bringing gravel there.

It's only fair to point out that not all geologists subscribe to Elliott-Fisk's theory. Terry Wright, for one, points out a possible problem concerning timelines. If, as I postulated based on evidence, the Russian River is less than 1 million years old, and if the final Sonoma Volcanics activity occurred about 2.4 million years ago, as seems to be the consensus opinion among geologists, then an episode of the Sonoma Volcanics could not be associated with altering the river's course.

Elliott-Fisk herself, when presented with Wright's objection, commented, "I believe that parts of the Russian River are older, probably much older, than 1 million years . . . perhaps as old as 20 million years." She added, "I also believe that . . . the Sonoma Volcanics include some activity as young as 1.2 to 1.5 million years." When I reported this to Terry Wright, he again turned to his USGS friend André Sarna-Wojcicki and then relayed the latter's view to me: "[André] says there's no hard evidence that he knows of . . . for this idea; the youngest age of Sonoma Volcanics is 2.4 million years ago." It remains, therefore, for a future generation of geologists to uncover the truth.

At any rate, the Russian River turned west. It did not hurt, as Terry points out, that the bedrock it encountered on its new course through the Russian River Valley was Wilson Grove stuff—soft, weak sandstone that had been formed underwater and through which moving water could slice with the ease of a hot knife through butter. "If that rock had been hard," Elliott-Fisk asks, "who knows where the river would have gone?"

No one can know for sure. But it is conceivable that a sprawling body of water might have filled the lowlands of what we now call the Russian River Valley. Instead of a valley, we might have had a Russian Lake, its shores studded with multimillion-dollar estates.

The river at Healdsburg does not make a clean turn west. Instead, it meanders, backbending and looping around itself in a tortured series of snaking twists and U-turns. It seems a rather indecisive waterway, resting a toe here, testing the ground there, unable to make up its mind which way it wants to go—much like the viticulture in this part of wine country.

The river makes a brief westerly sprint at the Chalk Hill–Alexander Valley AVA line, veers sharply to the northwest, and shifts west again below Seghesio's San Lorenzo Vineyard. Then, suddenly, it takes a hairpin turn to the southeast, loops clockwise around the massif of Fitch Mountain, and flows southwest to Healdsburg. Turning south, it tumbles past the J Wine Company and Rodney Strong and grandly down along the Middle Reach to Davis Bynum. Only there does it finally head west, in a more or less straightforward way.

I call this westward turn at Healdsburg "crucial," a word that has its origins in the Latin term for "cross," because it opens up the Russian River Valley to the winds and fog that arrive from the ocean, enabling the valley to be "Burgundian" in the wine sense. The term also seems appropriate because the turn occurs at the crux of four appellations: Dry Creek Valley, Russian River Valley, Alexander Valley, and Chalk Hill.

"Crucial" was my word, so when I heard Oded Shakked refer to the same region as the "crucible"—another old word associated in folk etymology with the cross, but which also has connotations of a melting furnace—my ears perked up. Oded is the winemaker at J Wine Company, a winery owned by Tom Jordan's daughter, Judy. Located at the junction of Eastside Road and the Old Redwood Highway, on the southern outskirts of Healdsburg, J is smack dab in the middle of the crucible.

I had first learned of Oded's existence not through the wines of J (although I knew and liked them), but through his own small brand, Longboard. I often stop in at the Wine Shop, right on the square in the center of Healdsburg, next to the Hotel Healdsburg. The owners always have some new local wines, and sometimes, if it's not too busy, whoever's working there will open a bottle or two and let me taste. That's how I stumbled

Oded Shakked, happy with his new Syrah vineyard on Westside Road.

across Oded's Longboard-brand Syrah and Cabernet Sauvignon, the latter with a Rochioli Vineyard designation on the front label. The Syrah alone
gave me plenty of reason to look up the winemaker, but noticing that he
was obtaining grapes from one of the most famous names in all the Russian River Valley further fueled my curiosity.

I called J and scheduled an appointment. On a fine autumn day, I drove
up to the modernish, art-filled winery, which shares a parking lot with Rodney Strong. Oded turned out to be a short, bald, bullet-headed, barrel-
chested Israeli American, with thick biceps and forearms and mallet-shaped
hands whose spatulate fingers looked like they could yank the cork out of
a bottle of wine. He had a big grin and laughed easily, and I immediately
liked him.

Most winemakers have interesting stories concerning how they arrived
at their professions, but Oded's is one for the books. This book, anyway.
The young-looking vintner was born forty-four years ago (as I write this)
in Israel. His father, a pilot in the Israeli air force, died in a tragic flying
accident before Oded was born. His mother remarried, and his stepfather
was a diplomat, so Oded grew up in a multilingual household with international influences. He did his own military service during Israel's 1982–
1984 war with Lebanon. It is an era he does not like to talk about, because
it was Israel's Vietnam, the first time the country's citizens, including its
soldiers, were split on a war, and the memories are still painful.

More to the point, Oded was a surfer. If you buy a bottle of his Longboard wine, you will find on the back label such pidgin Hawaiian surfing
terms as "howzit" (how's it going?), "sponger" (beginner), and "grom"
(young surfer). After he got out of the army, he got a job with a surf-
board company, being careful to work for only nine months of the year
so that he and his friends could spend their summers surfing the Euro-

pean beaches. "We'd start in Biarritz, then work our way down through Spain and Portugal," Oded says. "I was living the dream, which is still what I try to do."

Part of living the dream was a side trip to Pomerol to visit a friend. Wine snuck into Oded's life on little cork-padded feet; one thing led to another, and his interest blossomed. He was twenty-three, with ambitions of being an architect. "But then I thought: No. I never, even as a kid, wanted to end up at 'a job.'"

Wine, on the other hand, seemed . . . romantic. It was not "a job." Oded speaks of "the feel, on a gut level," that a young man or woman with utterly no background in wine may nonetheless develop for the juice of the grape. He got his hands on a book, Amerine and Singleton's *Wine: An Introduction for Americans*, which had been published by the University of California Press in 1965. He used it to instruct himself about grape varietals, the science of fermentation, winemaking, wine appreciation, and the Department of Viticulture and Enology at the U.C. Davis campus.

He went over to the American Embassy in Tel Aviv and managed to obtain the department's course catalog. He applied to the program and was accepted, the first Israeli in the department's history. (I asked Oded why he hadn't applied to a European school. "The surfing thing! California! What, was I going to surf in Geisenheim?" he asked incredulously, shrugging his shoulders with the irony of a standup comedian.) "I just had this feeling of destiny. There was no looking back." The night before he flew to California, he sat on a hilltop overlooking the Mediterranean and drank a bottle of wine.

Once at Davis, he worked the harvest at Domaine Chandon in Napa Valley and learned about sparkling wine. He also worked for a summer at Chateau Lafite and learned about Cabernet Sauvignon. He bought Pinot

Noir grapes from Robert Young (before the Youngs tore out the vines as unsuitable for the Alexander Valley) and made a wine, a few bottles of which are still in his cellar. He was learning.

Graduation day came in 1988. He needed a job. He opened a directory that listed all the wineries in California, closed his eyes, and randomly pointed his finger at one. It was Jordan. "So I sent my resume to them," Oded says. Two days later, Rob Davis called him in for an interview. Three days later, he was hired.

Oded became Jordan's assistant winemaker. He was thrilled to work under Rob Davis. "People would walk on fire for him," Oded recalls. "I knew he was someone I could learn from." Tchelistcheff was there "all the time." The young Israeli winemaker was watching, listening, absorbing . . . dreaming.

During this time, Judy Jordan was building up J, with her father's assistance. The aim was to make it a great sparkling wine house. Oded knew from bubbly. In 1990, he was shifted from Jordan to J, where he was appointed chief winemaker. Eight years later, he started Longboard—the word refers to the 1950s-era surfboards he collects and restores. At this writing, he is in his sixteenth harvest at J.

Why does Oded call the area around Healdsburg the "crucible"? "Because it's the melting pot of four AVAs, and Healdsburg is sitting smack in the belly button of them all," he says.

RHÔNES IN THE CRUCIBLE

The Alexander Valley may be Bordeaux, the Russian River Valley (as we'll see), Burgundy; the problem in trying to understand the crucible from a viticultural point of view is that anything and everything grows there. "It's neither fish nor fowl, sort of a mix-and-match. No-man's-land," says Forrest Tancer, straining for metaphors.

The difficulty in defining the area is compounded because it lacks its own AVA, a considerable disadvantage. In the modern way we think of a wine region, that lack casts it into a shadowy netherworld. The crucible is an appellation *manqué*.

Oded puts its unofficial boundaries as River Road in the south, Westside Road in the west, and Highway 101 in the east, a triangle that comes together at Healdsburg. (I might bring in the boundaries a bit here and there, but he's basically got it right.) What's interesting is that this triangle includes the northeastern Russian River Valley, the warmest part of that appellation, an area that shouldn't have been included in the AVA to begin with and is likely to be removed from it when the boundaries are redrawn. The Russian River Valley Winegrowers Association already has petitioned the BATF for a change that would "follow, more accurately than the original boundary lines, the historically identifiable borders of coastal cool fog."

When that happens, wines made from grapes grown in the crucible would not be eligible for a Russian River Valley, Alexander Valley, or Dry Creek Valley appellation; they would qualify only for a Sonoma County appellation. Viticulturally, this no-man's-land is reminiscent of the old-style California vineyards where everything grew cheek by jowl. Pinot Noir, Chardonnay, Cabernet Sauvignon, Merlot, Zinfandel, Sauvignon Blanc, Syrah, Petite Sirah, Grenache, Viognier, Sangiovese, Pinot Grigio, and almost every other varietal known in California all peacefully coexist, in a climate that is at once warmish-coolish but also neither and both.

I asked lots of people what they thought of the region. Pete Seghesio Jr. calls it "a transitional zone." Forrest Tancer seems airily dismissive of it; the crucible is something he drives through on his commute between cold Green Valley and hot T-bar-T. Dick Arrowood frowns and says, "We all want to be able to define it," by which he means not that Sonomans have some burning desire to pigeonhole the crucible, but rather that there is something in us, as intellectual beings, that longs for tidy definitions so that the world is less incomprehensible. It is an epistemologic "search for certainty" (in Descartes's words) of the kind the French, with their ironclad system of wine appellations and mandated grape varieties, bequeathed to us Americans and that we, for better or worse, believe in and subscribe to.

When I asked Oded which varietal did best in his crucible, he exhaled loudly. "That's a hard one."

A long silence, atypical for Oded. You could hear the gears working.

"It could be many things. Many, many things," he murmured, nodding his head sagely like a Talmudic scholar. "Syrah, I think, is a good possibility."

It was the answer I had anticipated. One could make a strong case for it. The argument has long raged in California, and still does, over whether Syrah likes heat or cold. The model is the Rhône Valley. In the northern, cooler part of that valley, Syrah, grown in places like Hermitage and Côte-Rôtie, is a big, dark, tannic wine, unblended or with a little Viognier mixed in. In the warmer south, at Chateauneuf-du-Pape and in the Côtes-du-Rhône, it is blended with up to a dozen other varietals and makes a lighter-bodied wine. The Syrahs of the north are far more expensive than those of the south; in recent years, the best Côte-Rôties, such as Guigal's, have commanded some of the highest wine prices in the world.

Syrah, in the year 2003, is the new "hot grape" in California. (Every few years, another varietal is baptized by the wine press.) Vintners are getting serious about it from Mendocino to Temecula, from the Edna Valley through Paso Robles to the Sierra Foothills. From this fever of activity, some spectacular Syrahs have emerged. But still, no one is yet sure where the best will come from: warm or cool?

Syrah was not always considered among the world's noble wines. When George Saintsbury, the great English literary critic and don, published his epochal *Notes on a Cellar-Book*, in 1933—possibly the most influential wine book ever written, certainly inspiring subsequent wine writers with its scholarly but humanistic approach—he did not even think to include a separate chapter on the Rhône Valley, as he had for Bordeaux and Burgundy.

But the professor did go to considerable lengths to describe a wine he calls "one of the three or four most remarkable juices of the grape, not merely that I ever possessed but that I ever tasted." It was an 1846 Hermitage, made shortly before his birth year. He drank it, as best I can tell, in 1878, when the wine was thirty-two years old. (Saintsbury, whose Victorian style of writing is curvilinear rather than direct, does not tell us these things straight out but scatters clues about his opaque paragraphs like a mystery novelist. The reader has to detect the date by sleuthing.)

Saintsbury in his time drank and praised 1858 Margaux, 1875 Mouton-Rothschild, 1869 Romanée-Conti, Perrier-Jouet 1857 (when the Champagne was twenty-seven years old), and Dow's 1878 Port. To call that 1846 Hermitage one of the best wines he had ever had is high praise indeed, considering the company, but Saintsbury still seems to have had his doubts about it. "If you want delicacy you don't go to the Rhône," he warned, clearly indicating that "delicacy" was what he and his fellow Victorian oenophiles wanted in a wine.

He was remarkably ambivalent about it. As much as it attracted him, he could not bring himself to put Hermitage up there with the Médoc and the Côte de Nuits in quality. Was he conditioned to believe that a Rhône wine could only be a brute? Yet in the whole of the *Cellar-Book* he devotes far more space to describing that Hermitage, four pages in all, than to any other wine. "You could meditate on it," he muses at one point. Later—it had clearly become an obsession—he tries drinking it from different glasses, "for it is quite wonderful what whimsies wine has as to the receptacles in which it likes to be drunk." (It went best, curiously, in flat-bottomed glasses "with nearly straight sides.") In the end, Saintsbury calls it "the *manliest* French wine I ever drank" (italics his), although by "manly" he did not mean to confer on it an undiluted compliment.

Of that particular 1846 Hermitage we know little; it may have been 100 percent Syrah, but it was undoubtedly a cool-climate red wine. Here in California, Syrah's warm-cold continuum is well illustrated in the Santa Ynez Valley of Santa Barbara County, which, because of the transverse nature of the Coast Ranges, has a sharp temperature gradient, from west to east. Under similar conditions, Syrah achieves a crescendo of greatness at certain small wineries in the western hills of Paso Robles.

Every generalization has its exceptions, but it's fair to say that cool-climate Syrah is meatier and more peppery, with thicker tannins, especially if it is grown, as it often is, on a hillside; also, that its flavors tend more in the direction of blue- and black-skinned fruits, such as plums and blackberries. Cool-climate Syrah also is more affected by the vintage and—theoretically—ages better.

Syrahs grown in a warm climate ripen more dependably and can be fantastically rich and tremendous in jammy fruit: cherries, red and black raspberries, and even sweet chocolate truffle. They are among the most delicious young California red wines you can find—and therein lies the reason for the faint suggestion of disparagement toward them that you sometimes detect in serious winemakers plying their trade in cooler waters. The implication is that the wines are a little *obvious.*

If cool-climate Syrah can be tannic and warm-climate Syrah can be fruity soft and sweet, what's wrong with mixing them together? Some winemakers who are able to blend—who have access to good grapes from both cool- and warm-climate vineyards—often prefer to do so, unless they simply enjoy playing the terroir game and releasing side-by-side kissing cousins for the sake of intellectual comparison.

Which brings us back to the crucible. *Degree days* are the cumulative number of degrees above the mean temperature of 65 degrees Fahrenheit during a growing season. Cloverdale has 1,127 degree days every year, on average. Santa Rosa has 526, and Healdsburg has about 853. Thus, the transitional zone of the crucible, measured by degree days, is right in the middle of Bordeaux and Burgundy—or perhaps the better comparison is in the middle of the northern and southern Rhône. You can grow a Syrah there that has attributes of both warm and cool climates.

At least one winemaker in the crucible focuses seriously on Syrah, and on Rhône wines in general. Philip Staley had been a longtime dentist with a practice in Hayward, a fast-growing bedroom community south of Oakland, when he purchased some land on Westside Road in 1988. His intention was to plant the grapes of the Rhône Valley; he'd fallen in love with the wines and dreamed of making some himself.

He knew he wanted someplace that was warm enough to ripen the grapes but cool enough to preserve vitality, something on a slope, with gravelly soil. He searched through Dry Creek Valley, the Alexander Valley, and the Russian River Valley before stumbling across an interesting piece of real estate on Westside Road. Although it was technically in the Russian River Valley, it was only a hundred yards from the Dry Creek Valley line and seemed to share characteristics of both. It had some fog and wind, some dry, sunny heat. It turned out to be not quite warm enough to fully ripen Mourvèdre or Roussanne, but it was potentially very good for Syrah and Grenache as well as Viognier. In a poor vintage, like those of 1998 and 2000, Staley's Syrah will suffer and be thin. But give the vines a great year like 1999, and they just explode with everything good about Syrah. Transitional zones are areas where vintages matter a great deal.

But the truth is, I've never had a great Syrah from the crucible; nor, for that matter, have I ever had a truly great wine of any kind that was entirely grown there. Oded makes a very good crucible Pinot Noir for J, but it does not rise to the heights of the best of the Russian River Valley. His Longboard Syrah has come from a crucible vineyard not far from J, off Eastside Road. It is very similar to Phil Staley's Syrah—good but a shade incomplete, missing that extra edge a wine needs for supremacy. Oded understands this and will enrich it in future years with Syrah grapes from a vineyard on Fitch Mountain that will provide greater depth and tannic structure. Oded also plans to blend in some Syrah grapes from his own vineyard, which he is developing in the Russian River Valley, that will bring a cool-climate character to the wine. The result, he hopes, will be complexity.

I have had fine Chardonnays, Sauvignon Blancs, Petite Sirahs, and many other good wines that were grown in the crucible. But it remains a vague place, Forrest Tancer's no-man's-land. Perhaps the quality of its wines has risen as high as it can go; not every place can make great wine.

But it would be far too early to write off this interesting area. Someday, somebody might come along—a grower like Jim Young who will bring a magic touch to his vineyards, or a master winemaker like Dick Arrowood—to craft the grapes into something special and wrest from the ground an amazing wine. I would not be surprised if this wine turned out to be Syrah, but we will just have to wait.

6

The Russian River Valley

PLAINS WHICH ARE TRULY BLESSED

The first time I ever visited the Russian River Valley was in the early 1990s, when my friend Joel Butler, one of the first two American Masters of Wine, invited me to drive up with him to the Rochioli place.

I'd been going to the Napa, Sonoma, and Livermore valleys for years to taste wine. But I had never been to this wild-sounding place, which conjured up images of tree-shaded riverbanks and scimitar-waving Tartars riding wild steeds. I found myself looking forward mightily to my inaugural visit.

Joel knew more about wine than anyone else I'd ever met. On the way up, he told me about Rochioli's underground sort of reputation, especially for Pinot Noir, and how practically no one except insiders knew about it at this point. I was impressed that he had managed to wangle an invitation to a winery that wasn't yet open to the public. (It is open today.)

I remember how pretty the valley was on that spring day. As soon as we left Highway 101 and turned west, civilization seemed to melt away as the countryside took over. The great old trees were budding, and their branches stretched over and sheltered Westside Road. Great forests of conifers clad the mountains. And then, of course, there was the Russian River itself. As we drove across the old steel bridges, it glinted with silvery flashes.

Roads in the Russian River Valley tend to follow the snaking meanders of the river and the creeks that feed it—Pieta, Big Sulphur, Dry, Maa-
cama, Mark West, Austin. They turn and twist with alacrity, and, if you
do not know them, you must drive slowly and be careful. Joel knew every
bend, or so I assumed—and hoped. Beyond that, my memories of that
visit are faded: Tom Rochioli tinkering with some equipment . . . old trucks
and farm vehicles scattered around a yard . . . could there have been chickens scratching in the dirt? Naturally, there were barrels of wine. Sadly, I
remember nothing of the wines we tasted—shame on me—but they must
surely have been Pinot Noir.

Since then, I have returned to the valley many times. It changes dramatically with the turning of the seasons. The valley of summer is all
Renoir pastels: the limes, emeralds, and pale greens of oak and laurel; the
rich orange-maroon of madrone bark; the lavender of the wisteria that
winds through every farmhouse arbor; the tangerine of California poppy;
the rich, royal purple of lupine peeping out from fields of golden grass.

In autumn, the air is filled with a dusky haze and the sweet-smoky scent
of burning vines. During crush time, the perfume of fermenting grapes
adds a pungent, heady note to the thick atmosphere. The sun, lower each
day in the sky, glints off the river through leaves turned russet and honey
gold, its beams casting long, diagonal shafts of mote-filled light. The vines
turn a fiery red, in the last, yawning days of Indian summer.

The colors of winter are dimmed. Creamy, eggshell-white ground fogs
are as dense and thick as cotton. Rains of steel and mists of zinc veil the
land under a ghostly shroud. Browns, too: the chocolate of mud and the
cocoa-colored ooze that slimes off the hillsides when it pours. But after a
winter storm, the clouds will scatter, tearing open the sky to a sunset of
blazing magenta and gold.

Spring is my favorite time in the valley because it is when life returns.

The new season seems to awaken the birds, although they have been there all along, hunkered down in the sodden forest: red-tailed hawks, great blue herons, and the small brown kestrels that ride the warming thermals under skies so blue they startle. The delicately scented, pink plum tree flowers come in January, followed by a succession of wildflowers. In the vineyards, mustard blossoms explode virtually overnight, filling the rows with a riot of buttery yellow; and if you walk the squishy earth and look closely at the vines, you will see the first tiny pea-green buds.

I also like the silence of Russian River Valley nights. I have lain in bed, alone in the darkness, in cabins deep in the woods and heard only the low, erotic cello-moan of tree limbs rubbing against each other, punctuated by the occasional eerie hoot of an owl hunting in the night forest. One falls into a long, untroubled sleep in such silence. The next morning finds beyond the window a fog-shrouded wood, dripping with water. Only if you perk up your ears can you hear the distant, muffled sound of cars driven by Russian River Valley commuters on their way to work.

The valley's viticulture has a long history—long by California standards, brief by European—and it originated from opposite directions. From the choppy Pacific waters in the west, Russian explorers arrived in the early nineteenth century, having pushed this far east in their explorations. They brought with them a love of wine and the vine. From the south and east came another wine-loving folk, the Spanish-Mexican Californios. Caught in the middle were the Native Americans.

After tentative forays along the coast, during which they scouted out a good location for a permanent settlement, the Russians finally dropped anchor in March 1812 on land that had not yet been claimed by any other

European great power. To the south, Spain owned the territories up to San Francisco. Across a wild continent that had hardly been explored, James Madison was president of faraway America, which three months later would be embroiled in a second war with its old nemesis, Great Britain.

The Russians established their settlement just north of Jenner, where they encountered a Pomo Indian colony that the natives called Metini. Not too far to the south was a great river, which these Russians called Slavianka, or "pretty Russian girl"; someday it would be named for them. Metini seemed a good place to live and farm. It was close to the shore, where they could build a fort and make a stand in the event of a crisis with the Spanish, which seemed likely in that intensely competitive international atmosphere. According to one account, the Russians offered a deal to the Pomo: three blankets, three pairs of breeches, two axes, three hoes, a handful of beads, and a silver medal for the local chieftain in exchange for Metini and its environs. The deal was accepted. The Russians named their new fortress-village Rossiya, after Russia's historic name for itself; the Anglos who came later dubbed it Fort Ross.

The fort was built from trees felled from the redwood forests that grew a half-mile inland, on the slopes of the coastal mountains. In 1821, the tsar issued an *ukase* (a decree) closing the Pacific Coast north of San Francisco to all but Russian ships—an act of chutzpah that was in part responsible for the proclamation of the Monroe Doctrine two years later.

Metini was an excellent place for a sailing people to settle. "Its harbor is the best in the vicinity, being perfectly secure from northers [storms]," J. P. Munro-Fraser claimed in his *History of Sonoma County*—a curious comment, since Fort Ross patently is not secure from storms. Curious, too, because there is no real harbor by the beach at Fort Ross, although there is one at Jenner. At least one archaeologist has suggested that the Russian anchorage was not at Fort Ross but rather at Bodega Bay (named after an early Spanish explorer). The people and heavy goods earmarked for Fort Ross would thus have been offloaded at Bodega Bay, which the Russians called Port Rumiantsev, named after Russia's trade minister.

Whatever they used for a harbor, the Russians actually lived at Fort Ross. They had come, ostensibly, to hunt sea otter, fur seals, and other animals and to grow food they hoped to send north to their hungry compatriots in Alaska. They had another agenda as well: to forge ahead with the colonization that had started under Ivan the Terrible, Russia's first imperial tsar, in the mid-1500s, at the height of European expansionism. Like Britain, Spain, France, and the Netherlands, Mother Russia wanted to be an imperial power. Unlike the ships of the other European powers, the tsar's royal navies had struck out not over the Atlantic but the Pacific, for Russia's only outlet to the sea lay to the east.

For two and a half centuries, the Russians had mastered their own vast continent, crossing the Urals, heading eastward along the Siberian steppes, conquering Sakhalin and the Kuriles. They did not cease when they came to the open sea. They built tall sailing ships and continued exploring and, when they encountered other native civilizations, conquering. As they came ever closer to the New World, Spanish officials, fearing the worst from the tsars, annexed Alta California to Baja, as a *cordon sanitaire*, in the year 1769.

And yet the Russian approach to California was fraught with difficulty and privation. They reached Bering Island, today a part of Russian territory (but, as a glance at a map shows, the westernmost of the Aleutian Island chain, geologically if not politically), in 1742; but it took them another three years to get as far as Attu Island, only four hundred miles to the southeast. When they did, they became the first Russians to reach lands that now are part of the United States. At Attu, their difficulties began to mount.

They landed on the Alaska mainland in 1784, and by 1799 had formed the Russian-American Company, similar to the great trading guilds established by European kingdoms to manage and exploit the riches of the New World. In 1804, they established Sitka as their official North American capital. They piled furs, fish, whale oil, timber, and other sources of natural wealth onto their sailing ships and sent them home to enrich Rossiya's treasury.

The Russians did well while times were good, but times did not stay good for long. The alien natural conditions of their environment, which they had not at first appreciated, soon became apparent. The weather in southern Alaska is cold and damp. Sitka's average high temperature in July and August is only 63 degrees; heavy rain is frequent year-round. Although Sitka is not a particularly cold place as far as Alaska goes, snow has fallen in every month except during high summer.

It was nearly impossible to grow crops. The settlers did not thrive. Scurvy and other diseases of privation took their toll. Something had to be done, and so the Russians, leaving behind a stalwart settlement to hold their claim, pushed on to the south, toward Alta California, seeking its sunshine and warmth, fabled perhaps even then. Seven years later, then, in March 1812, Captain Ivan Kuskov and his crew arrived at Metini and immediately encountered the Pomos, whose ancestors had lived in that location for four thousand years, if not longer.

The Pomos were the original inhabitants of the Sonoma coast and the Russian River Valley. They had long dwelt in what is now western Sonoma County, building villages of as many as a thousand souls and settling mainly in the rolling oak woodlands and grasslands along the river itself and the streams that empty into it—precisely where most people choose to live today. The footpaths where the Pomo hunting and trading parties trod were far enough above the highest flood points; those lanes are where today's local roads, even Highway 101, have been established.

The Pomos called the Russian River "Shabakai," or "long snake," for the meandering twists and turns it took. It is fascinating to learn that this same word is a very old Japanese one, derived from Sanskrit and used to describe the Zen Buddhist concept of a "world of endurance"—the opposite of the peaceful realm of Nirvana.

The tribe divided itself into family-based branches, each headed by a chief. The branch who lived out on the Sonoma coast—the ones the Russians encountered—were the Kashaya. (The word "Kashaya," in old Pomo, is said to mean "expert gambler.") At the height of their civilization, before the Europeans arrived, they occupied all the territories from Gualala, on today's Sonoma-Mendocino county line, southward to below the Russian River, a distance of thirty-five miles. Eastward, their holdings spread for twenty miles across four coast ranges, halfway to Healdsburg. That was a big spread for a family-based branch to own.

It was lush territory, rich and fertile, with mighty forests filled with game and a great river swarming with fish. The Pomo left no written records or descriptions, but the author of the *History of Sonoma County* wrote of the region's "great red-wood trees [that] shade its limpid waters, the favorite haunt of the salmon and the trout; the hills are full of game—deer, elk and bear." When German settlers arrived in the mid-nineteenth century, they found the region so rich and abundant in natural resources that they called it Valhalla, after the great hall in Norse and Teutonic mythology where Odin receives and holds feasts for the souls of heroes fallen bravely in battle. The name Gualala (pronounced "wa-*la*-la") may be a variant on that word.

The Pomo apparently avoided Metini during the cold, rainy winter months, for reasons the Russians were to discover, to their chagrin. But when summer came and the weather softened, this spot on the coast became a favored destination.

It also was a sacred spot for Native Americans. In the 1990s, anthropologists at the University of California at Berkeley launched an archae-

ological dig at Metini. The dig's leaders, who hoped to win the cooperation of the Pomo people still living throughout the region, were careful
not to be seen as irreverent pillagers and destroyers of graves and prayer
sites. The anthropologists promised "sacred respect" for Kashaya culture
and views. Their documents described Metini as a place "where power
forces from the center of the earth" focused. The anthropologists also made
sure that the young students who did the actual fieldwork participated in
Pomo ritual exercises so that their spirits would be clean before they set
foot on that sacramental ground.

However sacred Metini was for the Kashaya Pomo, their annual summer visits to the seashore must also have been simply enjoyable. While there,
the "people from the top of the land" (as they called themselves) aug-
mented their inland winter diet of deer, salmon, elk, wild greens, acorns,
nuts, berries, roots, seeds, and tubers with a fresh seafood diet of abalone,
mussels, fish, sea lion, and seaweed. They also manufactured sea salt on
the Metini beaches. It is not hard to imagine them relaxing there on the
sands on a sunny summer day, their children laughing and splashing in the
water—as children do today, if the weather cooperates.

One wonders what the Kashaya thought of the Russians, and vice versa.
Modern-day Kashaya, continuing an oral tradition, say that their ancestors, who had no boats, called the Russians "the undersea people" because
the arriving vessels, seen from the shore, seemed to rise up from below the
ocean. Yet for all the Russians' reputation for ruthlessness and cruelty, the
two cultures seem to have gotten along well enough. There are no records
of horrible acts or atrocities by either side.

The Kashaya learned to speak the Russian language, although the opposite does not seem to have occurred to any great extent. There were,
however, numerous recorded instances of intermarriage, which suggest that
spouses must have learned to communicate a bit in both languages. The

Pomoan language, which is still spoken in parts of Sonoma County, retains loanwords from the Russians: *chashka* (dishes), *chaynik* (teakettle), *chayu*
(tea), *kasha* (gruel), and *parus* (canvas). But other than these fossils of vo-
cabulary, the Russians, when they abandoned the New World, left little
behind to remind anyone that they had ever lived in Sonoma—only a few
place names: Sebastopol, Fort Ross, and, of course, the Russian River
itself.

For three decades, Fort Ross was a true melting pot of cultures and races.
A census conducted in 1821 counted 175 adults, mostly men, of whom only
24 were pure Russian; the rest ranged from Creoles to Siberians, Aleuts
to Alaskan Chugash and Kodiaks, Tlingits, Hawaiians, Miwoks, and, of
course, the Pomo.

The Russians had high hopes that they had found a more amiable climate than that of Sitka, but they soon discovered that conditions at Fort
Ross were only marginally more hospitable. Whereas at Sitka the average
summer high temperature barely managed to reach the low 60s, at Fort Ross
it was only a few degrees warmer, with an average temperature of 55 degrees
in June and only 57 in August. By early autumn, the first storms could come,
and they might blow until June. Even in the summer, fog was common.

Farming was difficult, and not only because of the climate. The steep
mountainsides, with their mudslides and rockslides and impenetrable
forests of Douglas fir and old-growth redwood, severely limited the land's
ability to support crops, particularly the wheat the Russians had hoped to
grow. Winter storms merely compounded the agony. Munro-Fraser's *History of Sonoma County* referred, in purplish but accurate Victorian prose, to
"veritable mountain torrents" that "rush seaward with relentless fury, and

everything in [their] pathway is swept into the broad bosom of the Pacific." Perhaps the final blow was when the hapless Russians depleted the coastal waters of otter.

Once again the Russians were desperate to find a warmer place to live. The lands to the south were out of the question, firmly in the hands of the Spanish. That left only inland, and eastward they turned, seeking someplace "out of reach of the coast winds," according to an 1885 article in the old *Sonoma Democrat* newspaper that described the tumultuous history of these pioneering coastal Russians.

"Out of reach of the coast winds." I thought of this one winter night in an old cottage near the coast. It was very cold, and the cottage was unheated. Silvery hoarfrost glittered on the hard ground outside the window under a fat, white December moon. Inside, I lit a log fire and, while waiting for the room to heat up, rummaged through some books that were gathering dust on a shelf, seemingly untouched by human hands for decades. One was a diary written by a young man who had made an auto tour of the region with two friends in the late 1930s:

> For hours we drove through a vapor tunnel, everything blotted out except for ten feet of the road ahead. Rarely, there were swift glimpses down from the road toward a patch of gray ocean, or up from the road to a patch of gray sheep on a gray hill. By noon the fog had drawn back a few feet from the roadside, bringing fences and trees into view. But we could stand it no longer . . . the temptation was too much. We abandoned the Coast, and turned our faces east, in search of sun.

For the Russians, too, the gray, dismal fog was too much. They abandoned the coast and turned east, in search of sun and warmth. Somewhere along the way, they put in grapevines.

They would have needed sticks of budwood, since grapevines are not planted from seed. No one is sure where they got them. According to one theory, some of the Russians sailed down the Pacific coast, perhaps as far as Peru, where they purchased vine cuttings in 1817 and planted them on their return. Another, simpler possibility—Occam's razor—is that the first plantings were of vines cultivated from a Franciscan Catholic missionary vineyard somewhere south of Fort Ross, in Spanish California. If this version is true, the grapes would have been of the Mission variety. Either way, it is almost certain that the Russians installed the first Sonoma County vineyard well before the Spanish did, since the earliest the latter could have planted was 1823, when they founded their Mission San Francisco Solano, at Sonoma Town.

We hear again of a Russian vineyard in 1836, in today's Green Valley, at the little town of Graton, whose original spelling, Graytown, is said to be after one James Gray (though perhaps it suggested what locals thought of the weather). The man who owned that vineyard was the last Russian to make a historical name for himself in the region—but what a name it was! Yegor Chernykh, who so powerfully lives across the pages of history, joins Cyrus Alexander as one of Sonoma County's great, colorful pioneers. (For information concerning Chernykh and others in this part of the county, I am indebted to historian Charles L. Sullivan, whose 2001 manuscript "A Miraculous Intervention: A Short History of Viticulture and Winegrowing in Western Sonoma County" was a valuable resource for this chapter.)

Among the Spanish Californios, Chernykh was known respectfully, and perhaps even affectionately, as Don Jorge. A trained agronomist, skilled in the economics and science of crop production, Chernykh had been sent to Fort Ross by the Russian government to help the struggling settlers with their farming. With the help of this agricultural genius, the Russians eventually did establish an orchard, located on a sheltered hillside near Fort Ross, where they managed to grow apples, peaches, cherries, pears, and, so we read, even some grapes. But not even Chernykh was able to get row vegetables, wheat, and other grains to thrive in that dank climate, and he more than met his match when he tried to establish a beef and dairy industry. Thoroughly discouraged, Chernykh sent a pessimistic report to his superiors in Moscow, around 1837, in which he acknowledged the utter failure of coastal farming.

However, he added, on a more hopeful note, "About a dozen miles inland from Fort Ross, there are plains which are truly blessed: excellent lands, various forests, and lakes and rivers with fish. Fogs could not affect the crops there." If you stick a compass point at Fort Ross and describe a twelve-mile-wide arc to the east, it runs through Guerneville and brushes Occidental—in other words, the western borders of today's Russian River Valley AVA.

When it came time to establish his own estate, the Russian Don himself settled in this blessed arc, in the vicinity of Occidental and Graton. There he built houses and barracks for his workers and grew the vegetables and grains he had been unable to raise on the coast. Somewhere along the way, in this burst of activity, he managed to become the first European to climb Mount St. Helena.

More important, Chernykh also developed a vineyard at his new farm. A French traveler, writing of his visit there in 1841, recorded that the "farm . . . of Don Jorge produces remarkable vineyards." Later, in 1889, a locally published history referred to "a small vineyard" that had been planted by "a Russian gentleman of leisure, by the name of Don Jorge," which contained two thousand vines, although we do not know what variety they were. Chernykh himself seems to have had mixed feelings about his vineyard. On the plus side, he wrote to Moscow, the "local grapes make good wine, but," he added, "in small quantities and [it] does not keep well."

Chernykh may have lived a gentleman's life of leisure, but the Russians, collectively, eventually realized the futility of their efforts to create a permanent settlement in California. In 1839, exhausted, outnumbered by the Californios, seeing Americans pressing into the area, and unable to reach a diplomatic accord with the Mexican government for recognition of their land claim, they gave up. The tsar commanded the liquidation of the settlement, and the Russian-American Company ordered the settlers to retreat back to Alaska.

They tried to sell off their lands, animals, ammunition, and other commodities to the Hudson's Bay Company, which the British had established in Canada, but were rebuffed, possibly because their title was suspect. A similar offer to the French also was turned down. Next, the Russians turned to the Mexicans—a proffer that, once again, was refused. In all likelihood, the Mexican government believed that, in time, they would get Fort Ross anyway, and for nothing, anticipating that it would fall into their hands like ripe fruit when the Russians left.

Instead, in 1841, the Russians unexpectedly sold Fort Ross lock, stock, and barrel—literally—to John Sutter, the colorful adventurer, for thirty thousand dollars. Sutter, who was still legally a Mexican citizen, was living at New Helvetia (Sacramento); it was at his Sierra Foothills lumber mill in 1849 that the discovery of a certain shiny yellow metal would lead to the Gold Rush and California's destiny. On New Year's Day of 1842, approximately a hundred Russians sailed out from Bodega Bay for the last time, headed north toward Sitka. With their departure, the Russian foray into California came to an end. In 1867, they abandoned North America altogether, selling Alaska to the U.S. government in the transaction that came to be known as Seward's Folly.

According to one account, Sutter took possession of Fort Ross in December 1841 on credit, for he was broke. He was nonetheless gobbling up land all over Northern and Central California as fast as he could—the first real estate speculator in the state's history. Fort Ross's deed of sale from the Russians listed two vineyards, in addition to cattle, sheep, "herds of swine," ammunition, and other goods.

While all this was happening, European settlers had been swarming into the eastern parts of Sonoma County and the Russian River Valley. In or around 1835, the last Mexican *commandante* of Northern California, the famous General Mariano Vallejo, whose name is connected with the rise of viticulture in both Sonoma Valley and Napa Valley, sent out a trio of young Scottish settlers from his headquarters in Sonoma Town to the far coast, promising to give them each a large grant of land provided they would "go and settle right upon the border limits of the Russians' claim." It was his idea to get as many Europeans as he could out to the coastal territories, to challenge the Russians and prevent them from encroaching any farther to the east.

The Scotsmen—James Dawson, Edward McIntosh, and James Black—settled on lands near today's towns of Freestone and Occidental; they were, except for the Russians, the first recorded white settlers in the area. On their ranch, they established a vineyard. They may have obtained their cuttings from General Vallejo's Sonoma vineyard, which had been planted around 1837, or from Chernykh's vineyard, or from another source.

Their expedition set off a frantic period of settlement in the west county. It would take a book in itself to record the next few decades of activity, as Scots, Germans, English, and French, as well as Italians, who made up the last great wave of European immigrants, flooded into the region. The Gold Rush brought matters to a boil; many of the discouraged thousands who failed to find a fortune in the mines of the Sierra Foothills trekked across the Central Valley and migrated west, seeking a better life. Between 1846 and 1850, the lands around Occidental, Freestone, Forestville, and Sebastopol were intensively occupied. And where the Europeans staked their claims to the land, grapevines went into the ground.

In the eastern part of the valley, a little creek, which may or may not have had a Native American name, flowed down from the west wall of the Mayacamas into the Russian River. Sometime in the 1820s, a Spanish priest, anxious to Christianize the "heathen" Indians, baptized a little Pomo girl in its waters. The devout padre was inspired to dedicate the creek to the "patroness of America," Rose of Lima, a Peruvian lady of great piety whose 1671 canonization by Pope Clement X had made her the first saint born in the New World. The priest called the rivulet Santa Rosa; the name stuck. By 1852, U.S. postal authorities named the town that was arising from its marshy lowlands Santa Rosa. Today, the burgeoning metropolis has a population of 154,000 and is the county seat of Sonoma. By the late 1830s, growers had already begun to plant vineyards there.

When the Gold Rush started, the eastern and western parts of the Russian River Valley contained many vineyards. But the central part, around Guerneville and eastward toward Healdsburg—the prime center cut of the Russian River Valley AVA—remained undeveloped. Guerneville "is purely a lumber-manufacturing center," Munro-Fraser asserted in 1880, a time when old-growth redwood still clotted the flanks of the mountains. The "Vineyards" section of his *History* contains not even a mention of anything outside the Sonoma Valley–Santa Rosa corridor. If anyone—Russian, Spanish, European, American—grew grapes around Guerneville and points east during this period, I have been unable to find any record of it.

That hiatus did not last long. In April 1881, a Guerneville newspaper reported on "a lively boom in another very important industry" (besides, presumably, lumber or maybe orchard fruits) "about here this spring, the setting out of vineyards." Suddenly, people were planting grapes; then, as now, it seems, when a new wine region was discovered, everyone wanted in. Eight months later, the *Russian River Flag* newspaper went so far as to recommend the proper varieties for the area. The breakdown was significant because it documents people's awareness that, even within this relatively small region, certain mini-climates, some warmer and some cooler, were suitable for different varieties.

The Burgundy-Bordeaux continuum had been discovered. The published recommendations were for Mataro, Chauche Noir, Black Burgundy, Petit Pinot, and (Pinot) Meunier for "Burgundy" wines, and Cabernet, Malbec, and Zinfandel for "Claret-style wine." The former were deemed suitable for planting in the cooler regions nearer Guerneville, the latter considered better around Healdsburg and points north and east—just as today.

With vineyards now dotting the region, it was time to build wineries. Then, as now, the demand was for wine to slake the thirst of San Francisco, just fifty miles south of Santa Rosa. Windsor, midway between Santa Rosa and Healdsburg, was the site of choice. It had previously been called Poor Man's Flat; a former Pony Express rider who became the town's first postmaster renamed it Windsor, as in Windsor Castle. (Perhaps to make it sound fancy and drive up land prices? He would certainly not have been the last to be so motivated.) The railroad had arrived in 1872, making Windsor perfect for locating big receiving, crushing, and bottling facilities. Plenty of cheap labor was available, especially when the Italians arrived in earnest, starting in the 1880s.

Along with most other commodity-based businesses in America, wine was becoming, as it were, industrialized. So great was the promise of profit that Munro-Fraser likened Sonoma's wine industry to the Comstock Lode, the 1859 gold and silver rush in Nevada that has been called the greatest precious ore strike ever. "There is no possibility of over production in wines," his *History* declared, words that must have caused entrepreneurial eyes to glitter with greed—however untrue they were.

By the early 1880s, two large wineries had been established that together would anchor Russian River Valley viticulture into the next century and whose lineal descendants remain today: the Twin Fir farm, near Forestville, eventually purchased by an Italian immigrant named Rafaelo Martini, which, several incarnations later, would be rechristened Martini & Prati; and the granddaddy of them all, and still the biggest, Korbel. Neither, however, ever achieved the stranglehold over local production that Italian Swiss Colony held over the Alexander Valley, and that too established a paradigm: whereas the Alexander Valley has always been a haven for big wineries, the Russian River Valley has been mostly about little ones.

The valley was burgeoning with grapes. By 1891, nearly 4,000 acres of vines had been planted (compared to 10,000 in 2002). That represented nearly one-quarter of the vineyard acreage in the entire county. As the economy grew, dozens of small family operations, mostly producing fewer than ten thousand gallons, opened their doors. Nearly all are gone now, but one of the class of 1896 remains: Foppiano. An influx of Italian American wine families soon followed, whose names still dominate Sonoma County viticulture: Sebastiani, Seghesio, Rochioli, and Pedroncelli, as well as others not so well known, including Bacchi, Domenichelli, and Frati. Guided and nourished by these Italian Americans, Sonoma's great wine culture was firmly established by the turn of the century.

These Italian American vintners worked primarily with the grape varieties they had inherited from the Europeans who preceded them. Once the awful Mission grapes had been rejected, the pioneers had planted their vineyards with "field blends," mixtures of primarily southern Rhône Valley or Languedoc grapes as well as Zinfandel. Back then, the naming of grape types was not very scientific; the same plant might have had several different names. But today we would recognize some of the varieties the Italian Americans farmed: Grenache, Mourvèdre (or Mataro), Carignane, Trousseau, Petite Sirah, Syrah, Negrette, and Alicante Bouschet as well as Zinfandel.

The field blend represented a realistic approach to an age-old challenge that has always confronted vintners, especially in a cool, marginal area like the Russian River Valley: how to beat the weather. A thin-skinned early ripener (such as Pinot Noir) might be ruined by August or September rains, frost, or hail, whereas a late ripener would squeak by undamaged. Even if the late ripeners encountered a harvest rainstorm, their thick skins generally immunized them against rot, especially if a few days of sun followed the storm, as is typical during October and November in this part of the world. (If you think about it, the *vignerons* of the Médoc did pretty much the same thing in establishing the five varietals that performed best in their vineyards.)

Then, too, the field blend afforded vintners a greater array of colors on their palates, so to speak. A dark-pigmented grape yielded desirable color to a red wine, while another lent acidity, another the tannins to age, another a fruity aroma and flavor, and so on. Why not, then, plant a whole range of varieties?

Which is what the European settlers did. If they put in the "Claret-style" Cabernet and Malbec recommended by the authorities in the *Russian River Flag*, these plantings failed to make much of a dent in the historical record, for by the turn of the century almost no traces of Bordeaux-type grapes could be found in the Russian River Valley. A few might have been planted during the 1880s, when news of the devastating phylloxera epidemic in France reached Sonoma and ambitious vintners perhaps hoped they could capitalize on the shortage of imported French wines and replace them with their own homegrown "clarets" and "Médocs."

But phylloxera struck Sonoma's own vineyards in the 1890s, and, as in France, the vines had to be torn out and replanted to resistant rootstock. In the process, the grape mix changed, exactly as it would in the North Coast after the phylloxera epidemic of the 1990s. Much of whatever Cabernet, Malbec, and other Bordeaux varieties had existed disappeared, to be replaced by what the Italians knew worked, and worked well: the field blend of southern Rhône varietals and Zinfandel. And then, with an indifference to legal niceties, they called their wines "claret" and "Médoc" anyway.

By the early 1900s, and for seventy years afterward, the field blend remained master of Russian River Valley viticulture. It is entirely likely that even the so-called Zinfandels of Asti were field blends (and today, anything called Old Vines, especially from Sonoma County, is likely to be such a blend). But by the 1960s, the field-blend vineyard had become an endangered species. The wine industry was lagging; America had become a beer- and spirits-drinking country. Entire vineyards were ripped out and replaced by housing developments and shopping centers, especially around Santa Rosa. Even when the boutique winery phenomenon of the 1970s arose rather unexpectedly, signaling a possible renaissance of wine drinking in the United States, growers budded over their field-blend vineyards to the handful of popular varietals, especially Chardonnay and Cabernet Sauvignon, that consumers were said to desire. But a few of the old vineyards remained, saved by accident or preserved out of love; and the story of one Russian River Valley field-blend vineyard now begs to be told.

THE TALE OF TWO ACRES

The most wonderful thing about the old field blends is the extraordinary wine they can produce. There is no other quite like it.

These wines are not for the faint of heart; they are bold and expressive. The nature of the particular grapes used is lusty and full bodied; Sonoma's sunshine adds a fruity extravagance to the mix.

Four or five hundred acres of old field-blend vineyards may still remain in the Russian River Valley—the estimate is mine; no one keeps track. Most of them are small to the point of tiny, in the backyard behind somebody's farmhouse, or along that little strip next to the barn that's had grapes since great-grandpa's time. Drive the backcountry lanes, and you can't miss these ancient, gnarled veterans.

Several years ago, during high summer in a hot part of California, I was at a big winetasting event inside an exhibition hall at a county fairgrounds. A thousand people were crowded inside, jostling elbows. It's always difficult to concentrate on the taste of a wine in a large and happy crowd. It's impossible to get near the most famous tables (which is not to say the best). The temperature inside was stifling, and I was tired. I decided to leave.

Next to the exit, set off by itself, was a tasting table. The winery did not have a famous name; it was stuck on the outer fringes of nowheresville. The young man behind the table looked lonely, as if he would pay someone, anyone, to stop by and sample his wine. When he saw me glancing his way, he put on his game face and smiled. Oh, well, I thought, one more can't hurt.

He introduced himself as Mike Officer, said his winery's name was Carlisle, and poured a glass of something from a bottle labeled Two Acres.

It was stunning. As tired as I was, this wine shocked my palate and brought it back to life like a jolt of adrenaline. It was clearly an extraordinary wine.

I arranged a visit with Mike and, that winter, appeared at the vineyard one late December day. As we sat in his car with the heat running (for it was wickedly cold), he told me his story.

Mike Officer at Two Acres Vineyard.

The vineyard is in the southeast corner of the Russian River Valley, hard by the Santa Rosa city limits and surrounded, literally, by ugly suburban tract houses all painted the same dull beige. Many of them had their Christmas lights up, which made the sight of the old vineyard in their midst even weirder.

The original vineyard had been a big one; it was subdivided and sold off in the early 1970s for three-acre housing parcels. Most of the new homeowners, having utterly no use for grapes, tore the vines out and replaced them with well-manicured lawns and flowerbeds. But one family left two acres of their vineyard intact, because they had been offered a good price for the grapes by the winemaker Sean Thackrey, who is famous for his old-vine, field-blended wines.

"We think the vineyard was planted in 1910, but we don't know much about the planter, except that he was an Englishman, and he was trying to re-create Chateauneuf-du-Pape," Mike said. By "Chateauneuf," he meant a wine made from a mixture of southern Rhône varietals—the equivalent of a field blend.

In the mid-1990s, Mike and his wife were living in San Francisco, where he worked as a software engineer for Wells Fargo. He'd been a home winemaker since the 1980s, and his interest in wine was increasing. Wanting to buy a house but not able to afford one in San Francisco, the Officers moved to Santa Rosa, where home prices are about half of what they are in the city.

Mike was out riding his bike one weekend when he stumbled across the vineyard. "It looked like it was on its last legs," he remembered. Trees had sprouted up through the vines, and it was overgrown with blackberry bushes and poison oak. "Some of the vines were squashed like pancakes. Just a total mess. It killed me, because these old-vine vineyards are historic treasures of Sonoma County, and they need to be preserved.

"I didn't know a thing about taking care of vines," Mike continued, "but I looked up the owner and asked if he minded if I renovated the vineyard. I knew that, at some point, if I continued making wine, I wanted my own vineyard, and this would give me the practical experience I needed." To Mike's surprise, the owner gave him permission, and Mike took over managing the vineyard in 1996.

The owner told Mike that the grapes were Zinfandel. "But in the spring of 1997, as the buds started pushing [out], I looked and thought, 'Hmm, this doesn't look like Zin to me.' Not only that, there seemed to be quite a number of different varietals there," Mike noted.

"So we had the University of California Agricultural Extension officer come out and take samples, which were sent to Andy Walker, Mr. Ampelographer." (Andrew Walker, associate professor in the Department of Viticulture and Enology at U.C. Davis, holds the Louis P. Martini Endowed Chair in Viticulture.) Mike recalled his surprise at what Walker discovered. The vineyard was mainly Mourvèdre (Mataro), with smaller amounts of Mondeuse, Petite Sirah, true Syrah, Valdepenas (or Tempranillo), and Alicante Bouschet. "There were exactly five Zinfandel vines," Mike smiled.

It was a classic field blend, and Mike knew that his work was cut out for him if he intended to restore the vineyard to health. He cleared the weeds and rehabilitated the vines. Mike also realized that to make the best wine he could, he would have to pick each of the varietals at the peak of ripeness, a process that could be spread out over a month or longer. He tied each vine to a stake, a different color for every varietal, "so when I have people helping me pick, I can just say, 'Today, we're picking all the yellow,' or whatever." Typically, Petite Sirah comes in first, Mondeuse last. (In the typical old-style field-blended vineyard, all the different varietals were picked and vinified together. Mike's approach, by contrast, results in an even richer, riper wine.)

Attention to detail in wine, as in other things, pays. Two Acres is a masterpiece, dark and lush, filled with exciting, even erotic, flavors; but despite its richness, it is balanced and firm. It has resemblances, in its density, to the fabulous Côte-Rôties that fetch hundreds of dollars a bottle, although Mike sold his 2000 and 2001 vintages for thirty-six dollars, a lower price than that commanded by many of the Napa Valley cult Cabernet Sauvignons that were not as luscious. He credits the wine's quality to the incredibly low yields of the vines; in 2002, the entire vineyard produced only a ton and a half of grapes, or three-quarters of a ton per acre. That is one-quarter, or even less, of what most of California's greatest vineyards yield.

As good as Two Acres and similar bottlings are, it was not the field blend that made the wines of the Russian River Valley famous, although in a reasonable world, it would have been. Instead, it was a totally unlikely grape, which no one—Russian, Spanish, or Italian—had ever dreamed of growing, because it would have been madness: Pinot Noir. In a reprise of the way viticulture itself came to Sonoma, this great grape of Burgundy arrived in the valley from two different directions: not east and west, but north and south, which then merged to become one. But once Pinot Noir found a home in the Russian River Valley, it became a superstar.

ROLLING ON THE RIVER

One August day, friends invited me to go rowing on the Russian River. My companions were the winemaker at Rodney Strong Vineyards, Rick Sayre; his vineyard director, Doug McIlroy; and our skipper, Rand Dericco, a vineyard manager who sold grapes to Strong.

It was to be an early start, so I arranged for a room in the Hotel Healds-

Captain Rand Dericco rolling on the river.

burg for the night before, in order to avoid the gruesome ride up through the morning rush hour. You encounter bottlenecks of gridlock all along the way up from Oakland; even when you reach Sonoma County and think you're safe, things jam up again at Santa Rosa.

Harvest was just starting, with Sauvignon Blanc and the sparkling varietals coming in. The little country lanes were choked with vehicles hauling bins of grapes. Along Eastside and Westside roads, you had to drive carefully lest some tractor or pickup truck come nosing out from a hidden driveway and cut short your travels with a crunch.

There had been a heat wave, with temperatures well above 100 degrees, and in Healdsburg that night the warmth lingered long past dark. Laughter and music bubbled up from the hotel café until well after midnight— one drawback of having a street-facing room. But when I awoke around

6 A.M., all was hushed, and I was wrapped in blankets. A soupy ground fog had rolled in, so thick that the redwood trees lining the square just across the street were barely visible. Overnight, the temperature had plunged by more than 50 degrees: hands-in-pockets weather.

The plan was to cruise the Russian River from Rodney Strong to the Wohler Bridge, along the stretch called the Middle Reach. I dressed in layers—t-shirt, flannel shirt, and denim jacket—thinking that if it were chilly now, on the water it would be downright cold. But by the time I reached Rod Strong, the sun was poking through the murk, and it was getting warm. Soupy ground fogs burn off early; it's the high stuff that sticks around all day.

We met in the parking lot and drove through the vineyard, then down a steep bank to the shoreline. It was thickly carpeted with small, smoothly rounded stones of an astonishing variety of colors: the famous gravel beds of the Russian River. Out from the stones grew an entanglement of small, spindly trees: red, yellow, and sandbar willow; cottonwood; California black walnut; ash; and box elder. They remain small because the frequent winter floods tear them out by their roots, preventing them from maturing. Dragonflies darted in the clear morning air, and fish leapt from the water and fell back in bursts of silvery spray. The sun was getting hot on my head, so I put on a baseball cap.

Beyond the bank, glinting and glittering with sharp flashes, was the river. I knelt and let the moving water brush my fingertips. It felt cool and was very clear.

We piled into the rowboat and drifted lazily downstream with the current.

My companions talked about the steelhead trout, bass, bluegill, and shad they caught in their secret spots (salmon are an endangered species and subject to special regulations) and about how the river will change its course following a storm because of something as seemingly insignificant as a fallen tree. Once or twice, the boat scrunched against a hidden sandbar with a lurching jolt, but mainly the journey was calm. We passed over a school of suckerfish. There were so many of the brownish, homely bottom feeders in the shallow water that you felt you could use them as stepping-stones to the shore.

The river's fauna were enjoying the sun as much as its human visitors were. Every now and then, we startled a blue heron, which would rise up with a loud whoosh and flap away to safety. Turkey vultures and red-tailed hawks circled overhead, wondering, I suppose, if we were to be lunch. Sharp-eyed Doug pointed out a giant turtle sunning itself on a log. It all reminded me of a boat trip I had taken the previous year along the Río Naranjo in Costa Rica, except there the wildlife had been monkeys, parrots, and caymans. But the idyllic, riparian quality was the same.

As we drifted on, the banks gradually rose in height until we came to a place where they reared up 20 feet or more. The uppermost half of this earthen wall was constructed of a fine, light-brown, silty sand. Below that was packed crunchy river gravel that continued underground for at least another 60 feet, or so I was told. The dividing line between the soil and the gravel was very sharp and perfectly horizontal, as if a carpenter had put in a wainscot. What we were looking at was the visible evidence of thousands of years of gravel deposition. When it ceased at that particular spot, silty sand, laid down by repeated flooding, covered it.

"That's Rochioli up there," Rand said, pointing up to the right. He was referring to the Rochioli property, perhaps the most famous of all Russian River Valley vineyards. He paddled to the shore, hopped out, and dragged the nose of the rowboat, with us in it, up onto the sandy beach. While Rand waited below, Rick, Doug, and I climbed the nearly vertical slope. The earth was very dry and crumbly, a type of soil aptly called riverwash by earth scientists. On this high-summer day, when the last rainfall already was a months-old memory, the earth was bone dry, and clods of dirt broke away from under our feet and tumbled to the bottom, exploding in bomb bursts of yellowish, powdery smoke. It was difficult to keep from sliding down; I grabbed onto bush branches and the stubby ropes of wild vines to haul myself up.

At the top, we stood at the edge of the large, well-tended Rochioli Vineyard. To the northwest was Westside Road. Beyond it and over the hills was Dry Creek Valley.

Nobody said anything for a while; there was a kind of reverent hush. "Terroir is such an interesting thing," Doug finally commented, giving voice to what I thought we were all feeling, for Rochioli's place is sacred ground.

I asked Doug what he meant by "terroir" and what made it so interesting. He might have said something about climate or soil or drainage or exposure or any of the thousand other technical minutiae that clutter every discussion about this untranslatable French term. Instead, he replied, thoughtfully, "It's really the power of observation in the person who's farming, and nobody does that better than the Rochiolis."

I would ask the same question of the Rochiolis themselves the next time I met them. Now it was time for us to continue our voyage, so we slid our way back down the bank to the beach, where we found Rand on his back on the sand, face to the sun.

Beyond Rochioli, the river assumes more of a westward flow. It narrows, too, and then come the rapids. True cliffs erupt, not sandy embankments but slabs of dark granite piled hundreds of feet high. The tallest of all was a dark stone mountain that rose up against the sky. It had rocky crags and a gothic peak crowned with spires of redwood and Douglas fir, their spiky shapes silhouetted against the sun-bright western sky.

"That's Wilson Grove," Rand said, paddling. "It's the first stand of conifers in the Middle Reach." We were entering another climate zone, rainier, foggier, and cooler. The water grew choppy as Rand maneuvered through the crests and troughs, the boat's prow lifting into the air and bouncing down again with a thud.

"You've got two mountain ranges that come together right here," he hollered over the noise, as cool spray hit our faces. "In another mile, the Middle Reach alluvial plain will end."

The big trees in Wilson Grove represent an important transitional zone along the Russian River's landscape provinces. Here, the fog is very nearly incessant, particularly during the summer months, while winter rains are heavy enough to give the giant conifers the huge volume of water they need. Indeed, these big coastal trees drink more water than any other living thing on earth.

The average annual precipitation at Healdsburg is 41 inches, about the same as in New York City. That is more than enough water for almost any growing thing to reach a good size, but only half as much as a mature redwood tree needs. Redwoods grow at Healdsburg, as they do across the street from my home in Oakland—average annual precipitation 20 inches—but they never assume the gargantuan dimensions of their coastal cousins. The farther inland you go, the smaller the redwoods become. By Cloverdale, about twenty-seven miles from the Pacific as the crow flies, they struggle. By the time you get to the Central Valley, the only trees are those whose genes have become adapted to drought.

But at Cazadero, slightly northwest of Wilson Grove, the annual rainfall is 85 inches. Although it is just twenty miles west of Healdsburg, Cazadero is the second wettest measuring station in California. This is a temperate rain forest, part of the primeval swath of Douglas fir, redwood, Sitka spruce, Western hemlock, and other big trees that once thrived from

Alaska down to Big Sur. After a century of logging, it survives now only in isolated pockets and parks. Nonetheless, the working ecological defini-tion of a temperate rain forest—over 1,400 millimeters (about 55 inches) of annual precipitation, cool summers, moderate winters, and a mean an-nual temperature between 4 and 12 degrees Celsius (roughly 39 and 54 de-grees Fahrenheit)—fits this part of Sonoma like a glove.

The tallest trees reach 300 feet and are fourteen hundred years old. It's not only the rain that provides them with sustenance. Even the author of the 1880 *History* understood, one hundred twenty years before science proved it, that the redwood is "a creature of the fog." "The foliage of the red-wood," Munro-Fraser wrote, "possesses the peculiar power of condens-ing this mist and converting it into rain," although he could not have sus-pected how or by how much. More recent research shows that fog drip in the Oakland hills accounts for the equivalent of 10 inches of annual pre-cipitation. In the temperate rain forest, where the fogs are much thicker and more persistent, drip undoubtedly accounts for far more. Redwoods also thin out the farther east you go in Sonoma County because the soils contain more serpentine rock; redwoods, like grapevines and other plants, cannot grow in soils influenced by that nickel-rich rock, which poisons them.

Back on the Russian River, we were getting hungry, and so we pulled onto a beach for lunch. Rand had brought collapsible chairs and a little camp-site table, and Rick, an accomplished amateur chef, had prepared our mid-day feast: Alaskan king salmon he had caught and smoked himself; home-made salmon pasta with vegetables from his garden; and a blackberry and peach pie, baked from scratch, with fruit he had grown. We had worked up a healthy appetite on the water. Now, under the warm sun, we ate the good food and drank Rick's Pinot Noir and Chardonnay, cooled in the river.

The men talked and laughed about things they knew and that made them happy: trapping coyotes in the back country, four-wheeling through canyons of juniper, wines they had drunk, and, of course, people. There are always good tales when you are with winemakers and vineyard men, who no less than women enjoy a juicy piece of gossip.

Doug stretched out and told the story about the hippie he once caught growing pot down by the river at the edge of Rod Strong's vineyard. The man had planted his marijuana bushes on little rafts he had made using grapevines chopped down for their wood, which he lashed together into rafts. He roped the rafts to trees in a looping section of the river hidden— so he thought—from view. On these floating hydroponic farms, the roots of the pot plants went straight down into the water, assuring them of plenty to drink all summer under the hot Sonoma sun. One fall afternoon— harvest time for the grapes as well as for the marijuana—Doug was out in the vineyard, when he happened to spy the young man loading a rented U-Haul truck with bales of new crop. The man was practically begging to be caught—and promptly was, after Doug called the Sonoma County sheriff, who drove out and busted him.

Doug related how, after the sheriff took the grower and the pot away, he discovered another six rafts chockablock with leafy marijuana. Good citizen that he was, he cut them down and piled them into the back of his pickup and drove into Healdsburg, intending to drop them off at the police station.

"Along the way, everyone stopped and stared," Doug said. "I just told them, 'Hey, pretty good crop this year!'"

Rand howled with laughter, and Rick leaned back in his chair, grinning. It was a good moment, but it was harvest time. Rick's cell phone rang.

He had a brief conversation. You could hear the crackly voice on the other side; it sounded urgent. "Cabernet," Rick said, disconnecting. "Gotta go." There was a crisis at one of Rodney Strong's vineyards in Alexander Valley. The grape sugars had soared 2 full degrees of brix overnight as a result of the scorching heat; the fruit needed to be picked, and Rick's presence was desired. The day had to come to an end.

Rand had arranged for a truck to be waiting for us a little farther downstream. As we hauled the rowboat up the bank, I asked Rick what he would have done in the old days, before cell phones kept him in constant touch with the outside world. He laughed and said, "I wouldn't have taken a river trip during harvest!"

7

Pinot Noir Comes to Westside Road

Rochioli's vineyard was indeed hallowed ground for Pinot Noir. The vineyard is located in the heart of a stretch of the Russian River Valley known locally as the Middle Reach, a term used by the mining companies not to indicate the river's geographic midpoint but to indicate the section that contained the richest deposits of gravel. It is also the most famous part of the appellation for the quality of its Pinot Noir. But if the Middle Reach is California's emerging Côte de Nuits, it was a long time coming.

For years, the "experts" had derided Pinot Noir, claiming that it was impossible to successfully grow it in California. Some considered California's climate too hot; others (particularly the French) believed that its soils were entirely unsuitable because they did not contain large amounts of the limestone that undergirds Burgundy. ("You can steal our vines, you can steal our methods, but you can never steal our terroir!" I was once told by a famous Burgundian *vigneron*.) Besides, it was once argued, Pinot Noir was not commercially viable. Even as far back as 1896, Eugene Hilgard, the agricultural genius who started the University of California's work in viticulture and enology, was warning grape growers against trying it. "No price that is likely to be obtained at present would justify" the effort, he wrote.

Even a mere generation ago, wine critics arched their eyebrows and pinched their noses when it came to Pinot Noir. "Thin-flavored and simple," sniffed one. "Deplorable," snapped another. And those were California wine writers, who might have been expected to show a little patriotic sympathy.

Europeans were even more savage in their attacks. The dean of British wine writers, the urbane, silver-haired Michael Broadbent, in the 1970s decreed that California Pinot Noir was "not to be compared with burgundy." Not content with this categorical injury, he added a gastronomic insult in describing it as "stewed."

Certainly, there was little to make Pinot Noir interesting, except to the most extreme fanatic. "In the 1970s, Pinot Noir had been written off in California," recalls Forrest Tancer, who made it at Iron Horse's Green Valley property from a vineyard earlier established by Rodney Strong but later acquired by the Sterling family, into which Tancer married. "There was a lot of miserable wine. I used to joke about 'eau de rubber boot' Pinot Noir." Rubber boots—stewed—pretty much the same thing!

Fortunately for us—perhaps unfortunately for them—some winemakers are attracted to Pinot Noir like moths to a flame. Every Pinot Noir story is a personal one, and here is mine.

I did not care much for it, at first. The earliest note in my tasting diary that mentions Pinot Noir concerned a 1979 Monterey Vineyard Classic California Red from the Central Coast. It was a "heavy, warm" wine, I wrote, but then, it cost all of three dollars. It is difficult, if not impossible, today to imagine a California vintner mixing Pinot Noir with Cabernet Sauvignon and Zinfandel, which was the composition of that long-ago mutant.

The next mention was Edmeades' 1983 Opal, a proprietary wine from Mendocino County's Anderson Valley, which at least had the virtue of being 100 percent Pinot Noir. But it continued the theme of cranky unconventionality by being, as the label boldly stated, a "dry white" (actually pink) wine. It cost four dollars forty cents, pretty fancy in those days for a rosé, much less one from Mendocino. Again, it is difficult to imagine anyone today making a rosé of Pinot Noir, because a red Pinot Noir (odd phrase) brings so much more money than a blush wine ever would. (Even as I write this, however, the notorious "grape glut" of the early 2000s is resulting in a sea of rosé wines made from all sorts of unlikely varietals, as vintners try to figure out new ways of repackaging old grapes.)

I mention these two oddities only to underscore the awkward position held by California Pinot Noir back then. It was sulky to grow, finicky to make, not understood by consumers, and, consequently, hard to sell. Distributors didn't want to touch it. Although California Pinot Noir from stalwarts such as Almaden, Beaulieu, and Paul Masson had been staples on restaurant wine lists in the 1940s and 1950s, by the 1970s it was harder to find. By then, a new culture of cuisine and wine appreciation, influenced by Pinot-bashing critics, largely short-circuited whatever progress the varietal had previously made. A sommelier who wanted a nice Pinot Noir for the wine list would get it from the only place in the world where that grape made good wine: Burgundy. Besides, as everyone then knew, the coming red varietal in California was Cabernet Sauvignon.

The first true, red California Pinot Noir I recorded in my tasting book was in 1985. It was—to reprise the theme of things that no longer exist—from the old Louis K. Mihaly winery in Napa Valley, the 1982 Private Reserve (a meaningless designation, then as now, as no law governs the use of those words). I came across it at the old Les Amis du Vin winetasting group in San Francisco and liked it so much that I promptly drove up and bought a half-case. I can't remember what I paid—five dollars a bottle?

What was that Mihaly Pinot like? "Fruity-cherry smell," I wrote. "Flavors of cherries and tar. Round, mellow, mouth-filling and deep. Terrific stuffing and complexity. Silky smooth. Long, rich aftertaste."

Silky . . . cherries . . . mellow. In other words, a wine we would recognize today as Pinot Noir. I recall a certain leathery smell (perhaps what I meant by "tar") that could have been caused by brettanomyces, a yeast that in small amounts can add complexity to a wine's aroma, but which in larger quantities can make the wine smell like a perspiring horse. (To this day, the subject of how much, if any, "brett" a wine can or should have launches critics into angels-dancing-on-pinhead debates.) It was the sort of Pinot Noir once planted in considerable quantity on the floor of the Napa Valley but hardly to be found there anymore, the victim of critical disdain and a conviction, now hardened into the detritus of conventional wisdom, that Pinot Noir does not deserve a place in Napa Valley, outside of the Carneros, which really oughtn't to be a formal part of Napa Valley anyway.

I liked that Mihaly, although in retrospect I can see that it lacked the delicacy and breed (such a nice word for wine) you want in a Pinot Noir. It might well have faded out of my mind forever in the endless Niagara of wines I have drunk, with more or less pleasure, since. But like a first date on which something significant happens, it turned out to be unforgettable. That wine proved to me that California Pinot Noir could be as distinctive as Cabernet Sauvignon.

After that, my Pinot encounters were scattershot. A 1982 Adelsheim from the Willamette Valley in Oregon intrigued me, and so did an early Saintsbury Garnet from Carneros, although you could not have asked for two more different wines—the former dark and earthy, the latter as lightly fruity as a fresh, carbonic young Beaujolais. I liked a 1985 Charles Krug for its soft suppleness. A 1986 Pedroncelli from Dry Creek Valley was heavy and tannic. I tasted through a range of the then-new 1985s from the Domaine de la Romanée-Conti and was a little ashamed at not being impressed. In the main, Pinot remained an afterthought. For every one I stumbled across, there were a hundred Cabernet Sauvignons, Zinfandels, Chardonnays, and—a passion at the time—German Rieslings. With Pinot Noir, the truth, now clear to me, is that you either love it or are indifferent. I was indifferent.

The first Russian River Valley Pinot Noir I find in my notes was a 1985 Lot #2 from Dehlinger. (Years later, I asked Tom Dehlinger what the name meant, and he replied, grinning, "A failed experiment in marketing!") It was a wine that intrigued yet puzzled me, and, judging from my brief and ambiguous written remarks, I wasn't sure what to make of it. It seemed to change before my very eyes (or nose), now beef-bouillony and vegetal and, yes, "stewed," in the sense of bringing to mind a gurgling pot of chunky tomato sauce. But then it seemed to inhale and breathe out from the glass a great waft of blackberries, blueberries, and cherries, as if some fruity essence had awakened deep within its slumbering soul, stimulated by a tickle of air. It straddled the line between ripeness and its opposite with the nimble-footedness of a high-wire acrobat performing without a net.

That was a wine to taste twice, or three times, or four, to pause between sips and mull over. It was not great, but it was, well, *interesting.* There was something elusive about it, like a flitting shadow or a butterfly's flight. For the first time, I understood why people used the word "tease" to describe Pinot's appeal. Tom Dehlinger has talked about Pinot Noir's "intellectual challenge," whereas Bob Cabral, at Williams Selyem, describes it as "a bully one minute and a passive baby the next." Both winemakers are referring, I think, to Pinot Noir's schizoid, changeling character.

LIKE FRANCE, A PINOT NOIR, A BURGUNDY

Rochioli's property is part of a chain of Middle Reach vineyards that runs for seven or so miles along Westside Road, from just outside Healdsburg down to the Wohler Bridge, where the landscape, as we saw on our rowboat ride, changes dramatically. (There is no precise definition of Middle Reach boundaries, since the region isn't a legal appellation—yet.)

The vineyards are on both sides of the river, but, to my mind, the best—certainly, the best-known—are to its northwest, on either side of Westside Road. They run from the river's edge onto the flatlands and benches and then, crossing Westside, extend a few hundred feet onto the flanks of the hills. Above that, the terrain, dominated by 1,652-foot Mount Jackson, becomes too rugged and remote to plant to any great extent. The temperature is hotter, too, as you move into Dry Creek Valley, which is patently too warm for Pinot Noir.

These Middle Reach vineyards and wineries, stretching from Philip Staley (who does not make a Pinot Noir) through Belvedere, Bacigalupi, and Hop Kiln, and then to Williams Selyem, Davis Bynum, and finally Porter Creek (all of whom do), are famous. None, however, is as historically connected to Pinot Noir as Rochioli.

Westside Road is a sleepy little country lane, rolling and curvy and picturesque as it wends its way past vineyards, farmhouses, and little wineries. To my esthetic sensibility, it is one of the most scenic wine routes in California. For more than a century, the Westside area, like all of Spanish-Mexican California, consisted of large ranchos, many of them thousands or even tens of thousands of acres. The regional Spanish-Mexican *comandantes* had issued these land grants within their jurisdictions to encourage agriculture and industry, reward soldiers, or provide for propertyless friends or relatives. Sonoma alone included scores of ranchos; Fitch's Sotoyomi Rancho, at 48,836 acres, was the second largest. Built on old Pomo trails, Westside Road was one of the lanes that connected the ranchos and the subsequent population centers. It gave people from Healdsburg and points north and east access to the river hamlets of Rio Nido and Guerneville and the far coast (and vice versa), allowing them to avoid the more circuitous southern routes along Eastside and River roads.

As chapter 6 described, the area was not heavily settled until the 1880s and 1890s, when Italian immigrants began arriving in large numbers. They came to seek their fortunes; word of mouth and letters back home spread enticing tales of a gentle river valley whose genial climate and hills were said to resemble Italy's own pastoral countryside. One of these families was a clan that originally came from the small village of Fornovolasco, outside Lucca. Their name was Rocchioli; they later dropped the second "c." Their story could stand for that of hundreds of others, except for the way it has ended.

Michele Rocchioli and his wife, Menichina, and their two children, Angela and Giuseppe, sailed past the Statue of Liberty to land in New York City on August 1, 1911, when Giuseppe, later to be known as Joe (and, still later, Joe Sr.), was eight years old. Over the next few years, Michele made his way across the country, working at odd jobs much as the young Cyrus Alexander had done. In 1914, he arrived in the Russian River Valley, where he found a position on the old Wohler Ranch.

At a mere 1,310 acres, the Wohler place hardly qualified as a rancho. It was a combination hopyard and vineyard, bordering the Russian River, that belonged to a landowner named Raford Peterson. ("Raford PETERSON was here Wednesday," the *Sonoma Democrat*, published out of Santa Rosa, proclaimed in an 1895 society brief, suggesting not only Peterson's importance but also the newsworthiness of the ten-mile trip between the Wohler Ranch and Santa Rosa in those pre-automobile days.)

As soon as Joe was old enough, he also started working on the ranch, and he did well. "He was one of the smarter ones and rose to the top," Joe Rochioli Jr. says of his father. By the late 1920s, Joe Sr. had become the ranch foreman, with a reputation for driving his field hands hard, although no harder than he drove himself.

In 1930, he married Neoma Baldi, the daughter of friends who also were from the Fornovolasco area. Joe Jr. was born in 1934. A few years later, the ambitious Joe Sr., longing to be his own boss, leased a 125-acre property near the Wohler Ranch, called Fenton Acres after the name of its owner. Joe spent the next thirty years there, raising his family and saving his pennies before eventually buying the property in 1957. The Fenton Acres site is where the Rochioli vineyards and winery are now located. Joe Sr. died in 1966.

Before he died, Joe Sr. put in his first vines, albeit reluctantly. Like many others throughout Sonoma County who planted grapes in those days, he did so on the advice of the University of California's local farm advisor. Joe Sr. considered himself a farmer of crops, especially hops, and apparently did not have any particular seriousness about grape growing, much less winemaking, beyond having another product to sell in a market that was reportedly expanding. He planted French Colombard, Gamay Beaujolais, and Valdeguie, the high-yielding varietals then in demand for the jug wines preferred by consumers. He sold them to the likes of giant wineries such as Gallo and Martini & Prati, where the grapes disappeared into blending vats of "Chianti," "Burgundy," "Rhine," and all the other purloined names.

Joe Jr. then entered the picture. He is a craggy man, earthy and voluble, with a penchant for salty tales and a good belly laugh. We sat one day on the veranda outside the winery tasting room, in our shirtsleeves although it was midwinter. The fragrant little pinkish-purple flowers on the plum trees had blossomed, and there were already bursts of wildflowers along Westside Road. We were in the January-February heat wave and minidrought of the 2003 vintage, and, although the weather was shortly to turn wintry again, on this day a soft southerly breeze shot the temperature to well over 70 degrees. In Guerneville, people were sitting in the cafés or sunning themselves by the old bridge; but Joe Jr. worried that the heat would wake up the vines too soon. If that happened, the rains and frosts that were bound to come could kill the tender shoots or start the grapes on the process of uneven ripening as a result of the physiological problem of grape shatter (loss of berries).

I asked Joe Jr. how he came to plant Pinot Noir. He settled back in his chair and spun the tale.

"We were gettin' the same prices [for grapes] as Lodi, Sacramento, and the [Central] Valley, and we just couldn't compete with 'em," he said. Prices for cheap inland grapes had sunk to extremely low levels by the 1960s. Along the coast, where the cost of production and the cost of living in general were higher, such prices were, in the long run, unsustainable. Beyond that, the local hops industry was in the throes of its final collapse. Joe Jr. understood that the farm's prospects were not good. "So I started thinkin', in order to survive, we're gonna have to do something special. And the future was varietal wines. I had read a little about France, and over there, they had all these varietals, and they kept the production [yield] down."

Joe Jr. got it into his head to plant some of those low-production French grapes. But Joe Sr. wouldn't hear of it. Like the other old-time growers, he was interested in quantity, not quality. But Joe Jr. was seeing something his father didn't.

Nor were the experts at the University of California particularly helpful. When Joe Jr. sought their advice, "They said, 'Jesus Christ, put in more Gamay Beaujolais! That's what you wanna put in!'" he recalled. "But I says, 'No! That's not what I wanna put in! That's ten tons to the acre. I want something shy-bearing! I want something quality!'"

"Something quality," in that unknown new world of varietal wine,

Joe Jr. and Tom Rochioli, père et fils, *the heart and soul of the Middle Reach.*

turned out to be Sauvignon Blanc. Joe Jr. planted some in 1960, using bud-wood he got from U.C. Davis's vineyard. He had walked through a dozen rows of grape-laden vines, each assigned with a different clonal number, tasted from each, and finally chose the grape "that really tasted different." But at that nascent time in the American wine industry, nobody wanted this strange new white grape for itself. Joe Jr. was forced to sell it, along with his French Colombard, as "mixed whites" to the usual suspects—Gallo and Martini & Prati. As he recalled this, Joe Jr. practically winced. He shook his head with sadness as he said, "The most beautiful grapes you ever saw. . . ." It wasn't until 1969 that a premium winery, Rod Strong's old Windsor brand, bought those Sauvignon Blanc grapes for themselves. (The story has a happy ending. Rochioli's old-vine Sauvignon Blanc is among the best of that varietal produced in California, year in and year out.)

Next, he tried planting Cabernet Sauvignon, but the grapes didn't seem to ripen properly in the cool climate. Then the idea of Pinot Noir popped up. It's hard to say just why. Joe Jr. hadn't exactly been a Burgundy buff; he barely knew what Pinot Noir was. "At home, we drank pretty much Zinfandel, the homemade stuff," he says, like most of the Italian Americans. But he now arrived at an firm conclusion: "We had to do it like France, a Pinot Noir, a Burgundy."

In 1968, he put in his first Pinot Noir vines, just a few hundred feet from where Rand, Rick, and I had climbed up, in a patch of the vineyard now known as East Block.

"Everyone thought I was crazy!" Joe Jr. laughed.

I asked him where he had gotten his Pinot Noir cuttings. In 1968, very little Pinot Noir was available in California, and the options for anyone seeking it were severely limited.

"I heard from friends that this old grower in Napa Valley had some," he recalled. I pressed him, wondering whether it could have been Louis K. Mihaly. Joe Jr. put his hand to his forehead and thought.

"To tell you the truth," he eventually replied, "I don't remember his name or even where he was, except that it was south of St. Helena." As Mihaly's place had been. Joe Jr. drove over the hill, struck a deal with that now-forgotten grower, and in went East Block.

Then I asked Joe Jr. what he had planned to do with his fancy new Pinot Noir. Wasn't it likely to have simply ended up in the "mixed red and black" blending vats at Martini & Prati and Gallo?

"To tell you the truth, I didn't really know," he said. "It was a matter of pride. I just thought something had to happen here, or there wouldn't be any grapes." Nor did it ever enter his head to make his own wine. "I was poor, very poor. I didn't have the money to buy equipment or anything."

Despite having no plans for his Pinot Noir, only a year after planting East Block, he planted West Block right next to it. This time, however, the source of the cuttings was well known. Joe Jr. recalled that he had been hauling some French Colombard down to Wente Brothers Winery in the Livermore Valley. The grapes from that rather bland varietal might have filled out one of the many white wines the Wentes were producing at the time. Joe Jr. had heard that his good friend Carl Wente had brought in some French clones of Pinot Noir, and Joe asked him for some budwood.

But Carl Wente said no. "'Joe,' he says, 'I paid a lot of money for these.' So I says to him, 'Carl, come on, now.'" (It's fun to imagine these two shrewd, veteran grape men, one a flinty-eyed Italian American, the other a wizened German American, in the vineyard, kicking the dirt, feeling each other out, bargaining.) "'Well,' Carl says, 'I guess I can let you have some.'" Joe Jr. laughed a deep, happy laugh. "He charged me five cents a bud. I bought five thousand buds. That was a lot of money!"

When our conversation ended, I shook hands with Joe Jr. and told him he must be very proud of how well things had worked out. After all, Rochioli's Pinot Noirs are among the rarest, most coveted, and most expensive in California—or in the New World, for that matter. He pointed with his chin to the winery building, with its fancy, stone-finished, wood-paneled tasting room, and said, "Oh, yeah. It's a gold mine." He did not miss the hard times during the Depression, when the family had been so broke they never left the Wohler Ranch and ate only what they could grow.

"But it's killin' me," Joe Jr. said. "I bought all this land for little or nothin', two thousand dollars an acre. Now it's valued so high, my estate's blown clear out of sight. They're sayin' my kids will have to come up with seven million dollars in inheritance tax!"

I guessed success was a double-edged sword, but I did not think that Joe Jr. was complaining.

Technically speaking, Joe Jr.'s Pinot Noir was not the first to be planted in the Russian River Valley, or even along Westside Road. In the 1930s, the old Fountaingrove Winery, north of Santa Rosa, grew some, or is said to have grown something called Pinot Noir. Mary Frost Mabon, in *ABC of America's Wines,* thought so highly of it that she called it "one of the top wines of California"—and, moreover, noted that Fountaingrove's '35 vintage was actually labeled Sonoma Pinot Noir. Where exactly the grapes were grown I do not know, but, in 1948, the American writer Julian Street said that Fountaingrove's Pinot Noir and its Cabernet Sauvignon were "identical in color, bouquet, and flavor," which is exactly the problem when Pinot Noir is cultivated in a too-hot climate—it becomes too full bodied.

The Bacigalupi family, just up Westside Road from Rochioli's place toward Healdsburg, definitely planted some Pinot Noir in 1964, also get-

ting their budwood from Wente Brothers and also following the advice of
the peripatetic farm advisor. A few miles farther west, after Westside merges
with River Road just before Guerneville, Korbel had tinkered on and off
with Pinot Noir and actually vinified a varietally labeled one in the 1950s.
Paperwork in Korbel's archives dating back to 1955 records something called
Sonoma Pinot Noir, Santa Nella Vineyard, the old name for the vineyard
just across River Road from the sprawling Korbel campus. (There's still
a little inn nearby, the Santa Nella House, built in the 1870s by a physi-
cian friend of the original Korbel brothers.) But Korbel's focus was on
sparkling wine, and the winery missed out on the chance to become known
as a Pinot Noir pioneer. Not that it has hurt them. Korbel has become
one of the most successful sparkling wine producers in the world, and the
profits from his bubblies have enabled owner Gary Heck to buy other
wineries in Sonoma County—Kenwood, Valley of the Moon, and Lake
Sonoma. And, in fact, Korbel's Pinot Noir program, now resuscitated, produces very good wine.

Once the Rochiolis started growing Pinot Noir, they needed to find
a winery to make it into wine. They didn't have to look very far. Just a few
miles down Westside Road was another adventurous family whose claim
to fame in this little tale is that they were the first to make a wine from
Rochioli's Pinot Noir grapes—and in so doing made history.

That family was headed by Davis Bynum. Davis, who had been the garden editor at the *San Francisco Chronicle* and a home winemaker, was hooked
up with the old Berkeley food-and-wine crowd that included Alice Waters,
of Chez Panisse restaurant fame. He began making and selling wine in 1965,
using purchased grapes, in a storefront on San Pablo Avenue in Albany, just
north of Berkeley, a traffic-choked street of auto repair shops and Chinese
restaurants. Davis's ambition was to own his own winery, and he eventually purchased the old Whitehall Lane vineyard, on Highway 29 in Napa

Hampton Bynum with two barrels of organically grown Pinot Noir.

Valley. "We wanted to build a winery," his son, Hampton, recalled, "but the Napa Planning Commission wouldn't let us. So we thought, 'This is a joke. Let's find someplace else.'"

"Someplace else" turned out to be a run-down hop mill on Westside Road. The hops industry had been huge in the Russian River Valley; the annual hops harvest employed more pickers than any other crop in the county, and the beer factories of Santa Rosa were the biggest employers around. But even by the early 1950s, the hops industry was going down-hill—one reason why Joe Sr. was looking around for a new crop to plant—and by the early 1960s, it had completely collapsed. In 1962, the little hop mill on Westside Road shut down.

Davis bought it on the cheap, although it required a huge amount of work to convert the dilapidated old stone building into a winery. (In the small world of Russian River Valley wine, one of the young men Davis hired to work on the project was the Pinot Noir winemaker Gary Farrell, then a student at Santa Rosa Junior College, who later had his own eponymously named winery on Westside Road. Farrell had started a construction company to put himself through school. Later, he made wine for the Rochiolis. In the spring of 2004, Farrell sold his winery to the spirits giant Allied Domecq, although the deal called for him to remain as winemaker.)

"Joe was selling his Pinot Noir to Martini & Prati and Gallo for practically nothing," Hampton Bynum recalled. "Those grapes were going into Hearty Burgundy. So we went to see him, and we said, 'Joe, you're getting a hundred fifty dollars a ton for your Pinot Noir. We'll give you four hundred fifty a ton for it.'" It was an offer Joe Jr. couldn't refuse.

Once they got the grapes, the Bynums needed a full-time winemaker; Davis was still living in the Bay Area, visiting the winery only a few days a week. That turned out to be Hampton. Young, bearded, and handsome, with long blond hair, Hampton knew next to nothing about making wine. But Davis appointed him to the job anyway. "When Dad informed me that I was now the winemaker," Hampton says, grinning with irony, "I just said, 'Well, Dad, that's great!' But he was nice enough to hire Bob Stemmler to hold my hand." Stemmler was an experienced winemaker who had worked at Charles Krug and Inglenook and who went on to establish his own winery in Dry Creek Valley.

As things turned out, the day they crushed their first grapes, the Bynums' permit to operate a winery arrived in the mail. Also on that day, Farrell and his construction crew finished putting a new roof on the winery building. Hampton (whom Farrell calls "a very good instinctual winemaker") made the wine. That 1973 Davis Bynum Rochioli Vineyard Pinot Noir was the first vineyard-designated wine ever made in the Russian River Valley. Despite its historical significance, one critic, writing of it in 1976, said that it "deserved no standing ovations." On the other hand, Joe Jr.

claims that the best Pinot Noir he ever had was a 1978 Davis Bynum, also made with Rochioli grapes.

I asked Hampton why Davis decided to put Rochioli Vineyard on the label; the *hommage* of vineyard designation was almost unheard of in California at the time. "Because my father was raised in the European tradition," Hampton replied, "and he fancied that, perhaps, this might be the New World Burgundy." The label also listed the Russian River, not the Russian River Valley.

Step by step, Russian River Valley Pinot Noir was happening. Serious growers were growing it, serious reviewers were paying attention to it (if not always favorably), and serious wine lovers were drinking it. Davis Bynum served his Pinot Noir to his Berkeley friends, who in turn told *their* well-connected friends about it. Word was spreading.

From these chance occurrences, a Burgundian-centered vision began manifesting itself along Westside Road. The pieces and players were now in place for the revolution that was erupting in the Russian River Valley.

It is a testimony to how slowly things actually developed, however, that even by the early 1980s, Rochioli Pinot Noir grapes remained very cheap. When Gary Farrell released his first commercial wine, a 1982 blend of Rochioli West Block and Three Corner, it could fetch a price of only eighty dollars a case. "At that time, no one knew who Rochioli was," he says. The same wine today, if that blend were made (it isn't), would cost eighty dollars a bottle.

But the critics—insiders like Joel Butler, who were always on the lookout for something new and compelling—eventually discovered wines made from Rochioli's grapes. By the late 1980s, demand for these grapes had become so intense that Joe Jr.'s son, Tom, became convinced that the family had to build their own winery and make their own wine. "Everybody else was using our name and making great wine," he recalls. "Davis Bynum was doing well with it, Williams Selyem was getting some, Rod Strong was doing good things with the Sauvignon Blanc, and several others. So I told Dad, 'Let's try to do it on our own! Rochioli is who we are, and that's what the label's gonna say!'"

Joe Jr. was reluctant to take such a giant step. "He kind of hemmed and hawed," Tom recalls. Joe Jr. had been a pioneer, but not a reckless one; the financial investment of starting a winery carried an extraordinary risk. But around this time, he delivered some grapes to a certain winery and discovered the entire crush crew stoned out of their minds on pot. When he returned the next morning, the crew was still high—and the grapes were still sitting there in their bins, untended and oxidizing, crawling with fruit flies. That place "made an awful wine that year," Joe Jr. says. That episode helped to convince him that Tom was right: they had to do it on their own. They got Gary Farrell to help them design the new winery and select the equipment. He also made the first few wines, but Tom quickly took over the job as winemaker.

They were now producing a Rochioli Pinot Noir. The next step came in 1990, when Tom visited Burgundy for the first time and the scales fell from his eyes. The father had been determined to grow Pinot "like France, a Burgundy." Now the son decided to do it like the quintessential Burgundy vineyard, the Domaine de la Romanée-Conti.

The Domaine, of course, is famous for being divided into seven mini-vineyards, or *climats*, six of them devoted to Pinot Noir and one to Chardonnay. The various vineyards are separated by little more than donkey paths, but for centuries they have been the subject of fascinated speculation. Why are the wines made from each vineyard so different? And why, for that matter, are the various *climats* not blended together to make a single wine, as is the custom in Bordeaux? The six Pinot Noir vineyards at Romanée-Conti (Romanée-Conti, La Tâche, Romanée St. Vivant, Richebourg, Grands Echezeaux, Echezeaux), added together, total just 175 acres, about half the size of, say, Lafite. But it would be absurd to suggest carving Lafite up into separate bottlings. Why do they do it at Romanée-Conti? And why is Pinot Noir never blended with other varietals, as are the wines of Bordeaux?

The answer has partly to do with Burgundian inheritance laws and local tradition, but it also involves the nature of Pinot Noir. Something about this wine is, to use a word commonly associated with it, transparent. That is, it is an almost perfect mirror of the conditions in which the grapes are grown; it seems to reflect even the tiniest subtleties of weather and soil, in a way that a fuller-bodied red wine such as Syrah, Merlot, or Cabernet Sauvignon does not. (Riesling and Sangiovese are the only other major varietals that are similarly transparent, and they, too, are delicately structured wines.) A chemist might point out that Pinot Noir grapes contain as little as one-tenth the quantity of anthrocyanins—pigments that add body and strength to a red wine—in Cabernet, and thus that subtler influences from elements other than the grape will have a greater impact on the resulting wine. But Beaujolais also is low in anthrocyanins, and it is never referred to in the same hushed tones as Pinot Noir, which is why, in 1395, the Duke of Burgundy ordered all "wicked and disloyal" Gamay Beaujolais vines uprooted from his vineyards and replaced with Pinot Noir.

I have asked many Pinot Noir winemakers about this transparency, and while all agree that Pinot Noir is the most site-sensitive of varietals, no one is quite able to say why. "For some reason, it's just a more translucent filter of what's coming up through the plant from the ground," says Ehren Jordan, who makes Pinot Noir at his Failla winery on the Sonoma coast. Dan Goldfield, at Dutton-Goldfield, expresses a similar thought. "That's the difference between Pinot and Cab. What makes Pinot so unique is there's no grape that expresses a singular piece of land more straightfor- wardly." Then he adds, "Because with Pinot Noir, there's no such thing as the best quality. It's all about personality."

It is an astounding thing to say that "there's no such thing as the best quality" when it comes to Pinot Noir. Would anyone ever say that about Cabernet or Chardonnay or almost any other varietal? But that is the essence and the charm of Pinot Noir: minute differences between the wines fascinate us. To a Burgundian, the wine is an expression not of its variety but its origin; that is why the Pinot Noir always must remain un- blended, as a highly pedigreed show dog must breed only with its own kind. Romanée-Conti's co-director, Aubert de Villaine, has said that a Pinot Noir wine is "like somebody's personality or face." Each wine, that is, a window into an authentic and independent soul, each different in its own way, and each revealing a different facet of—well, of whatever its essence is. Richard Olney, who wrote about the Domaine in his little 1991 book *Romanée-Conti*, said that, after every bit of science has been applied to un- derstanding Pinot Noir, its "chthonic mystery . . . remains intact." (And it took a trip to the dictionary to find the meaning of "chthonic": "dark, primitive, and mysterious," from a Greek word designating the underworld of the dead.)

I don't mean to suggest that there is universal agreement on the issue of whether the best Pinot Noirs must be single-vineyard specimens. "Who's to say," muses Farrell, "that a combination of, say, Rochioli West Block and Three Corner wouldn't create a more complex wine?" For that matter, who's to say that a blend of Russian River Valley and, say, Santa Rita Hills Pinot Noir could not make a great wine? But no one is likely to create such a composite (except, just possibly, Jess Jackson), which would be entitled only to a California appellation.

Farrell hits one nail squarely on the head with his suggestion that the single-vineyard Pinot Noir trend "is more market-driven than winemaker-driven," and this statement is certainly not undermined by the fact that he makes quite a number of single-vineyard wines himself. Collectors who are willing to shell out fifty or sixty dollars and more for a bottle of Pinot Noir want to see a vineyard name on the label, and that is what vintners happily give them. I used to joke (and it's truer than ever) that every extra word a vintner can squeeze onto the front label is worth an additional five dollars. Apply this formula to a hypothetical wine—Jones Winery 1999 Brown Vineyard South Block Bobby's Corner Lily's Row Clone 9 Old Vine Grandad's Special Estate-Grown Pinot Noir—and be prepared for sticker shock.

At any rate, and in so many ways, the Domaine de la Romanée-Conti estate reminded Tom Rochioli of his own piece of land. His first Pinot Noirs had been blends assembled from various parts of the estate. Now he arrived at a momentous decision: to create separate bottlings of Pinot Noir, each based on a block designation, or a vineyard-within-a-vineyard—a *climat*—the way they did it at Romanée-Conti. Whereas Joe Jr. had honored the Rochioli Vineyard en masse, Tom would award each subsection its own *hommage*, if he believed it deserved it. Chutzpah? Shrewd marketing? A true idée fixe? Probably, in Tom's case, a combination of all three.

The teardrop-shaped Rochioli vineyard consists of 128 planted acres. The section closest to the Russian River, where we climbed up the crumbly bank, is called Riverblock. It was planted to Chardonnay and Pinot Noir in 1989.

Riverblock seems to have been the Rochiolis' response to increasing consumer demand for their grapes and wines. The soil is not ideal for Pinot

Noir, and nothing might ever have been planted there had the market not tightened and economics not dictated. Tom himself calls Riverblock "a mess" and admits, "I don't think it's the best of my group."

In fact, lots of people with land immediately adjacent to the Russian River planted grapes there only in the late 1980s and 1990s. "Prior to 1996, you couldn't even sell Pinot Noir from down there," says Simi's vineyard manager, Jerry Chong, referring to riverbank Pinot Noir. "You were lucky to get six hundred dollars a ton. But the explosion of the Pinot market has allowed these people to sell Russian River Valley Pinot Noir. I'll tell you, in the long run, that's not where the best ones are going to grow."

But such remarks do not take into account the obsessively perfectionist viticulture that a fanatical grower like Joe Rochioli Jr. practices in his vineyards. The soil in Riverblock is very rich old riverbottom. It consists of deposits of fine-grained sand and silt left behind by the river's endless flooding and receding (hence the name riverwash) and is relatively high in nutrients and organic material left over from decaying leaves, fish poop, microorganisms, and the like. (Below that, as we have seen, is that 60-foot-deep well of gravel.) Left to themselves, grapevines would grow too vigorously, which is why Joe Jr. and his crew have to fuss endlessly to reduce yields. "If you miss," Tom says, "you get that tomato, veggie quality"— Broadbent's "stewed" character.

(But I want to say here that Joe Jr. does such a good job at viticulture that the winemakers who vinify Riverblock's grapes—such as Cabral at Williams Selyem and Tom Rochioli himself—consistently produce some of the great Pinot Noirs of California. In the summer of 2004, at another of our big blind tastings, my *Wine Enthusiast* colleagues and I went through more than three hundred California Pinot Noirs from the 2002 vintage, and Williams Selyem's Rochioli Vineyard River Block, as they spell it, was the second highest-scoring wine.)

Next up from Riverblock is the section Tom calls Mid 40. It is a true bench, separated from Riverblock by a step in the earth, about a foot high and stretching across the entire vineyard. In a homely phrase, Tom calls this step "the Hump." Mid 40 contains East Block, West Block, and Three Corner, the third-oldest Pinot Noir vineyard on the estate, planted in 1974. These *climats* are the crown jewels of the Rochioli estate and are priced accordingly.

The soil changes abruptly at the Hump. It is less rich in nutrients, a well-drained sandy loam common throughout Sonoma County's valley-floor agricultural lands, ideal for grapes and almost any other crop. In the Côte de Nuits, for a thousand years, the best grapes have grown on a slice of hillside, midway up the slope. Go a little higher or lower, and the quality is not so good. One is tempted to think of Mid 40 as such a tenderloin strip. The vines there grow well but not too vigorously and do not require as much fussing as those down in Riverblock. They ripen "almost automatically," Tom says.

Another reason why Mid 40 is different from Riverblock is the fog. Coming in from the south, southeast, and southwest during the late afternoon or early evening, it crosses over Riverblock first and reaches Mid 40 a little later. By mid-morning the next day, the pattern reverses, making Mid 40 warmer and sunnier than Riverblock—not by much, but on such thin margins is Pinot Noir's personality built. This delicate balance of sun and fog seems to impart to the grapes the beautiful acid-tannin-fruit complex they possess. Vine age no doubt also has something to do with it.

As you leave Mid 40 and approach Westside Road, you notice how red the soil becomes. There is nothing like it farther down toward the river. This is not rivery silt and sand anymore, although streaks of it are folded in. Rather, it is iron-rich stuff, formed inside volcanoes, eroded and rusted, and washed down from the mountains. And beneath it is that bottomless pit of gravel. This soil is very dry and not particularly rich, and consequently growers find even lower vine vigor.

These roadside vineyards represent an ambiguity. Tom Rochioli himself seems unsure about which varietals do best there. "There are so many inconsistencies, it's hard to nail," he says, when I ask him about it. The Rochiolis have hedged their bets in these vineyards, planting not only Pinot Noir and Chardonnay but also Syrah, Gamay Beaujolais, Sauvignon Blanc, Zinfandel, and the Cabernet Sauvignon grapes Oded Shakked buys for Longboard.

In fact, Westside Road marks an important transitional zone at Rochioli. "It's on the edge of the hundred-year flood plain," says Cabral, whose winery is across the street, just down Westside Road. "On the river side, you see all this alluvial plain of silt and sand that sits on top of gravel that goes down to kingdom come. As you cross the road, you get into more clays and metamorphosed sandstone and rocks that were held under intense pressure and heat for a long time, that cooked the soil down below it."

In Rochioli's case, this Westside Road transitional zone marks the boundary between the sandy soils of Riverblock and Mid 40, on the one hand, and the true hillside vineyard Tom calls Sweetwater, on the other.

Hampton Bynum had told me, "Tom's favorite, of all the plantings, is Sweetwater," and I certainly got the feeling that it was his pride and joy. Planted only in 1999 and 2000, it is his youngest vineyard, his little baby. As the last vineyard he may ever get to install, it occupies a special place in his heart.

We four-wheeled up there one afternoon, and Tom beamed like a proud papa. "Now *this*," he said, as we bumped along up a steep incline, "is really new." Sweetwater looks different from the flatland vineyards, not only because of its rugged slopes but because the vines are bunched much more closely together, in so-called European tight spacing. This accomplishes several tasks. In such nutrient-poor dirt, the vines' foliage of leaves would otherwise be very thin, allowing the grapes to get sunburned. Clustering the plants together creates a communal canopy that helps shelter them. It also forces the plants to compete for whatever water and nutrients are available, further stressing them. Then, too, tight spacing represents an economic decision that maximizes the land's value, an important factor because developing a new vineyard can cost tens of thousands of dollars an acre.

The Sweetwater soils are the most complex on the estate, of a type found in Sonoma only on mountainous uplands in the northern half of the county. The land here has been folded, faulted, uplifted, shuffled, and reshuffled endlessly over the eons, the soils constantly metamorphosed, broken down, recycled, and eroded. There is practically no consistency at all from one spot to another, except that, in general, the dirt is meager. Runoff is very high, bringing with it the danger of erosion and landslide. Vigor is the lowest on the estate, and the berries on the vines predictably are very compact, far smaller than at Riverblock, and with thicker skins.

I tasted Rochioli's 2000 West Block, 2000 Riverblock, and two 2002 Sweetwater Pinot Noirs on a Bulwer-Lyttonian dark and stormy night at the Farmhouse Inn, a country inn and little restaurant run by an old Sonoma Italian American family, the Bartolomeis, in Forestville. The inn is on River Road right where Wohler Road meets it at Mark West Creek, an intersection that dependably floods during big storms. While the wind howled outside and the creek rose ominously, I lit a cozy fire and popped the corks.

The 2000 vintage wines were in bottle and had already been commercially released, but the two Sweetwaters were barrel samples. Tom initially had been reluctant to let me try them, because a barrel sample is only an embryo of a wine, and it can be too easy to come to premature conclusions regarding such an undeveloped infant. But he eventually relented and gave them to me in 375-milliliter bottles, half the size of a regular bottle. They were made from the Dijon clones 777 and 115 and were the first Sweetwater Pinot Noirs ever vinified, which lent them a certain historical interest.

The Riverblock and West Block wines, I wrote that night, "share the same characteristics," which were a ripe full-bodiedness and power, combined with delicacy. Both were delicious from the get-go, but there was no getting around the fact that Riverblock was a shadow of its neighbor. But what a shadow!

The smell of West Block reminded me of a "meat-centered entree." Certain California Pinot Noirs can be overly fruity; they are delicious but have a Lifesaver candy one-dimensionality. Not so the West Block, which contained scents of veal and tobacco, mushrooms and bacon, herbs and anise, as though a Mediterranean stew were bubbling happily on the stove. "Then dark fruits and berries emerge," perfuming the air: cherries, blackberries, the deepest, ripest, smokiest blueberries. Dark chocolate and roasted coffee bean, too.

Riverblock, by contrast, was "undeniably thinned down." Tom himself earlier had used the word "floral" to describe Riverblock, and "floral" in a Pinot Noir is not particularly a compliment the way it is in, say, an aromatic Riesling or Gewurztraminer, or even a violetty Merlot.

Both Sweetwaters were dense, dark, and tannic, the result of the grapes' thick, mountain-grown skins. Clone 777 was all fresh, young, jammy fruit: raspberry tart, red cherry pie (including the baked, buttery crust), a sprinkle of white chocolate powder and cinnamon, a drizzle of sweet vanilla. Clone 115 by contrast had sharper acids and was earthier and more herbal.

It seemed only natural to make a blend of the two Sweetwaters, something I assumed Tom Rochioli might do, in one ratio or another. Mine was fifty-fifty and produced a fabulously wholesome, complete Pinot Noir. It was different from West Block, livelier and fruitier, without as much depth, silkier, and perhaps less serious, but precocious and sensual, with a good grip of tannins on the finish. It was a Lolita of a Pinot Noir, a warm, sexy nymph. You couldn't have asked for anything more seductive, and I marveled that it would only get better—not simply this vintage when additional months in oak conferred upon it a smoky sweetness, but in the future, as the vines aged.

Every winemaker talks up his or her latest project. In this case, it was obvious that Tom Rochioli's happiness about his sweet new baby was entirely justified.

PINOT NOIR'S RIVER ROAD ROUTE

While the Rochiolis and the Bynums were busy on Westside Road, a nearly simultaneous development took place on the opposite side of the river, to the south. In the rolling hills below River Road, a retired airline pilot named Joe Swan, who had flown for the old Western Airlines, bought some vineyard land for his retirement and decided to make wine.

River Road is the valley's main crossing, the nearest thing to a highway it's likely to get. The road used to be a backwater, but with so many young workers settling around Forestville and Sebastopol these days, it can get trafficky during rush hour, with commuters driving to and from the industrial parks and office complexes paralleling Highway 101. Near River Road's eastern end, in Santa Rosa (across Highway 101, it becomes scenic Mark West Road, which climbs across the Mayacamas into Napa Valley), is the Egg Basket general store, which marks the unofficial boundary between city and wine country.

As the crow flies, River Road is only a few miles from Westside Road, but in some respects it might as well be in another county. Particularly in the old days, valley folk tended to stay on their own side of the river. With only a few bridges, and those just as likely to be flooded out during a big storm, travel wasn't so easy; besides, there was a certain provincial "my neighborhood is better than yours" attitude.

As a result, and even though they were thinking and working along similar lines, Joe Swan and Joe Rochioli Jr. were barely aware of each other's existence. "Swan was doing his own thing a couple of hills over," Tom Rochioli said, motioning his arm in River Road's general direction as though he were gesturing toward Japan. As for Joe Jr., he just says, "Well, I knew Swan was plantin' some vineyards over there, but we didn't really communicate."

Swan, who died in 1991, was a fanatical Burgundy lover. According to his son-in-law, Rod Berglund, who makes the wines at Joseph Swan Vineyards, Swan always intended to grow Pinot Noir, even before André Tchelistcheff recommended that he plant it because the weather along River Road was so cold.

Swan's land is in the southeast part of the appellation, actually not too far from Two Acres, in a part traditionally known as Vine Hill. Berglund calls it Laguna Ridges, a take on the old Laguna de Santa Rosa name from Spanish rancho days. (He also expresses hope that Laguna Ridges will someday be an AVA.) Because it is farther south, and more open to the broad floodplain running down through the Petaluma Gap to San Pablo Bay, Laguna Ridges is chillier, foggier, windier, and rainier than the Middle Reach. Joe Rochioli Jr. used to deride it as "swampland" more suitable for Gravenstein apples than the fine French varietal grapes he was interested in. The bottomlands, especially right along the Russian River, are not really so good for grapes, although lots of them grow there. The best vineyards are located south of River Road, and especially on the well-drained slopes of

Rod Berglund holding the reins at Joseph Swan.

low hillocks in a compact area that some, including Merry Edwards, call the Golden Triangle. Merry, a vivacious and energetic woman with a keen sense of humor, describes this as her "nickname" for the land bounded by Vinehill Road, Laguna Road, and Guerneville Road. It's not really shaped like a triangle, more like a bowling pin. But a glance at a map shows that it occupies the geographic heart of the Russian River Valley AVA.

When Swan bought his property, it contained the usual field blend, dating from the 1880s, but he ripped out the old vines in 1968. (In retrospect, it's a shame he didn't keep a few rows.) In 1969, he planted Pinot Noir and Chardonnay, exactly one year after the Rochiolis. But the first commercial release of a Swan Pinot Noir was in 1973, the same year Davis Bynum put out his Rochioli Pinot Noir. Talk about synchronicity!

Two things make the Laguna Ridges area distinct. One is the climate; the other is Goldridge soil. The climate is coolish, although some areas in the Russian River Valley, especially the Green Valley, are even chillier. As for the soil, "Goldridge" is as serious a buzzword as you'll find in California wine country. Burgundians may boast of their vaunted Kimmeridgian limestone, Germans of their slate, the Chateauneuvians of their rounded stones; Sonomans slap the Goldridge trump card down and reach for the chips. Of course, every wine region, of necessity, finds something to brag about. If grapes grew in Manhattan, people would praise asphalt.

Tom Dehlinger says that, of his sixteen acres of Pinot Noir, "maybe four acres are absolutely stunning, year after year, our top spots. And they tend to be Goldridge and a variant of Goldridge, Altamont." Davis Bynum agrees: "Grapes love it. It's mostly sand and doesn't have a lot of nutrients."

In a 1972 study of Sonoma's soils, the U.S. Department of Agriculture and the University of California described Goldridge as "fine sandy loams" with "a sandy clay loam subsoil . . . underlain by . . . sandstone."

"It's almost like talc, it's so light," marvels Rod Berglund. That sandy structure ensures excellent drainage, which is what vintners like about it.

"I can tell you what makes Goldridge so easy for farming," says Ehren
Jordan, at Failla. "There aren't a lot of rocks, [and] it drains incredibly
well. You can get twelve inches of rain in one day and then drive a truck
out into the vineyard the next day. That's why I call it the rain forest desert."
Yet this same quality "makes Goldridge highly erodable," Forrest Tancer
adds, warning that "you have to be really careful it doesn't all wash away
after a rainstorm."

You can't pin the excellence of the Laguna Ridges area for Pinot Noir
merely on Goldridge soil, however; as Dan Roberts, Dr. Dirt, points out,
"You could have Goldridge in Fresno, but you couldn't grow Pinot Noir
there!" It seems to be the combination of climate *and* soil—terroir—that
does the trick.

Joe Swan's Pinots were big, tough wines. Tancer used to go over to taste
with him, and he recalls them as being "masculine. You'd almost want to
question if it really *was* Pinot Noir. It had that very herbal, spicy, tannic
quality. I didn't find them particularly charming."

But they aged well. A year or two after Joe Swan died, Alice Waters
asked Rod Berglund to host a tasting of Swan Pinot Noirs at Chez Panisse,
starting with the 1973 vintage and going up to the 1989. For the occasion,
she prepared a Mediterranean lamb dish; recalling it now makes my mouth
water. Although I no longer have my tasting notes, I remember the wines
as being delicate and fine. Some were richer than others, with that taffeta
mouthfeel and mocha-raspberry liqueurish sweetness you sometimes get
in a mature California red of almost any varietal—Pinot Noir, Petite Sirah,

Zinfandel—whose tannins have fallen out. They were light but very pretty, although I wasn't entirely sure they made the case for twenty years of cellaring. But they did show that the best California red wines can age.

I met up with Rod Berglund again in January of 2003. It was the day of the annual Winter Wineland event, designed by the Russian River Valley Winegrowers Association to lure tourists during a season when they normally don't come. Swan's tiny parking lot was packed, and the rustic little tasting room was jammed with a swirl-and-sniff crowd that, fortunately, was buying. Rod, a tall man with a shaggy mane of reddish hair, a lopsided grin, and an easy, languorous personality, was busy chatting up visitors, while the cash register ka-chinged. Later, Rod joked that he once had been able to take January off and go someplace warm after the harvest, but no more. What with the increased marketing and public relations duties a winemaker is expected to shoulder in these competitive times, even dull old January has become just another work month.

Sadly, many of the details of Joe Swan's viticultural history died with him. He was not, it turns out, a garrulous man. "If you asked him a question," Rod recalls, "he didn't pontificate. He'd give you a simple 'yes' or 'no.'" Tancer referred to this same reticence when he described Joe Swan as "mysterious."

As a result, there are different versions of where Swan obtained his Pinot Noir budwood. "According to one," Rod relates, "André Tchelistcheff gave him the cuttings from Beaulieu's original vines, in Rutherford." Joel Butler, who now works for Diageo, the company that owns Beaulieu, says that those vines had been planted in the early 1900s by Georges de Latour "from cuttings he imported from France," although no one seems to know from precisely where. "But," Joel adds, "there's also speculation that M. de Latour might have gotten plant material from his next-door neighbor, Gustave Niebaum, at Inglenook."

(Our friend Mary Frost Mabon, in *ABC of America's Wines*, tells of her visit to Inglenook in the summer of 1941, when she tasted wines with its then-owner, John Daniel, Niebaum's grand-nephew. Among them were two Red Pinots [*sic*] from 1936 and 1937, both with a Napa Valley appellation. Here is her description: "Both . . . have a good deal of body, although they are by no means coarse. The '37 is softer and quite velvety; the '36 will remind French winedrinkers of an Hermitage, and like that wine should age well and so be laid down in their cellars." That '37 rather sounds like the Mihaly I once liked.)

Rod Berglund continues the narrative: "Later, when Beaulieu's vines were ripped out and André wanted to replant Pinot Noir in Carneros, he had to come back to Joe for the cuttings." Butler adds, "André began to pull out the Rutherford Pinot blocks starting in about 1952 or so. Combination of vines dying off . . . and also André just didn't think the character and quality of these Pinots were as good as what could be produced in a cooler area. And there was pressure to plant more Cabernet in Rutherford anyway."

But that's only one version. "Others," Rod tells me, "say Joe got his cuttings from Mount Eden Vineyards, in the Santa Cruz Mountains," which Martin Ray had established in 1942. (Ray had worked at Paul Masson and made a '36 Pinot Noir there. The American writer Julian Street, in 1948, called it "the first American red wine I ever drank with entire pleasure.")

Merry Edwards, who crafts a range of single-vineyard Pinot Noirs from the Russian River Valley at her Meredith Estate, happened to be working at the Martin Ray winery when Joe Swan was alive. At dinner one night in her Forestville home—a brilliant meal of five courses, each composed of wild mushrooms, and each accompanied by a different Pinot Noir of hers— she said, "I can tell you where Joe got his first Pinot cuttings: from Mount Eden. Joe used to come down and visit me all the time. The reason Rod doesn't know is that he came into the picture a lot later than I did.

Merry Edwards, a true pioneer of Russian River Valley Pinot Noir.

"After that," she continued, "Joe would go to France every year and always bring [budwood] from Burgundy in his pocket." Bringing in such uncertified "suitcase clones" (sometimes called "Samsonite clones") has long been illegal—the last thing the U.S. Department of Agriculture wants is for some contagious plant disease to be smuggled into the country and start an epidemic—but that has never stopped covetous vintners from doing it, to this day.

Joe Swan's enthusiasm for Pinot Noir spread to his neighbors in the Golden Triangle. Two years later, Elmo Martini planted some at Martini & Prati, a remarkable turn-around for a winery that for nearly a century had produced jug Chiantis and faux-Burgundies. "Dad thought it was going to be the next big thing," his son, Tom, recalls. (By coincidence, as I write this, the Martin Ray Winery has just announced that it is buying Martini & Prati.) Martini & Prati never made a name for their own Pinot Noir wine, though, because they preferred to sell their grapes to others.

In 1975, Tom Dehlinger came along, obtaining his cuttings from Joe Swan's vines and making his first Pinot Noir wine, the 1977, in Swan's winery. Also around that time, Forrest Tancer really got rolling with Iron Horse, and Marimar Torres arrived in the Green Valley. Among others who pioneered the southern part of the valley were Steve Kistler, Merry Edwards, Lynmar, and Paul Hobbs. Today, the south Russian River Valley makes Pinot Noirs that differ from those of the warmer Middle Reach, wines that perhaps trade ripe and fruity voluptuousness and warming alcohol for a crisper elegance and, possibly, greater ageability. Just as in Burgundy (although in a different way), the north-versus-south dichotomy of the Russian River Valley offers alternatives for Pinotphiles as well as a lifetime of happy arguing concerning preference.

8

Clones, AVAs, and Storms

A Divertissement

I was struck by all the pioneers who had schlepped down to Wente Brothers for Pinot Noir. Getting to the bottom of that story raised the interesting subject of clones and selections.

Of all the classic grape varieties, Pinot Noir has the greatest number of clones, thus offering the greatest number of promises beyond "what is." The reason Pinot Noir is so clonally promiscuous (my term), explains Professor Carole Meredith, the famous grape DNA researcher, who retired in 2003 after teaching at the University of California at Davis for twenty-three years, is that the older a varietal is, the more clones it has had time to develop.

And Pinot Noir is very old, older even than Syrah, which Meredith has reliably dated as at least two thousand years old. Compared to that, Cabernet Sauvignon, which seems to have spontaneously appeared only four hundred years ago—and is a cross between Sauvignon Blanc and Cabernet Franc (so why didn't they call it Blanc Franc?)—is a Johnny-come-lately.

You don't have to be a rocket scientist to understand the difference between a clone and a selection, although the two words are often used synonymously, even by winemakers (who sometimes call selections "old-school clones"). When Tom Dehlinger got his Pinot Noir from Joe Swan—which means that he took a little pruning knife and sliced budding twigs off selected grapevines and then grafted the individual buds onto rootstocks he had previously planted in his own vineyard—what he got was a cross-section, or a *selection*, of who-knows-what. Any given Swan vine might originally have come from Beaulieu or from Mount Eden or from Wente or from some unknown, unknowable vineyard or nursery in Burgundy, by way of Joe Swan's suitcase. And even then, buds selected from the same vine, according to Meredith, can differ dramatically in their genetic properties. All you know about a selection is that it came from a particular vineyard. If you have a clone, however, you are getting the viti-cultural equivalent of Dolly the sheep. A *clone* is genetically identical to its parent and sister clones.

But thirty years ago, there were no Pinot Noir clones to be had. Sci-ence hadn't yet developed them. If you wanted Pinot Noir, you went to the producer you trusted most and cut off a selection from the vines in that vineyard. That's why so many people drove down to Wente for Pinot Noir. The original brothers, Ernest and Carl, both now long deceased, had planted it in the 1930s, although not even Phil Wente knows where his fa-ther and uncle got *their* cuttings. "I wish I'd asked," he says.

Of course, you could have tried your luck buying Pinot Noir at a plant nursery, but even if you found a nursery that purported to have Pinot Noir, what you got might have been the real deal, or it might have been some-thing else—almost anything else, as it turns out. "We never used to pur-chase any plant from a nursery, because we didn't trust them," states Phil Wente.

After the Sterling family bought the Iron Horse Green Valley prop-erty from Rodney Strong in 1976, they had the vines, which had been planted by Tancer in 1970–1971 when he worked for Strong, analyzed. The supposed Pinot Noir turned out to be "a mix of everything under the sun, from real Pinot Noir to six different varieties of Gamay Beaujolais to who knows?" Tancer recalls. "You scratch your head and go, 'How in the world could they have called all that Gamay Beaujolais Pinot Noir?'" Strong had bought his ersatz Pinot Noir from nurseries.

In the January 2001 issue of *Wines & Vines*, three U.C. Davis grape scientists—Lynn Alley, Deborah Golino, and Andrew Walker—described the difficulty of obtaining clean, pure plant material in the bad old days: "Planting ... was often done with little knowledge of or concern for variety identity ... the same variety was often given separate names (synonyms) in the different regions in which it was grown. .... Confused nurserymen would sometimes dispense with attempts to identify a variety correctly and simply tack a pet name onto saleable vines."

French vintners and growers had pretty much the same problem. They also had, in their cool, damp climate, many serious vine diseases, which is why French grape scientists began working to develop true, certifiable, virus-free clones in the 1960s. They were far ahead of their American counterparts. "We never had a clonal program here in California," Professor Meredith explains, "because there was never any money."

The so-called Dijon clones of Pinot Noir (and Chardonnay) were developed in the 1970s and 1980s in Dijon, Burgundy, by local researchers (not at the University of Dijon, as is often claimed). They are true clones, exact replicas of their parents, bearing the same genetic properties. They are also far more likely than selections to be disease free, although this is not necessarily a positive. Lots of winemakers believe that a little virus, like a little brettanomyces, can be a good thing, quality-wise; for example, certain viruses, such as Eutypa, limit vine yield.

When Pinot Noir vintners from Oregon traveled to Burgundy in the late 1970s and 1980s and found out about the new Dijon clones, they smuggled them into the United States—suitcase clones that, inevitably, found their way south of the state line. California had very strict import con-

trols on vine material at that time, and vintners were tired of the quaran-
tine hiatus that had been imposed on the new Dijon clones. They had heard
about them through the rumor mill or seen them on their own visits to
France and wanted some for themselves.

"I'd gone to Burgundy in 1977," Merry Edwards remembers, "and when
I came back, I was telling everyone about clones." A little later, David
Graves, the co-founder of Saintsbury, planted some of the new clones at
his Carneros vineyard. I asked him where he got his budwood. "Let's just
say someone left it on our doorstep," he replied, with a wink and a nod.
In a suitcase, I presumed.

By the 1990s, a kind of clonal frenzy was spreading throughout California. Wineries boasted of their Dijon clones the way you might show
off a Picasso on your living room wall, a sign of your discernment and
good taste. Every serious Pinot Noir vineyard in the state, to my knowledge, is growing them; and the newer the vineyard, the more Dijon clones
it is likely to have. Hugh Chappelle, the young winemaker at Flowers Winery on the Sonoma coast (he left in early 2004, to go to Lynmar), calls
this craze "clonalmania"; Graves himself refers to "the spirit world of
clonal stuff."

Clonalmania got out of hand. Saralee Kunde, of the Russian River
Valley grape-growing family, grows an astounding twenty-three different
clones and selections of Pinot Noir just north of River Road at her Saralee's Vineyard, a major grape source for wineries throughout Sonoma
County. She recalls the frantic atmosphere when clonalmania first struck.
"We grafted, what? fourteen million vines to them," she laughs. "Everybody felt, if it wasn't [Dijon clones] 114, 115, 667, 777, it wasn't anything."
Things got so crazy that, one night, a thief snuck into her vineyard and
chopped the branches right off an entire row of clones that she was growing

Hugh Chappelle at Flowers, before he left to work at Lynmar.

for Rod Berglund at Joseph Swan. "People were scrambling for budwood," Saralee says, "and there wasn't any to get."

Hearing all this reminded me of another, remarkably similar craze that occurred during the same period: the mad, irrational rush by investors to buy Internet stocks, on the assumption that anything with a dot-com affixed to its name would go up in value forever. As experience showed, that turned out to be an example of the triumph of hope over common sense. But what about clonalmania? Are the Dijon clones all they're cracked up to be?

I remember a time around 1994 when some Pinot Noir winemakers from California and Oregon were having a clonal taste-off down in Santa Barbara. As we trudged up a hill through a vineyard to the little cottage where the tasting was to take place, my companion, a winemaker, predicted, "The Dijons should be the best," adding, "The Martini clone should be the worst."

In fact, the consensus chose that ill-regarded Martini selection—it wasn't actually a clone—as the best wine of the tasting, rich and ripe compared to all the rest. It was yet another example, if one were needed, that when it comes to wine, the conventional wisdom isn't always true.

In today's Russian River Valley, as throughout Pinot Noir regions everywhere, opinions about Dijon clones diverge. True clonistas, such as Merry Edwards and Rod Berglund, hold fast to their conviction that the Dijon clones eventually will prove their worth beyond dispute. But others continue to believe that terroir, not clones or selections, is the most important element. These debunkers include Tom Dehlinger, who thinks that, given a good soil, a Swan or Pommard selection will make as good a wine as a Dijon clone. Gary Farrell agrees: "If you have a site that is producing great Pinot Noir, then almost any clone will be successful. When I see a great vineyard, it won't just be the 777 that's fantastic but the Pommard and everything else."

David Hirsch, whose Sonoma coast vineyard has been the source of acclaimed Pinot Noirs from the likes of Williams Selyem, Siduri, Kistler, and Littorai, actually prefers the old selections to the new clones, although he grows both. He puts forth an interesting reason for his semi-aversion to the Dijons: "The old clones [selections] haven't been subjected to genetic manipulation. They have gypsy blood in them, a complexity that a great site can create." The new clones, by contrast, "are geared to industrial efficiency."

"There's a potential danger," warns Chappelle, "that with everyone putting in the same clonal mix, a lot of these wines will taste the same." The risk is that Pinot Noir's eccentric and unique personality may become homogenized. There can be a curious similarity among young-vine Dijon clone Pinot Noirs from regions as scattered as the Santa Rita Hills, the Santa Lucia Highlands, the Sonoma Coast, Anderson Valley, the Carneros, and the Russian River Valley, especially cooler subsections such as Laguna Ridges and Green Valley. I know that this tends to belie all the statements about Pinot Noir transparently showing its terroir, but, in the case of the clones, they can be so clean and laboratory pure, so powerfully fruity, that they trump even terroir. At the Santa Barbara Pinot Noir blind tasting I referred to earlier, few if any of the winemakers present were able to identify even their own wines because all of the wines bore such a close family resemblance. One reason for that certainly could have been that so many were produced from three or four Dijon clones.

Most growers, if you can get them to open up, admit that they put in the new clones because they were in fashion. Everybody else was planting them; nobody wanted to be the last one on the block. Maybe the Dijons actually were better than the old selections—who knew? "Roll the dice!" exclaims Bob Cabral about clones. Besides, in a worldwide wine glut where selling individual brands has never been more difficult, there is an ongoing search for some way to spin wine as a consumer product; and the words "Dijon clones," in a press release or on a label, play approximately the same role as "New and improved" on a box of detergent.

Most growers are planting what Professor Meredith calls "a palette of clones," a spectrum that, in theory, should produce a richer, more intricate, and nuanced wine, the way the many colors in a Renoir painting create warmth and richness. Berglund, in a pretty metaphor, likens things to a Bach mass, a single clone or selection being the soloist, and a blend the chorus. "First, you hear this beautiful voice singing, and it's the most beautiful thing you've ever heard. Then suddenly the whole choir joins in, and you think, 'My Lord, what have I been missing?'"

CARVING UP THE VALLEY

It's a sign of midlife crisis when a California wine appellation, after all the effort required to get itself approved in the first place, thinks about dividing itself up into smaller AVAs.

Napa Valley winemakers famously did just this when they created Oakville, Rutherford, St. Helena, and Yountville in the 1990s (and, as I write, they're petitioning the feds for Calistoga). For a while, it looked as if we'd have various Napa "benches" as well. So it was probably inevitable that Russian River Valley winemakers, always sensitive to what their friends and rivals over the hill are up to, would eventually get around to doing the same thing.

After the 2001 harvest, a group of them began gathering to taste the wines from different parts of the appellation. Their focus, obviously, was on Pinot Noir. These men and women tended to be the more sociable joiners, not the iconoclasts who have little patience for meetings and agenda items and the chit-chat of social discourse. Dehlinger, Farrell, and Tom Rochioli, for instance, were not among them.

Bob Cabral, of Williams Selyem, who did attend, explained the gatherings: "Our purpose [was] to answer the questions, What is Russian River Valley Pinot Noir? What do we see as being unique?" Dan Goldfield, always quick with a wry quip, called the group's effort "Russian River Valley self-exploration, so to speak." The object was to see whether it made sense to carve up the valley into sub-AVAs, based on organoleptic distinctions. (It is true that some winemakers object to the term "sub-AVA," asserting that there is no such thing, that every AVA is legally legitimate in its own right. They're correct, of course, but the *concept* of a sub-AVA, an appellation-within-an-appellation, seems valuable.)

A secondary, less visible agenda was concerned with marketing. The

Pinot Noir wineries from Oregon's Willamette Valley and those in the Carneros had been extraordinarily successful during the 1980s and 1990s in convincing consumers that their regions were hog heaven for Pinot Noir. By the mid-1990s, Santa Barbara County winemakers, under the banner of their well-funded Vintners' Association, had done the same. The success of these rival appellations frustrated the old-time Russian River Valley Pinotistas, who after all had been the first. Their fame had always been spread via word of mouth, transmitted through the wine underground by the Joel Butlers of this world. But the strengthening competition led many to believe that some PR was in order and resulted in the birth of the Russian River Valley Winegrowers Association in 1993. Its prime movers were people such as Saralee Kunde, Rod Berglund, and Dan Goldfield's grower-partner, Warren Dutton.

The Pinot Noir tasting group that convened in 2001 was an unofficial extension of the association. In addition to Cabral and Goldfield, it included, at various times, Berglund, Merry Edwards, Greg La Follette (of Flowers, Hartford Court, and his own Tandem), and Dutton as well as winemakers from La Crema, Lynmar, and a few others. These vintners would get together every so often for a few hours to taste and see whether they could detect consistent differences in the wines. In the winter of 2003, the group, perhaps predictably, dissolved because of the participants' lack of time. But that has only slowed, not stopped, the momentum for sub-appellating the valley.

Exactly where these divisions are and what they should be called are years away from being determined. As we saw in the Battle of Alexander Valley, these things aren't easy. The Russian River Valley Winegrowers Association itself has suggested three sub-AVAs: the Middle Reach, Laguna Ridges and the Santa Rosa Plain (counted as one), and Green Valley, which has had AVA status since 1983. You can think of this as a warm-cool-cold continuum.

Some people, such as Berglund, separate Laguna Ridges from the Santa Rosa Plain; it's the old hills-versus-flatlands argument. Berglund would also add a cooler Sebastopol Hills and a warmer Windsor Hills AVA. Goldfield has suggested dividing Green Valley into Upper and Lower, meaning not north versus south, but hills versus valleys—another warmer-colder continuum. Cabral leans toward a West River AVA, which would pick up where the Middle Reach trails off beyond Porter Creek and the Wohler Narrows and would probably include Gary Farrell and, possibly, Korbel.

Minute distinctions aside, three elements (other than soil) distinguish one Russian River Valley region from another: their distance from the ocean, the conduits of cold air that can reach the region from the ocean or from San Pablo Bay, and elevation. The wind and fog do not reach everywhere. The summertime fog bank on any given day peaks at about 800 or 900 feet. Sonoma County has dozens of hills greater than 1,000 feet in altitude, and many taller than 2,000 feet. (Sonoma's highest mountain is 4,349-foot Mount St. Helena, which it shares with Napa and Lake counties.) The result is that different places in the Russian River Valley have different temperature and fog patterns. The tendency is to think of the valley as a uniformly chilly place, but this is not true. It's a huge area with tremendously complicated weather and climate distinctions.

The Middle Reach, as the warmest, sunniest part, clearly differs from the colder parts to the south and southwest. It also has a historical continuity, which the authorities like when they consider a new appellation. But it is by no means one consistent place. "This Middle Reach, I don't know," Gary Farrell mused one day. "It's one thing in the valley, but if you get up into the hills around Rochioli, you get into drastically different situations."

As we saw, conditions are very different at Rochioli Riverblock than they are at Sweetwater. Nonetheless, the Middle Reach does deserve its own AVA status. Some day down the road, further distinctions might have to be made for flats, benches, and hills.

As for the cooler parts of the Russian River Valley, we already have the done deal of Green Valley. Probably it makes sense to carve something out of the River Road area; maybe Laguna Ridges is a good place to start. But why rush things? After all, it took the Burgundians a thousand years to get a handle on their real estate, and it's been only thirty-five years since people told a farmer named Joe Rochioli Jr. that he was crazy to plant Pinot Noir in the Russian River Valley.

WINTER STORMS AND FLOODS

Some years, summer seems to linger forever in the Russian River Valley. Autumn officially arrives on September 21, but that is simply a date on the calendar; the best is yet to come. October is usually warm and dry, with everyone still running around in shorts and shirtsleeves. The sun may lean a little lower in the sky, casting longer shadows as the hours tick away toward the winter solstice. But even in December, on certain days, people say to each other, "Isn't the weather great?" and congratulate themselves for having the wisdom to live in California.

In such a season, the streets of Guerneville are thronged. There are the bikers on their hogs, long hair and bushy beards blowing sideways in the wind, the backs of their shiny black leather vests bearing the names of their clubs. Hippie dudes and teenage boy dopers gather by the old Guerneville Bridge, shirtless in the sun, showing off their lean bodies to midriff-bared teenybopper girls, whose belly buttons, and sometimes noses and lips, are pierced with golden rings and studs. A passerby will sniff a certain acrid, smoky scent in the air, and it's not always patchouli oil. Crewcut lesbians stroll arm in arm on their way to tea and pastries, while the gay boys gather in the bars, which already are blaring thumping disco music at ten in the morning. Guerneville—originally called Stumptown, until postal authorities in 1870 decided to name it after George E. Guerne, who owned a big sawmill there (with, coincidentally, Tom Heald, brother of the founder of Healdsburg)—hasn't changed much over the years. It retains the funky, alternative-lifestyle flavor it always seems to have had.

The drift into winter is slow. But when it comes, it arrives with malice, as if to say: "You thought I would spare you this year? Think again." Away go the tank tops and Birkenstocks; out come the flannels and boots.

Winter came late in 2002 after a long, glorious harvest. For months, it seemed the warm sun could do nothing but shine. In mid-November, I'd paddled the Russian River with Terry Wright, and the weather had been so pleasant that we ate lunch on a gravel bar (beef stew from his thermos). Afterward, I searched the rockpile for odd stones for him to identify.

One day in December, suddenly, summer ended. The storm door opened up with a vengeance, and it rained for the better part of a week.

At first, Napa bore the brunt. Napa Creek flooded, the sandbags piled up, residents evacuated. Then it was the Russian River's turn. The National Weather Service issued a flood warning for Guerneville, where the river already was up to 34 feet, 2 feet above flood stage, and still rising. Tom Rochioli emailed to say that Riverblock was underwater, along with a good portion of Mid 40; but "we're used to it," he added.

The storms were stacked up all across the Pacific, with a new one scheduled to hit every day for the foreseeable future. El Niño, it seemed, was back in town. In the midst of all this, Terry Wright emailed.

"River's up bigtime. I'm going out again tomorrow. Want to come?"

Was he serious?

"I love bad weather," he replied. "I eat big storms for lunch."

I decided to spare Terry the opportunity to risk my life. But I made plans with Catherine, the innkeeper, to spend the night at the Farmhouse Inn. I wanted to be in the valley when the river was rising and to see Guerneville, California's most famous flood town.

The night before, the forecast was frightening. Rain, heavy at times, and windy with a chance of thunderstorms. Highs from the mid-40s to the lower 50s. South winds twenty to thirty-five miles per hour, gusting to fifty. Chance of rain near 100 percent.

When I left that morning, the rain was coming down so hard that, even with the windshield wipers on high, it was difficult to see. There was a high-wind warning for the bridges; on the Richmond–San Rafael span that crosses to Marin County, the car was buffeted left and right, and it was hard to stay in the narrow lane. On the long, slow, traffic-choked drive, I had plenty of time to think about the weather.

Coastal California is drought-stricken for six months of the year. It almost never rains between May and October. The average July precipitation in San Francisco is zero, and just a fraction of an inch in June and August.

Rainfall decreases south of the city (except in the coastal mountains), and increases north of it. San Diego gets a paltry 10 inches a year. San Francisco gets double that. But in the Russian River Valley, the average rainfall soars to 40 inches; and in northwest Sonoma, it's 70 inches. The highest peaks of the northeast county, where the Mayacamas Mountains wring water out of the storm clouds as though they were squeezing soggy sponges, get more than 80 inches in a typical year. Sonoma is not the wettest place in California—Humboldt County gets that honor, or curse. But it is a very wet place indeed; some weather stations there have recorded more than 110 inches in a single year.

The winter storms arrive from one of two directions. The infamous Pineapple Express brings warm torrents in from the southwest. Like a hose running from Hawaii to the Pacific coast, it will spew for days on end. Storms that come out of the northwest are much colder and equally wet. The gales can line up like airplanes on a runway, four or five at a time, stretching from the Gulf of Alaska to Japan, riding the jet stream and repeatedly striking like bullets from an automatic weapon. Both types of storms bring flooding rains to the swollen rivers and creeks, and the northern ones frequently bring snow, sometimes heavy, to the peaks. On some winter days, Mount St. Helena is shrouded like a Swiss Alp and Sonoma Mountain is buried under a blanket of white. Even Laguna Ridges will get a dusting.

Whether Pineapple Express or northern gales, storms are carried along by the jet stream, which migrates south in the winter. Of course, the jet stream has fluctuations. In a strong El Niño year, it warps in an extreme southerly direction—in the winter of 1997–1998, for example, Los Angeles had more rain than San Francisco, a rare meteorological event. But regardless of where the jet stream goes, Sonoma County seems to get hosed.

The wettest recording station in the county is at Cazadero (Spanish for "the hunting place"), a tiny settlement, just a bend in the road, really, with a general store and a few cabins set deep in a dense redwood forest, on the winding banks of Austin Creek, seven miles east of the Pacific. Cazadero gets an average of 85 inches of rain every winter, compared to Guerneville's 49 inches. In 1937, precipitation there totaled 143 inches.

All that rain and the dense fogs enable the big trees to thrive and encourage the undergrowth and ground cover of native grasses, berry bushes, ferns, and wildflowers. During the summer months, when much of this plant life withers and dries out, fire season arrives, and it can last until November. The wildfires can be spectacular. In the drought year of 1923—the same year a large part of Berkeley burned to the ground when a wildfire raged out of the hills at Strawberry Canyon and took aim straight at downtown—a massive fire raged from Guerneville to the coast. People still talk about 1978's notorious Creighton Ridge fire, which started on the back side of Cazadero and also reached the sea. It torched 12,000 acres, destroyed scores of structures, and injured dozens of people, although, because the area is so sparsely populated, no one died. Four years earlier, a rare snowstorm, the last big one to strike the region (drifts at Cazadero were six feet deep), had downed many tree limbs, and the deadfall fed the flames of the 1978 fire.

Most wildfires are started by lightning, but sometimes they are sparked by humans. One day I was up in the mountains above Fort Ross, driving around with Hugh Chappelle. From a high ridge, he pointed to the west, in the direction of a brushy canyon where a settlement of squatters who had arrived in the 1970s still lived (we could not see them from the roadside). "They're the ones who accidentally started the Creighton Ridge fire," he said; someone had been using a welding torch, which ignited the dry grass. The squatters were using grape grower George Bohan's land to access their house. "George got so fed up with them," Hugh said, "that he blocked off their access." Such are the culture wars of the far coast.

Curiously, the biggest storms, and the worst floods, don't necessarily correspond to El Niño years. That's because, when it comes to flooding, timing is everything. Flooding occurs after a series of high-intensity storms with little time between them, which can happen any winter. But it's also a fact that the Russian River Valley's worst recorded flood occurred during a big El Niño year.

That was in January 1995. For the month, Guerneville had 33.6 inches of rain; farther inland, Cloverdale practically floated away under 17 inches of rain in just three days. Two months later, Guerneville received another 25 inches. (Its annual total reached 90 inches that year; Cazadero had 117 inches.) By far the biggest storm, or storm series, occurred during the week of January 8, when 13 inches of rain fell. The Russian River experienced a classic hundred-year flood, but it was not the only one of the state's rivers to rampage. The same winter saw the costliest flooding in California's history. Some of the floods were not mere hundred-year events, but thousand-year ones.

I was not in Guerneville in 1995, but anyone who was near a television set or a newspaper saw the appalling images. River Road and downtown were under 4 feet of water. A thousand people, caught unawares as the river rose up around them, had to be plucked from their roofs, or from floating debris to which they were clinging, or from hilltops poking above the flood-waters like isolated islands in the sea. California National Guard troops flying Chinook helicopters hauled them up by rope baskets. An operations post was set up in Santa Rosa that looked like a war command center, which in a sense it was. The U.S. Army put in emergency water-purification systems to clean up raw sewage that was freely spilling into the river, which provides much of Sonoma's water supply. It was an ugly, dangerous mess.

Maybe people should have known better than to live directly on the river. Following the '95 floods, many of them learned from experience and put their houses up on stilts. The first time I cruised the Russian River, I was struck by all the structures, especially west of Wohler Bridge, that had been raised up another 20 feet or so, balanced (rather precariously) on wooden beams. Some river denizens find stilt-house living romantic, and it makes for nice photos, but the real estate offices now advertise houses as being out of the flood zone—reason alone for commanding a premium price.

By the time I got to the River Road turnoff, the rain was coming down in torrents, and it was almost as dark as night. Ahead, with the rising river and streams, lay who knew what. It was like being in a hurricane hunter airplane, flying straight into the teeth of the storm.

It was still early, and no one was at the Farmhouse, so I drove on into Guerneville. The road was littered with downed trees, branches, leaves, and pine cones. The Rio Nido bridge was still open, but the churning, brown water was scraping its underside. The gravel bar where Terry Wright and I had had lunch just a few months earlier was nowhere to be seen in the rushing, brown water.

In Guerneville, the streets were empty. At the Coffee Bazaar, a few hapless souls had braved the elements, and the counterman kept up a steady flow of cappuccinos and lattes. I wandered into the bookstore next door, where the carpet was soaked from a leak in the ceiling. At the magazine rack, you could pick up your copy of *Cannabis Times* or *Mother Earth Review,* but there was not a *Time* or *Newsweek* to be found, in this mother of all countercultural towns.

I decided to drop in on my friends along Westside Road: Hampton Bynum, Bob Cabral, Tom Rochioli. In some spots in the low places, a boat would have been more convenient than a car. Small creeks had jumped their banks, and the high shoulders were pouring down cascades of muddy water. At Davis Bynum, I learned that Hampton was on a well-deserved vacation

Bob Cabral stirring up a vat of Rochioli River Block grapes at Williams Selyem.

in Thailand. The lady who worked at the tasting bar didn't have much to do; no customers were arriving that day. We stood at the pot-bellied stove, making small talk and warming our hands.

At Williams Selyem, I found Bob Cabral with his crew; it was business as usual, despite the deluge. He greeted me excitedly, with news: "River-block is underwater!" Then he added that Wohler Bridge was closed.

"How do you know?" I asked, wondering whether it had been announced on some local emergency radio broadcast.

"You don't know," Bob laughed, "until you get there!"

We went into his office. His hound, Layla, rose up with a groan, sniffed my pant leg, gave her tail a friendly little wag, and collapsed back down onto the floor.

Pictures of Bob's nieces and nephews were on the wall, along with a framed note from Ed Bradley of 60 *Minutes* thanking the winery for "finally" including him on the mailing list and one from a frustrated Jerry Bruck-heimer, the Hollywood producer *(Black Hawk Down, Pearl Harbor, Top Gun)*, practically begging to be added (he eventually was). To judge from her effusive thank-you letter, Hillary Rodham Clinton apparently hadn't had any trouble getting some Williams Selyem 1990 Rochioli Vineyard Pinot Noir for a state dinner (smoked breast and terrine of duckling and wild venison) she and Bill gave for Boris and Naina Yeltsin, the Russian president and first lady.

On the shelves were mementos: assorted empty bottles of wines Bob had enjoyed—Veuve Clicquot, La Grande Dame, a 1900 Madeira—Fresno State University pennants, and NFL footballs autographed by former Oakland Raiders stars Jim Plunkett and Fred Belitnikoff. It looked as though Bob had inhabited his cozy little corner of the universe forever, but that was far from the truth. He'd been hired only in 1998, when Williams Selyem's founding owners had sold the winery to a New York businessman, John Dyson. Burt Williams had chosen Bob as his successor, but Dyson had to sign off on the deal first, so Bob flew to New York to be interviewed by his prospective boss.

He was nervous, as might be expected. The winemaker's job at Williams Selyem was one of the most prestigious in California. For a young, relatively unknown cub to be hired into that august position was like Dwight Eisenhower's being leapfrogged ahead of dozens of ranking generals to lead the invasion of Europe during World War II.

Bob told me a funny story about the interview. Things seemed to be going well, when Dyson asked whether he had any preconditions for taking the job.

"Well, I do have one," Bob replied. Dyson shifted in his chair and looked uneasily at his lawyer. What was this brash young man going to ask for? A spectacular salary? A huge house? A Porsche?

"I would like a case of every wine Williams Selyem makes each vintage," Bob said.

"You could see the smiles of relief on their faces," he added, chuckling. He got the job, but there was plenty of second-guessing among writers and critics, and a certain amount of brutality as well. Some people couldn't wait for him to fall on his face. A *New York Times* article cautioned, "If Williams Selyem stumbles, plenty of able competitors are waiting to lure its customers." Williams Selyem did not stumble. Its wines are better than ever.

Bob had placed on a side table a few dozen little sample bottles of the 2002 Pinot Noirs, which were still in barrel. Each bore a scribbled label. Some were from vineyards along Westside Road, including Bacigalupi's, that normally went into the winery's Russian River Valley regional blend. There were also different Dijon clone samples from a new Williams Selyem estate vineyard in Guerneville, the first wines ever made from it. Bob would be tasting them for the first time.

Dyson had come up with a novel idea: to create a new tier of Pinot Noir, midway between the top-level vineyard-designated wines (Hirsch, River Block, Rochioli, Allen, Precious Mountain, Weir, and the others) and the regional blends, such as Russian River Valley, Sonoma Coast, or Sonoma County. Having three tiers would be similar to the Burgundy system of Grand Cru, Premier Cru, and ordinary village wines. Bob mentioned that this new middle tier would be called Neighbors, or something with that word in it, since it would come only from Westside Road vineyards.

For the next two hours, as the rain came down and the wind howled outside, we tasted. Bob was not only putting together Neighbors; he was crafting his Russian River Valley blend at the same time. The tabletop and all the paperwork on it became spattered with red drops of wine.

Some of the samples were stunningly rich, some less so, while others were dull and uninspiring, as is often the case with Pinot Noir. Just because it comes from Westside Road or the Russian River Valley and ends up in a Williams Selyem barrel doesn't make it great. Only the top wines from the blending session, including from the new Williams Selyem vineyard, would go into Neighbors.

Bob would pour and taste, occasionally asking me for a comment. If he particularly liked something, he put a little bit of it into a glass, which gradually became fuller and fuller. Finally, before us on the desk, was the result, a blend of a dozen or so of the little vials: the prospective Neighbors.

It seemed, to me, to be a particularly luscious Pinot Noir, and I asked Bob what he thought.

He leaned back, crossed his arms across his stomach, and stared up at the ceiling, looking rather like a contemplative Buddha. "You know what?" he said. "It's pretty close."

He put the glass to one side, placing a small crystal disc on top to keep airborne particles or fruit flies from falling inside. It was his notion to re-taste it at the end of the day and then again the following morning to see what the steady assault of time and air did to it.

"I am looking," Bob said, "for perfection."

(Six months later, back at Williams Selyem, Bob told me, "Mr. Dyson changed the Neighbors blend. He didn't like the first one." I asked to taste the new version, and it didn't seem all that different from the old one. I remarked as much; Bob tactfully smiled and said nothing. *Droit du seigneur*, as they say.)

I learned something else about Bob when I visited during the storm. After the blending session, I joined him for an appointment to meet an arborist a little way down Westside Road, at the site of another new vineyard Williams Selyem was developing. The rain had temporarily let up, but it was very cold, and our breath turned to steam in the raw air.

The new vineyard had been torn apart by earthmovers to get ready for spring planting; huge boulders and piles of rock were everywhere. A pair of two-hundred-year-old coast live oaks on the property, right by the roadside, framed the earthen driveway like an arch. They were grand old veterans, their bare, intricate branches forming dark spidery patterns against the leaden winter sky. But both seemed in sad shape. Some of the upper limbs were shattered and splintered, as though they had been blasted by lightning, and a few smaller branches had fallen to the ground. Bob had called in an expert to evaluate whether the trees, which were obviously ill, could be saved. The arborist picked up a fallen branch and showed it to us; you could see and feel the pulpy rot inside.

The arborist said that the trees were dying of old age. Sooner or later, they would topple over, probably during a big wind storm. If someone happened to be below at the time—a field worker, a passing motorist— it could be disastrous. The choice, or responsibility, was Bob's, she said, but it seemed clear that she favored having the trees felled.

The three of us stood there, looking up at the old giants. They had been seedlings when George Washington was president, veterans when the Civil War was fought. I saw the agony—that's the word—on Bob's thoughtful face. It was impossible for him to make a decision that day— and the decision would be entirely his, not Mr. Dyson's.

Six months later, he told me he had kept the trees, at great expense to his boss. "I had to," Bob said.

It's a good sign when winemakers are looking to save old trees and other flora and fauna in their vineyards. It means that they love beauty and life, and that reverence will show up in their wines.

The next storm rolled in; it started to pour again. At Rochioli, Tom was on the bottling line, but he came out to say hello. We stood on the covered veranda overlooking the vineyard. The rain pelting the stone walkway sounded like sticks battering a steel drum. Beyond, Riverblock and half of Mid 40 was a rippling sea of white-capped brown water. It was hard to believe that the river had risen all the way up and over the bank and flooded this far into the vineyard. I asked Tom how the 2002 Pinots were coming along. "Oh, that Sweetwater's going to be some wine!" he beamed.

I drove into Healdsburg. The temperature on the dashboard thermometer was 39 degrees. The radio was reporting snow in the hills, but the hilltops were lost in the low clouds and fog. At Veteran's Memorial Beach, the river rumbled past like a brown freight train.

I downed a quick lunch at the Oakville Café and then drove back along River Road to the Farmhouse. The rain tapered off again, and when the clouds lifted, the snow-capped Laguna Ridges sprang into view. The standing water in the vineyards, wind-rippled, sparkled brilliantly under the sharp winter sun.

Catherine invited me for dinner in the restaurant that night, an honest Sonoma winter meal of rabbit, bitter greens, and root vegetables. It was good to see my friend Joseph Bain, the Paris-born sommelier, again.

Joseph is a passionate wine lover and is famous throughout the Russian River Valley for his friendliness and warmth. Everyone eats at the Farmhouse, and part of the allure is Joseph. (In 2004, he took a position at the Chalk Hill Winery, a sad loss for the Farmhouse and the Russian River Valley.)

For many years, Joseph has worked on his magnum opus, a thick notebook written in his own scrawl, entitled "L'Histoire des Vins de

Joseph Bain striking a pose reminiscent of his
"event of the millennium" speech at the Farmhouse.

Bourgogne" (not, I think, that he has any intention of ever trying to publish it; it is strictly a labor of love). In between his sommelier and cheese cart duties, he will take a few minutes to read entries to an enthusiastic listener. Now, with a spare moment on his hands, "Ergo bibamus!" Joseph sang out; the phrase, "Thus, let us drink!" was from Goethe's drinking song:

> For a praiseworthy object we're now
> gather'd here,
> So, brethren, sing: ergo bibamus!
> Tho' talk may be hush'd, yet the glasses ring clear,
> Remember then: ergo bibamus!

And then he read his own translations of Pliny and Columella on the grape-growing practices of the Romans and finished up with a dissertation on papal drinking habits.

I'd brought along a couple of Pinot Noirs I hoped he would enjoy: a Swan Saralee's, a Gary Farrell Star Ridge, a CL Kanzler Sonoma Coast, and a Saxon Brown with a Russian River Valley appellation. Joseph sniffed them all, inserting his nose deep into the glass and inhaling loudly. He took little sips, slurped, savored, swallowed, considered. After one of them, he frowned and said, "This is not Pinot Noir." But when he came to the Saxon Brown, his eyes lit up. "Burgundian!" he cried in triumph. He seemed about to break into an ecstatic dance.

Standing there, holding the glass of wine aloft like the Statue of Liberty's torch, Joseph declared, with a solemnity befitting the occasion, "That the Pinot Noir should find such a great home in Russian River Valley is the event of the millennium!" His voice filled the little dining room. Other customers, including Merry Edwards, turned and stared. Here we were,

on the verge of war in Iraq, with the threat of terrorist attack and the economy in meltdown, and the most important event of the last thousand years,
according to this mad, lyrical, romantic, passionately opinionated French-
man, was the planting of Pinot Noir in the Russian River Valley. That is
Joseph, I smiled to myself—and then (the wine flooding my brain) I
thought, no, it is not just Joseph. It is Russian River Valley, it is Pinot Noir,
it is wine!

9

Into the Fog, and Above It

The Sonoma Coast

Beyond Guerneville, grape growing enters a real no-man's-land. The distance from Guerneville to the coast is only about a dozen miles as the crow flies, but it's light years away in almost every other respect. Guerneville, with its cafés and souvenir shops, is San Francisco in the redwoods. Fort Ross, as Don Jorge and the Russians discovered, is more like a remote outpost in the Aleutians.

"It cannot be practically farmed," declared J. P. Munro-Fraser, author of the *History of Sonoma County,* concerning the coast, "and the mountains . . . afford only timber." But what timber it was, and in what vast quantities! Because of its density, redwood is the most insect- and rot-resistant wood known, and old-growth redwood in particular is the most dense. It is also a beautiful wood to look at, with its warm, sunglow-red hue. San Francisco, Santa Rosa, and other Gold Rush cities had to be built (and rebuilt following the 1906 earthquake and fires), and the millennium-old redwoods provided seemingly endless quantities of smooth, long boards and strong, solid beams. By the late 1850s, the call of tall timber was luring ambitious loggers to the far coast for the first time since the Russian abandonment.

The logging industry thrived from Mendocino down to Big Sur—the so-called Redwood Empire—but its epicenter was on the slopes and mountaintops of the Sonoma coast, where, by the 1860s, entire settlements were being founded around single sawmills: Salt Point, Fisk's Mill, Stillwater Cove, Fisherman's Bay.

After California became a state, in September 1850, the legislature formed counties, including Sonoma. Back in those days, counties were further divided into political divisions called townships. Before 1856, Sonoma County had only a handful of townships: Petaluma, Sonoma, and Russian River; they were the places where civilization was coming in, where villages were arising, in the eastern part. By the 1860s, Vallejo and Santa Rosa had been added, then Cloverdale and Knight's Valley. As more and more inhabitants gathered on the coast, the county formed another township in November 1870, its fourteenth. They named it Ocean.

Ten years after Ocean Township came into being, Munro-Fraser's *History* celebrated its bustling progress. His account hailed the "new roads of easy grade leading into the interior [that] are in course of construction." These were the logging trails, stretching from the coastal lanes up and over the mountain passes to Cazadero and points east. When completed, Munro-Fraser predicted, these corridors would "bring [the interior] within easy access of a large portion of back country. We bespeak for it a brilliant future."

From the deepwater harbors and coves off Ocean Township, schooners— the *Mary Zepher*, the *Euphemia*, the *Eden*—ferried cordwood, bark, railroad ties, and fence posts out to the nation's markets. (The *Eden* capsized off the coast in 1877 in a great winter gale, proving that the coast was not as "secure from northers" as some had thought.) In 1885, county officials opened a railroad line that ran as far west as Cazadero—from there, you could continue on the new roads out to Seaview and Fort Ross via stagecoach. For all anyone knew, another San Francisco could have been springing up right there on the Sonoma coast.

In the middle of all this hustle and bustle, wine began to creep into— or back into—the coastal hills and dales on little pips-feet. Columbus A.

Robinson reported to the 1870 census taker that he had made twenty-five gallons of wine. Ten years later, the census records indicated that Charles Haupt was farming 10 acres of vineyard at Plantation, above Fort Ross. East of Bodega Bay, the 1890 census reported a total of 830 acres around Forestville and Occidental. By the early 1900s, a family by the name of Charles was growing Zinfandel and Golden Chasselas up on scenic Fort Ross Road, northwest of Cazadero.

But as things turned out, the coast never developed the way so many had hoped. The loggers denuded the Fort Ross mountains, stripping them of old-growth trees, and then went elsewhere to cut. The new railroad went broke. The coastside settlements were abandoned. With the Great Depression, the Sonoma coast fell into a dark age.

The few families who remained on the ridges from Plantation down to Bodega turned to the only possibility that remained to make a little money in the dreary economy: raising livestock—sheep and cattle mostly. On the clear-cut high meadows, they found open space for large flocks and herds; and it turned out that grazing animals thrived on the barren, windswept rangelands, with their perennial oak-grasses and wildflowers.

One of these families was the Bohans, the same clan that had shut off access to the squatters involved in the Creighton Ridge fire. I'd been told that the Bohans were central to the story of modern viticulture in the Fort Ross area, and so, in early 2000, I looked them up.

Getting to Jenner is no problem. It's a straight shot west from Guerneville out Route 116 and then a right turn north along the coast on Highway 1. The trouble starts when you turn inland and head up steep, winding Meyers Grade Road into the mountains. This is California's hinterlands, a backwater of old logging roads and fire trails, where your only directions are based on local markers—a cattle crossing, a pond, a green barn, a blue water tank—that are easy for an outsider to miss.

Eventually, I found the Bohan ranch, replete with a clutch of Bohans. Their spread was right out of an Andrew Wyeth painting: a sturdy, lonely farmhouse set in a grassy field, with a few old trees and a couple dozen sheep milling about, blocking the narrow road. Beyond, an expansive horizon of mountains and big sky stretched. The ranch was situated on the aptly named Bohan Dillon Road, where early in the twentieth century a logging railroad ran all the way up to Gualala.

It was lunchtime, and Mick Bohan, who was quite elderly, invited me in for sandwiches and salad and a glass of wine. Afterward, his son, George, took me on a bumpy truck ride across the property and described how his father came to be the first in modern times to plant grapes in such an unlikely spot.

"Our family has been on this ranch for one hundred thirty years," George related; the first Bohan arrived the year Ocean Township was created. "After World War II, we were mainly in the sheep business. But by the early 1970s, the sheep industry was not doing well." It was the same old story. Prices for veal and wool had leveled off; costs were rising. To make matters worse, the sheep increasingly were being killed off by coyotes. "We needed a new gig," George said.

This was the period when pioneers such as Joe Swan, Joe Rochioli, and Hampton and Davis Bynum were getting started. Even on the coast, word had filtered out that one could earn a little extra money, maybe even good money, at this business of grape growing. The Bohans decided that their "new gig" would be a vineyard.

"On the recommendation of a friend, a viticulture and enology graduate of U.C. Davis," George continued, "Dad planted some vines in 1973: an acre of Zinfandel. That winter, at the age of fifty-five, he put in another seventeen acres, this time of Pinot Noir, Chardonnay, and Riesling, because they were early-ripening varieties." In that marginal climate, where, as the Bohans knew well, the first winter storms can hit by October, it was important to get all the grapes in before the rains came.

"At first, everyone told us we were crazy to plant grapes out here— too cool, the climate wasn't right, a million and one reasons," George said. I recalled that Joe Richioli Jr. had met the same reaction.

"We sold our grapes to Sea Ridge. I, myself, was a commodities broker, living in Tahoe. By 1987, Dad was in his late sixties. He was doing it all himself, and he wanted to retire. Someone needed to take over. So I made the decision. I had no viticultural knowledge at all, but I knew something had to happen." George grabbed hold of the reins and still runs the family business.

Today, the Bohan ranch has a large plantation of vines, but the Bohans have chosen not to go the production route, preferring instead to sell their grapes to others, who blend the Bohan grapes into their wines. That is why most consumers, even those familiar with Sonoma Coast vineyards and wines, have never heard of the Bohans, although they may well have drunk wines made with Bohan grapes. But the Bohans were the Christopher Columbuses of this new coastal world of wine; they were the first.

The Sonoma Coast AVA was officially declared in 1987. It is a large appellation, at 480,000 acres and 750 square miles, half the size of Rhode Island. It is the biggest appellation in Sonoma County, more than twice the size of the Russian River Valley, Alexander Valley, and Dry Creek Valley AVAs combined.

Like other huge appellations—San Francisco Bay, Central Coast, Northern Sonoma—it is cumbersome and unreliable to the point of being misleading, encompassing such a complex range of soils and climates that even most of those who farm here concede that it is too big. Dan Goldfield calls it "a mega-appellation," Forrest Tancer "the Sonoma Coast silliness." Hartford Court's winemaker, Mike Sullivan, says he would "pull it in, possibly halving the entire appellation." Ehren Jordan, asking, "Where is the real Sonoma coast?" answers, "The true coast is Annapolis, Fort Ross, Occidental Ridges, and all the stuff going on toward Freestone"—which is to say, only along the immediate coast.

The common belief among such vintners is that the AVA was manufactured by Brice Cutrer Jones, who founded his Sonoma-Cutrer Vineyards in 1973 and today owns the up-and-coming Sebastopol winery GoldRidge-Pinot (named after the soil type). Jones was a great marketer; for years, California Chardonnay was virtually synonymous with Sonoma-Cutrer. The winery had two major Chardonnay vineyards, both designated on the label. One, the Cutrer, was in the Russian River Valley AVA; the other, Les Pierres, was in Sonoma Valley. People claim that Jones wanted both vineyards in the same appellation and moreover wanted an appellation that suggested cool-climate viticulture (which Sonoma Valley does not). To these ends, the story goes, he developed rather creative boundaries for an AVA that sounded cool and included both vineyards.

Sonoma-Cutrer "created Sonoma Coast, pushed it through. It was their effort," declares Daniel Schoenfeld, the owner of Wild Hog, whose vineyard, planted in 1981, is above Fort Ross. "It's the screwiest damned thing," he says, "to call Carneros and Windsor 'Sonoma Coast.' It's so big as to be meaningless."

Jones does not deny that he utilized some poetic license in drafting the appellation's boundaries; he even concedes that he "gerrymandered" it. At the same time, "it's an honest appellation," he insists.

The AVA begins in the northwest where the Sonoma and Mendocino county lines meet, at the shoreline of the Pacific Ocean. From there, it

Ehren Jordan near the deer fencing he put up
to protect his Failla vineyard from hungry critters.

sweeps south past Fort Ross along the coast to the Marin County line and then turns eastward along San Pablo Bay to the Napa County line. From there, it travels northwesterly along the Mayacamas Mountains, reaching the top of Sonoma Mountain and extending well to the east of Highway 101. By a circuitous route, it rises to the peak of Fitch Mountain, runs through the southern part of Healdsburg, turns abruptly to the southwest, hits the confluence of the Russian River and Dry Creek, runs down to Sebastopol, and then veers northwest again before finally winding its way back to the starting point at the beach.

The idea of a Sonoma Coast AVA contains a certain validity, as Jones has pointed out: the word "coast" implies fog and maritime influence, and you certainly get both in these parts. But on any given summer day, fog, however you define it (anything from high clouds to the soupy ground stuff), can extend clear across, and up and down, the state of California, except for the deserts and mountains. On some August days, the fog bank runs from Humboldt County clear down to the Mexican border and extends for dozens of miles inland. In fact, every single grape-growing region in California within a hundred miles of the coast prides itself on its maritime influence—as the claims of "cool coastal breezes" by Lodians and even Temeculans suggest. So the concept of being "coastal," in and of itself, is not a reliable basis on which to draw an appellation, unless it's understood to be one of those mega-appellations, like "Bourgogne," that can mean practically anything.

Because of this, vintners like Ehren Jordan who ply their trade in places hard by the Pacific colloquially refer to the "true" or "real" Sonoma coast, with a dismissiveness toward the official appellation. This real coast consists of a thin ribbon of land stretching from the beaches to about four or five miles inland and takes in the first two ridges of the Coast Ranges and possibly the west-facing slope of the third ridge as well—ridges with names such as Bohan Dillon, Kings, Smith, Mohrhardt, and Camp Meeting. (This last name often appears on official maps as Campmeeting; the Pomo used to summer there, and so did Christian revivalists in the nineteenth century.)

Because of their feeling that the official Sonoma Coast appellation is too broad, vintners in and around Fort Ross have been meeting for years to establish their own AVA. I followed the process and was amazed at how contentious it was, although perhaps I shouldn't have been surprised, considering what the Alexander Valley crowd had gone through in the 1980s. Winery owners and grape growers, with all they have invested in their projects, both finances and egos, can be as fractious as lawyers, which many of them are. Different people had different opinions about where the new lines should be drawn and what the new AVA's name should be. Finally, in 2003, they agreed on boundaries and a name whose politically correct inelegance suggests a hammered-out compromise: Fort Ross Seaview.

Fort Ross's origins were described earlier, in chapter 6. Seaview is a tiny old logging community, named (as Sea View) by U.S. postal authorities in 1883 but discontinued in 1914. Little remains of the community today except memories in the minds of old-timers. In their application, formally filed with the Regulations Division of the BATF in February 2003, the petitioners noted a neat distinction between the two place names. "Seaview has more meaning to local residents and growers," they wrote, "while Fort Ross has been used to define the area on a more regional level."

The proposed boundaries of the AVA would demarcate, with a few exceptions, an area above 920 feet in elevation, just above the fogline. It thus would be one of the few California appellations governed by elevation, although this consideration is becoming increasingly important. The boundaries were much easier to determine in the west, where the fog-sun interplay and temperature gradient are as dependable as clockwork. But the petitioners noted that "the eastern boundary is much more difficult to define than the western edge." In the east, temperatures gradually increase, but they do so erratically, depending on the lay of the land. The almost complete absence of reliable climate measuring devices on these isolated ridges and in the lonely hollows and *arroyos* further obscures the issue. Rather in despair, the petitioners finally drew their eastern boundary following the climatic line where coast redwood and Douglas fir trees give way to gray pine, which cannot thrive in conditions of cool fog and is found only in the warmer inland.

The late 1970s were the tail end of an era when droves of hippies, despairing of city life, flocked to isolated pockets of rural Northern California, including the Sonoma coast, seeking new places to live. The '67 Summer of Love had turned violent; bad drugs came in; the national political and social mood lurched to the right; and the longhairs, in reaction to all this bad karma, launched their back-to-the-land movement. Communes sprouted up all through the secluded mountainous forests of western Sonoma County.

"A lot of people bailed out of the Haight-Ashbury and came up here," remembers Greg Adams, the vineyard manager at Flowers Vineyard and Winery. Some of the hippies had enough money (from whatever source) to buy land, which was cheap, and wanted only to be left alone. They built their little wooden A-frames with pot-bellied stoves for heat and cooking, put up barns, planted vegetable gardens and fruit trees, and raised a few pigs, ducks, and chickens. They learned to cultivate edible mushrooms and herbs and to make cheese and bread and paté and confits and all the other artisanal foods that Sonoma today glories in and that form the basis of a true regional cuisine.

The area around Cazadero was a particular hippie hotbed. Just as the Alexander Valley had its north-versus-south dueling cultures, so Sonoma County developed an east-west dichotomy. Slowly but surely, a distinct west-county culture—or counterculture, as the case may be—formed. Whereas the east county and the Alexander Valley were increasingly conservative, the west was an amalgam of hundreds of years of Pomo and Hawaiian, Russian and pioneer fur trapper, logger, recluse, squatter, outlaw, and hippie, and if it had a political orientation in its basically anarchic, outsider soul, it was to the left.

David Hirsch arrived in this cultural melange in 1978. He bought a spread just down Bohan Dillon Road from the Bohans, where he wound up being the person who can in fairness be credited with single-handedly launching the Sonoma coast's reputation for Pinot Noir, especially in the Fort Ross area—although that was far from his intention.

"Originally, I bought this ranch to have some elbow room," Hirsch says. He'd been living in Santa Cruz, running an import business—clothing, gifts—"but I felt the walls closing in. I wanted to live in an area that was unsettled, where land was cheap." He spent a few years exploring in Idaho, Humboldt County, the Tomales Bay area in western Marin County, and along the Big Sur coast before discovering the hills above Fort Ross, where he fell in love with the littoral environment of redwoods, fog, and rain forest.

"This place had been a sheep ranch," he said, as we walked his property one brisk fall day. "When I came, there was no electricity, the roads were very suspect. But that was fine with me. All I wanted was some peace and quiet.

"Of course, I'd heard that Mick Bohan, down the road, had some vines, but I had no intention of planting grapes myself. I did not come from the wine world. I mean, I couldn't grow a tomato! But I was friends with the guy who owned Felton-Empire Winery, and one day he comes up to visit."

Hirsch smiled and reverted to the present tense as he recounted the scene that had occurred more than twenty years earlier.

"So this guy is walking around the place, and all of a sudden, he looks at me and says, 'Plant Pinot Noir here, and this will be a very famous vineyard.'"

At this recollection, Hirsch laughed out loud. "Believe it or not, I planted Pinot the very next day! What did I do with the grapes? There used to be a little winery near here, Sea Ridge. It was a pretty rustic operation. I sold to them." For a while, Sea Ridge actually vineyard-designated a Hirsch Vineyard Pinot Noir, at Hirsch's request.

It was the second mention of Sea Ridge I'd heard. At home that night, I pulled down an old wine directory from the bookshelf and looked it up. There it was, its Fort Ross location described by the writer as "near the border of Lunacy." The winery was started in 1979 by a pair of scientists who liked the wines of Burgundy. According to the book, the owners at first made their wine with grapes grown "on an old sheep ranch," which undoubtedly was the Bohan vineyard. Sea Ridge was one of those small, interesting wineries that attract some insider interest but then, for whatever reason, go out of business, which it did in 1991. But for a while, it was famous, in an underground sort of way. Ehren Jordan, who used to work for the well-known vintner Helen Turley, told me that Turley planted her Pinot Noir vineyard in the Fort Ross region, for her Marcassin winery, because of the quality of Sea Ridge's wines.

At any rate, it was David Hirsch, not the Bohans or Sea Ridge, who made a name for Pinot Noir in the Fort Ross area. His first cuttings came from Pommard selections he obtained in Oregon. At first, though, Hirsch encountered problems selling his grapes, just as the Rochiolis had.

"There were no local wineries committed to independent growers like me," he said—no Davis Bynum to drive up one day and propose a deal.

Hirsch continued, "I wanted to find some small village winery that would take my grapes and whose sole purpose was to promote their character and quality. I knew how good my grapes were. The problem was finding good winemakers."

Hirsch struggled for years to locate that village winery with good winemakers. His dream, as he put it, was "to get enough momentum out here to really start to build a little cottage industry." But when Sea Ridge went out of business, Hirsch was back to square one. He sold to Jess Jackson's Stonestreet brand for a while. But his big break finally came in 1994, when a trio of small, prestigious wineries—Littorai, Kistler, and Williams Selyem—decided that they wanted his fruit.

"That was it," Hirsch says. People—the right people—finally were buying his grapes. Hirsch had landed squarely on the boutique winery map, bringing with him, indirectly, the Sonoma coast, the same way the Rochiolis and Bynums had dragged the Russian River Valley onto the wine stage.

The young entrepreneur who wanted only a little elbow room to live among the fog-shrouded redwoods has come a long way. From not being able to grow a tomato, Hirsch nowadays sells his Pinot Noir grapes for upwards of five thousand dollars a ton—if, that is, he likes the buyer—a price that is comparable to the very best vineyards of the central Russian River Valley. Such has been his success that, a few years ago, he rather abruptly stopped selling Pinot Noir grapes to some of his oldest clients, including Williams Selyem, so that he could keep the best of the best for his own, new Hirsch Vineyards label, which he launched with the 2002 vintage.

I think of the "true coast" in much the same way as Ehren Jordan. It is clustered in three areas close to the shore: Annapolis up north, near the

Mendocino County line; Fort Ross in the center; and (merging these two areas into one) Occidental Ridges and Freestone, in the south (which some people refer to as the Bodega plantings). Fort Ross, which was developed earliest, today contains the largest vineyard acreage. The southerly plantings came later, installed, in most cases, by wealthy people already in the wine business, such as the Wagners of Caymus, Joseph Phelps, and Jess Jackson. They recognized the potential value of far-coast Pinot Noir and Chardonnay, in terms of both quality and price. In the economic boom of the 1990s, which seemed as if it would go on forever, these growers developed their own Burgundian vineyard community in the south, where land was still available, as ranchers and others sold it off.

Up north, the Annapolis area is the least planted, the most isolated, and so sparse in vines and finished wines that it is difficult to assess. For the purposes of this book, I have concentrated on the Fort Ross area, not only because of its history but also because it is nearest to the Russian River. In addition to Hirsch, Flowers, Bohan, Wild Hog, Marcassin, and Ehren Jordan's Failla, it includes Jason Pahlmeyer's Wayfarer Vineyard, the Martinelli properties, Donnie Schatzberg's Precious Mountain Vineyard, the Nobels Vineyard, W. H. Smith's vineyard, Peter Michael's Sugar Loaf Farms, and others.

Above the immediate coastal strip, the landscape is a massif of ridges rising to more than 2,000 feet, riddled with deep valleys and *arroyos* through which creeks and streams—Marshall, Sproule, McKenzie, Carson—wander on their way to the Russian River or to the sea. This is serious San Andreas fault country, tortured and repeatedly torn apart by giant, land-altering earthquakes. The towns, such as they are—Cazadero, Duncan's Mills, Seaview, Annapolis, Plantation, Bodega Bay, and, a few miles inland, Bodega, with its pretty little white church, where Alfred Hitchcock filmed *The Birds*—are little more than human outposts in the deep wilderness, separated by miles of almost impenetrable forest. Even today, roads are negligible, except for Highway 1, a twisting, looping roller coaster of a ride with grievously hairpin turns and fall-offs hundreds of feet down to the rocky, wave-whipped shoals, to which careless motorists regularly plunge. In recent years, especially in summer, the coast road has become choked with SUVs and camper-driving tourists.

Despite the visitors, the region is still very remote, and living there poses special practical and psychological challenges that not everyone is prepared to shoulder. In the winter of 2003–2004, when David Hirsch was looking to hire a full-time winemaker, he ran into difficulties for this reason. "Trying to get someone to live out here is a big obstacle," he acknowledged. Greg Adams, at Flowers, smiled when he told me, "My friends ask me what I do for a social life, and I go, 'What's a social life?'" You can buy small items at the Sea Gull Market, twenty-five minutes away in Jenner, or do more substantive shopping at the Cazadero general store, a good forty-minute drive from Bohan Dillon Road, but for your major needs, you must go all the way to Guerneville or Sebastopol. Under the circumstances, locals are careful about keeping accurate shopping lists. "I write everything down three times," Ehren Jordan jokes.

Yet those who live here declare that there's no place quite like it. Adams, whose tiny house in Flowers's vineyard is way up on the top of a mountain, can see down past Bodega Bay to the Golden Gate Bridge from his hot tub. "I've worked in Napa, and it's great there for Cabernet Sauvignon, but if you're a human being, you suffer. To be in a location this beautiful is good for the soul."

Almost every vineyard in the Fort Ross area is located miles up a narrow, twisting dirt road. During summers, these roads are pitted and rutted, with your car raising such thick, suffocating clouds of dust that you have to shut the windows. In winter, during the rainy season, these same trails may be hubcap-deep in mud.

The people who live here are a different breed. Along the Sonoma coast, time marches more slowly than it does in Healdsburg or even Guerneville; the pulse of business beats erratically, when it beats at all. I once made an appointment to visit a Fort Ross vintner. We made arrangements; he sent me a map; it took nearly three hours to reach his handmade wooden house. When I arrived, no one was there. After waiting for thirty minutes, I drove back to Oakland, leaving a note stuck in the door. At home, a phone message was waiting. "Sorry, man, I blew it! Totally forgot!" But that is very coastal. There are no fancy wineries and tasting rooms, no secretarial staffs, no PR firms, no amenities at all, outside of a few inns at Jenner. But there is, obviously, an inverse relationship between these modern accoutrements and the coast's wildly primitive, soul-stirring beauty.

Some of its inhabitants are determined that western Sonoma will remain forever young and untarnished, and sometimes they are prepared to act on their beliefs.

A few years ago, when Marimar Torres began to develop her new Doña Margarita Pinot Noir vineyard, down near Freestone, some folks tried to scare her off. One night, they spray-painted all the road signs leading to her property with slogans such as "Wino Poison" and "Wine Is Evil." Another time, they turned her horses loose. Twice, they shut off her wells.

Local law enforcement and civic leaders were less than helpful when a frightened Marimar turned to them for assistance. "This has been a very difficult property to develop," she said one showery winter afternoon, as

Marimar Torres's dog, Brandy, is her constant companion at the winery.

we walked a hill at the edge of the sleeping vines, picking our way around the muddiest spots. Marimar is a lovely, aristocratic woman, born to an old Spanish family, and no shrinking violet when it comes to asserting herself; but against the "tree huggers," as she calls them, she found herself helpless.

Marimar wanted to show me her new drainage system and water purification pond, built at enormous cost in order to ensure that any runoff would end up in the right spot and be clean enough to drink. It was impermissible, she insisted, for anyone to accuse her of allowing even a drop of dirty water into the watershed—it was a matter of pride for Marimar herself. She also wanted to show how well-tended her vineyard was, how she had left old trees standing that she could have cut down, and how she had gone the extra mile to be respectful of the land. No ugly signs, no garish outbuildings; even her new horse barn looked as though it had been there for a hundred years.

All to no avail, however. The vandals struck again, and the officials once again were unable to do anything. For self-defense, Marimar had been forced to erect a chain-link fence around her property—something she hated to do, and which only enraged her antagonists all the more. She finally invited some locals to her house and cooked them a splendid paella. The attacks have since stopped.

I have friends who live in West County, and it is difficult for them to accept any planned use for the land at all. This point of view is certainly understandable in view of the pristine beauty of the environment. But most of the land is privately owned, and it is impossible to stop owners from developing their property if it is done in accordance with local ordinances. It also seems to me that a pretty little organic vineyard is far preferable to, say, a housing development or a tacky motel. Steve Domenichelli, who considers himself "both east and west," praises West Sonomans for having "a great mentality when it comes to the environment." But, he adds, "they can be extreme."

"We've got guys living out here who are completely off the grid," says Greg Adams, at Flowers. Here and there, in hidden clearings in the forest, marijuana plantations are zealously guarded by shotgun-wielding thugs, and unwary people who accidentally stumble on the pot farms risk being shot and even killed. During the growing season, everyone—hunters, mushroom gatherers, ordinary hikers—is on high alert (or should be) while prowling these woods.

The marijuana guards are not the only dangers. Bigfoot, or Sasquatch, is reportedly seen from time to time, lumbering his—or her—way through the forest. Everyone knows about the 1980 incident at Occidental, when two local teenage brothers, camping out overnight on some remote acreage their parents owned, had a terrible misadventure. Someone, or something, attacked their tent in the middle of the night, shaking it so violently, they later said, that they were terrified for their lives. The boys crouched in a corner of the tent, holding on to each other and wielding an axe to protect themselves should the intruder enter. Finally, when things quieted down, they cautiously made their way to their truck and drove home. The next morning, the entire family returned to the area, searching for clues, and supposedly found small redwood trees snapped in two at the seven-foot height. The mother was quoted as saying, "[The Sasquatches] have been here long before us and are probably just as curious of us as we are of them." A very West County libertarian attitude, indeed.

I remember a West Sonoman I met in the high hills above Fort Ross while I was driving the coastal byways. There had been a terrific winter storm; many trees were flattened, presumably by the wind, not Bigfoot. I was driving up the mountain on a one-lane dirt road (little more than a fire trail) in my old Volkswagen; it was a bumpy ride. On one side of the trail, the mountain rose up like the wall of a skyscraper, only to disappear far above in a dark clot of redwood and fir; on the other side, it plunged down five hundred feet to a brush-choked ravine.

The road broke out onto a ridge, leveled off, and widened. Suddenly, I found the way blocked by a large tree limb that had toppled. An old pickup truck was pulled over in a clearing. A tall, skinny, bearded man, with hair well below his shoulders held by a red headband, was cutting the branch into pieces with a chain saw.

We chatted while he sawed. The man said he was on contract with the county to keep the roads clear. He had lived in the area since the 1960s but was planning to move on.

"Where?" I asked.

"Alaska."

"Why?"

He grunted. "Gettin' too crowded." The chain saw bit noisily into the wood, sending out a spray of dust.

Too crowded? We were in the middle of nowhere. I remembered something that Julie Martinelli, whose family owns 2,000 acres in the Fort Ross area, had said. "Out on those old country roads, you pass one car and you think, 'Oh, my God, there's too much traffic!'"

The man complained about an onslaught of newcomers, tourists, city folk (I blushed a little at this), and—worst of all, from his point of view— rich grape growers, who were flocking to the coast in order to plant their damned vineyards. His voice oozed annoyance and resentment.

"Every day now, you hear 'em overhead in their helicopters, vrooom, vrooom, lookin' for a spot to grow grapes. Not peaceful anymore. It's get-tin'," he spat the words out, "like San Francisco!"

I took his point.

Later, I told this tale to Daniel Roberts. In his coolly laconic way, Dr. Dirt said, "He was probably growing dope."

And what of the wines? Depending on where they're grown, the vintage, and how they're made, they fall along a continuum, ranging from a tomatoey, rhubarb-and-beet unripeness through ripe fruitiness to a super-ripe style that can verge on Port. Depending on where they land on this continuum, the wines can be exciting, but they also can be vexatious.

The coolest part of the AVA is probably down around Freestone and Occidental, where the vineyards are more or less open to the sea. In a cool vintage, coming from a cool vineyard, these Sonoma Coast wines can simply be unripe.

Fort Ross, by comparison, is warmer. It is to the Sonoma Coast what the Middle Reach is to the Russian River Valley. Up at Fort Ross, for the most part, getting the grapes ripe is less of a problem—especially in recent vintages, which have been getting warmer. This ripeness shows in the successful wines, such as Failla's 2001 Hirsch Vineyard Pinot Noir. Here, Ehren Jordan crafted one of those jammy wines in which you can taste the September sunshine in every sip of savory black cherry and raspberry. At the same time (credit those nighttime temperature plunges), there are darker, more somber overtones—or, rather, a chillier undertow—of grilled meat and beefsteak tomato. It is an exciting, complex Pinot Noir, the kind that reminds me, pleasurably, of the fascinations of that old Dehlinger 1985 Lot #2.

But up in the Fort Ross hills, things can go too far in the ripeness direction, and the character of Pinot Noir can be compromised. I began to worry about all this as I completed this book. At first, it was hard to put my finger on just what was the matter. As I went over my Pinot Noir notes from 1999, 2000, and 2001, I began thinking that the wines had been getting a little, well, *brawny*.

That was good—wasn't it? We didn't want pale, thin Pinot Noirs; we wanted substantive ones that might even improve with age. Didn't we?

In the summer of 2004, a couple of *Wine Enthusiast* editors and I had a big blind tasting of the 2002 California Pinot Noirs, and the results were eye-opening. Many of the wines, including some from the most famous estates, didn't fare well. They were too extracted, overly alcoholic, and too tannic and heavy for a varietal whose name is—or used to be, or at least should be—synonymous with delicacy. Slatherings of new, well-charred French oak, far from concealing this flaw, only seemed to exaggerate it. After the tasting, the bothersome question of why so many old favorites had been so disappointing rattled around my brain.

Questions, first posed a generation ago, seemed to be still echoing off the winemaking walls, yet to be resolved. What is California Pinot Noir? What should it be? What do consumers have a right to expect, especially at high prices? What is Sonoma Coast Pinot Noir? What special features does it possess that wines from other appellations do not?

It turned out that no less a figure than David Hirsch himself was wrestling with his Pinot Noir angels. His first challenge dealt with something largely beyond his control: growing conditions on the coast itself. "Viticulture out there is more extreme than anywhere else," he said one rainy winter day. I'd run into him in Healdsburg, where he'd come to get permits for his new winery building.

He told me about the hundred-mile-an-hour winds that had wracked the vineyard the previous week, about the snow that had fallen the week before that, about summer temperatures that can hit 105 degrees. "And don't even ask me about rain. In the spring of 1998, we had a hundred fifty inches, and the sun didn't shine until June.

"It will take us at least two generations to 'get it,'" he candidly predicted.

Winter wind, snow, and rain are one thing; the vines are dormant then and don't particularly care what the weather is doing. Bad springs, however, are something else. Late rains and cold can cause shatter, resulting in diminished yields (although that's not necessarily bad for quality). If the spring rains continue too long, they will bring rot to the vines.

But summers are absolutely key. A reading of 105 degrees is not a temperature at which Pinot Noir thrives. The grapes grow high up in the mountains, generally well above 1,200 feet, easily exceeding the normal fogline, which was the rationale for the 920-foot elevation boundary for the Fort Ross Seaview AVA. On ridges like Bohan Dillon, you'll find true summer weather—and powerful solar radiation. "I would never want to camp down here," Julie Martinelli noted one gray day in her little office on the second story of the famous big red Martinelli barn on River Road, hard by Laguna Ridges. "It could be two in the afternoon, and we're still all fogged in here, while up on that ridge, at ten in the morning, we're in our bathing suits." Martinelli's Fort Ross vines, on average, get considerably more hours of sun than ones in the Russian River Valley.

In a warm year, it can get downright hot in the Fort Ross hills. Bob Cabral remembers that, in the vintage of 2001, "the fog never even came in on those coastal ridges. I had never picked Hirsch [Vineyard] in September before, but we ended up picking it all before Labor Day." That was earlier than any of Williams Selyem's other vineyards in the Russian River Valley, even in the warmish Middle Reach, and far earlier than almost any Pinot Noir vineyard on the Central and South coasts—odd, given the Sonoma coast's reputation as a cool growing region.

I have now tasted scores of Fort Ross Pinot Noirs from recent vintages, and there's little question in my mind that something is happening. One of the first red flags was the Flowers 2001 Andreen-Gale Cuvee Pinot Noir. I liked it, but, as I noted at the time, it was "a bit hot in alcohol [and] definitely full-bodied for a Pinot. . . ."

Whereas three years ago the big challenge seemed to have been achieving ripeness, many of the more recent wines have been big, dark, and ripe to super-ripe, high in alcohol and dense in body—the hallmarks of sun and heat. A few were more like a big Syrah. In the most problematic cases, the wines had flavors of raisins. One 2001 Hirsch Vineyard Pinot Noir, from a winery I don't want to name, was so overripe that it smelled and tasted like Port.

But it's not just the weather (or climate) that's pushing the grapes to excessive levels of ripeness. It's also the vintners. The same thing that's happening to Cabernet Sauvignon—letting the fruit hang and hang on the vines until the grapes are practically oozing sugar—is happening to Pinot Noir. Growers, on orders from winemakers, are pushing the harvest days and even weeks later than they used to, in order to let brix, or grape sugars, ripen to the max. At some point, you have to wonder how much is too much.

After our big blind tasting of the 2002 Pinots, I was puzzled and disconcerted. The evolution of Pinot Noir had seemed so straightforward, so progressive, for so many years. Had it now hit a speed bump? I turned to some winemakers I respect, to engage them in conversation, pick their brains, and ask them about what I was beginning to call the Incredible Hulk-ization of Pinot Noir. Were they seeing the same trend? If so, what did they make of it?

Farrell was one of the first I asked. I knew he preferred a leaner, more acidic style of Pinot Noir, the kind often described as elegant. I also knew that he had a keen sense for detecting when the camel's nose of market-ing was snuffling in under the tent-flap of winemaking. I was beginning to suspect that the marketers—the legions of PR and sales wizards that so many North Coast wineries hire—were driving the phenomenon of super-ripe Pinots.

"I'm definitely seeing the same trend," he immediately responded, "and I think it's driven by"—and here he mentioned two well-known wine writ-ers (yes, *those* two)—"who favor that style and give those kinds of wines high scores. And frankly," he continued (I'd obviously pressed a hot but-ton), "we're seeing a lot of this from young winemakers who are trying to make a statement early in their careers." Farrell, then in his twenty-second year of making Pinot Noir, no longer had anything to prove. "Some of us," he concluded, "are bucking that trend. But I'll be honest with you: it's costing us the big scores."

In nearly identical language, Greg La Follette, who'd just been hired as De Loach's new winemaker (but still produces his own Tandem wines), said in no uncertain terms, "A lot of winemakers are gonna hate my guts for saying this—especially since I helped establish the style at Flowers—but we need to buck the trend of these huge-alcohol, dark fruit, late-picked, hundred percent new oak Pinots." That formula can work for Syrah, for Cabernet—look at the glorious 2001 Napa Cabs. But it's not right for Pinot Noir.

The vintner Rick Longoria, who makes great Pinot Noir in Santa Barbara County, also made a prescient observation. "Pinot's not a Rhône wine," he stated. "That's not what it's all about." Leaving Pinot Noir grapes to hang on the vine in order to achieve high sugars is a sound strat-egy in a cool-climate growing region, such as the Santa Rita Hills or the Santa Maria Valley, but it can result in tactical failure in an overly warm region in a hot year. The late-picked phenomenon, Longoria asserted, "is a huge mistake."

Even Bob Cabral, who flirts with the new style and occasionally gives in to it, pointed out that "in the evolution of Pinot Noir winemaking, where we found that, physiologically, grapes get riper at higher brix, some people are pushing things too far, for such a delicate grape." When I asked him what would motivate some people to go too far, he replied, "They're chasing the wine writers."

"Does that bother you?" I wondered.

"Not at all," he laughed. "But I think it's insane."

So what's a Sonoma Coast Pinot Noir vintner to do? There's no road map as there is with Cabernet Sauvignon. These vintners have parachuted into terra incognita and are on their own, looking for some clue that might give them direction.

It's easy to see why even a guy like Hirsch, who started on second base by owning a famous vineyard, would be puzzled over how to knock a new brand out of the ball park. Do you go with the critics? With your heart? With some intellectual, Platonic ideal of Pinot Noir? When it comes to making great Pinot Noir, how do you know what to do?

On my final visit to Hirsch's place, he described how the people to whom he sells his grapes are urging him to let the grapes hang longer and longer on the vines with each passing vintage, "so you don't take a chance on having anything that's unripe." They wanted him to "farm for flavors," in the current parlance, to let sugars run up as high as he dared before the rains came—far higher than he had ever dreamed of doing, in more than twenty years of grape growing. (Between 1995 and 2003, the average brix of Pinot Noir grapes crushed in California increased by 9.5 percent, according to the state's Department of Food and Agriculture. That was statewide; it's a slam-dunk that it went up more than that, probably far more, in the best vineyards of Sonoma County.)

Hirsch was, in fact, seeing the rules change before his very eyes at the critical moment when he was starting up his own commercial brand. It must have been confusing, I commiserated, made all the more difficult by the inherent challenges anyone faces in creating a new label.

He agreed. Even though the name Hirsch is well regarded in Pinot Noir connoisseur circles as a result of the vineyard designations, that regard didn't automatically translate into sales of a Hirsch wine. At that time, David joked, he had a total of three names on his mailing list and wasn't about to sit back and wait for the phone to ring with orders. "I can't afford to," he laughed. "I'm thinking of throwing a bunch of wine in the back of my truck and going around," which is the old-fashioned, tried and true, wear-out-the-soles-of-your-shoes way of selling wine.

David had just bottled his first estate Pinot Noir, the 2002, under his Hirsch Vineyards label, and he wanted to show it to me. He'd given it his best shot, but I think he knew that it wasn't what he wanted it to be, or what it could and would be someday. It seemed an indecisive wine, reflecting the way David himself was feeling his way through the dark. He apologized for it being too young and then explained that it had been crushed and bottled at the deLorimier Winery, in Alexander Valley, because David hadn't completed his own winery until 2003. He was quite honest. "Just because we know how to grow fruit doesn't mean we know anything about making wine!"

Someone recently said to me that "Pinot Noir is like a gawky teenager whose body is growing too fast." The implication was that, as an adolescent varietal, one that (to stretch the metaphor) has just hit puberty, it will surely go through phases, some more awkward than others, before it decides what it wants to be when it grows up. Sonoma Coast Pinot Noir, at its best, is fabulous wine, but it isn't always at its best. We shouldn't be surprised that a varietal that only twenty years ago was considered freakish for California is going through growth pains. But we may be permitted to hope that the current infatuation with size—Pinot envy?—may be nothing more than the sort of temporary aberration California winemakers occasionally experience in their search for style.

Leaving Hirsch, I looped back south of Jenner and continued a mile farther, across the Russian River Bridge, where the Sizzling Tandoori Restaurant, perched precariously on a cliff above the river, always is such an odd sight. Just beyond it was the entrance to Goat Rock Beach. This is the point where Highway 116 ends at Highway 1 and where the river ceases its westward course and instead turns abruptly north for its final two-mile sprint to the sea. Separating it at this point from the Pacific is a hilly peninsula that gradually lowers and narrows until, opposite Jenner, it becomes a mere spit of sand that dissolves into nothingness. That is where the river and the ocean merge and become one.

The Pineapple Express had opened up, and it had been raining for more than a week in Northern California. Guerneville had flooded again, not seriously, but enough to drive a few dozen people from their homes. Although the sky was blue now, a monster gale was a thousand miles away, far out over the Pacific, and already lines of dark clouds were gathering ominously on the farthest stretch of the horizon.

From the Goat Rock parking lot, it's another half-mile or so by foot to the end of the beach. I walked along the heavy, wet sand. There was no one else in sight, although here and there the beach was torn up by the deep tire tracks of dune buggies. To the left, the surf pounded and exploded in cascades of foamy white. To the right, just across the estuarial lagoon, were the cottages of Jenner, looking like little white Monopoly pieces scattered on the hillside. The beach was littered with logs, tree branches, sea sponges, stones, driftwood, and, mysteriously, piles of stalky bamboo. From where?

The beach grew narrower, and crunchier, too, as the sand was replaced with pea-sized gravel. I came to some old wooden pilings and a crumbling foundation—the remnants of the railroad that used to run all the way up to here. It was like an archaeological ruin. Finally, there it was: the end of the peninsula. It was a mere wedge of sand, a little platform two feet high, the prow of a ship, surrounded by churning water. There were birds everywhere, thousands of them, wheeling and cawing and careening through the sky and crowding the sand; here, where the fresh water of the Russian River met the salty Pacific, were masses of fish and shellfish for them to feast upon.

The river was rumbling out to sea, while the mighty ocean was rushing inland; and where the two forces met, a titanic struggle ensued. Great swirling whirlpools and geyserlike bursts of current gurgled up from below, erupting in plumes of white spray. Eccentric waves seemed to arise from nowhere and fall back in on themselves as the riptides tore the water into roiling eddies. This was where the gods of river and sea wrestled in epic, never-ending struggle.

I could only look and listen. Suddenly, a huge wave, the kind they call a sleeper, easily twenty feet high, came in and exploded, one of those rogues that gather strength above long offshore troughs and then break with tremendous force against the steep beach face. This one was so near that it soaked my pants. Startled, I backed off and headed home.

It was sunny when I left. At Cazadero, the sky suddenly darkened and the rain came pouring down—but that was exactly as it should be. Ten minutes later, at the Farmhouse Inn, the sun reemerged and lit up the vineyards, bare of grapes till next year.

Recommended Wines
and Producers

It goes against my grain to recommend specific wineries or wines in a book. By the very nature of publishing, the time between the day of writing and when that writing appears in print is very great; in that duration, anything can happen, and it often does. After a book sits on a shelf for some years, the information it contains may be entirely outdated. Wineries may go out of existence or, through a change in ownership, winemaker, or vineyard source, may fail to maintain their quality; conversely, they may improve. Meanwhile, new wineries and vineyards spring into being all the time. All these shiftings conspire to make recommendations at best misleading, at worst an anachronism from the start.

Having said this, certain generalizations can and should be made, if for no other reason than to pay respect to the wineries that, year in and year out, battle against the vagaries of time to successfully produce splendid wines. In that spirit, here are some recommended wineries and wines, sorted by appellation. As is to be expected, the warmer Alexander Valley stars Cabernet Sauvignon and its late-ripening allies, while the Russian River Valley brims with cool-climate Pinot Noirs. Chardonnay and Zinfandel, those chameleons of wine, find the limelight anywhere and everywhere. Syrah pops up unexpectedly throughout the play.

I include only wineries physically located or headquartered in each AVA and wines sourced from that appellation. Thus, for example, a Napa Valley winery that makes a wine from Alexander Valley grapes would not be included.

ALEXANDER VALLEY

Alexander Valley Vineyards—Juicy, succulent Bordeaux blend Cyrus; ripe, oaky Chardonnay; Sin Zin classic

Chateau Souverain—Good, seldom great, reserve Cabernet and Chardonnay

Clos du Bois—Complex, often flinty Calcaire Chardonnay; rich, ageworthy Marlstone Bordeaux blend and Briarcrest Cabernet

deLorimier—Notable for Mosaic, a Bordeaux red blend, and Merlot

Ferrari-Carano—Buttery, complex, oaky Chardonnay; complex, tannic Cabernet

Forefathers—New winery with stunning debut Cabernet Sauvignon

Geyser Peak—Reserve Alexandre always rich and ageworthy; Kuimelis Vineyard Cabernet Sauvignon dense and tannic; good Zinfandel and Merlot

Iron Horse—Sleek, streamlined Sauvignon Blanc and Viognier (sometimes blended together as Cuvee R); good and sometimes great Cabernets, especially those labeled T-bar-T and Benchmark; polished Sangiovese [*see also* under Russian River Valley]

Jordan Vineyard & Winery—Lean, balanced, and elegant Cabernet ages well

Lancaster Estate—Intense, complex mountain Bordeaux blend

Murphy-Goode Estate Winery—Polished, soft Cabernet and Merlot; succulent varietal Zinfandel; crisp, rich Sauvignon Blanc; ripe, oaky Chardonnay

Robert Young Estate Winery—Chardonnays of supreme power and complexity; Scion is an oaky Bordeaux blend of great style and finesse

Rodney Strong—Plush, oaky Alexander's Crown Cabernet; powerful Alden Vineyard Cabernet; Sauvignon Blanc a good value

Sausal—Good Zinfandel, especially old vine

Seghesio Family Vineyards—Superb Zinfandels; extraordinary Venom and Chianti Station Sangioveses

Simi—Reserve Cabernet often compelling, especially in a great vintage; Landslide Cabernet dense and cellarworthy

Stonestreet—Christopher's Alexander Mountain Estate Cabernet Sauvignon, dense, tannic in youth, ages to complexity

RUSSIAN RIVER VALLEY

Carlisle—Two Acres old-vine field blend of fantastic density and monumental size, as well as complex, huge-fruit Syrah

Davis Bynum—Laureles Merlot ripe and flavorful; various Pinot Noirs true to type, always interesting and complex

Dehlinger—Estate Pinot Noirs always compelling; firm, ageworthy, interesting cool-climate Cabernet

De Loach—OFS wines best, including rich, complex Zinfandel; single-vineyard Zins; good Chardonnay; Pinot Noir; rich, spicy Viognier. New French ownership promises improvement

Dutton-Goldfield—Grower/winemaker duo turns out intricate, terroir-driven Pinot Noir, Chardonnay, and Zinfandels of power and weight; peppery Syrah bows to northern Rhône

Foppiano—Petite Sirahs of power and ageability are the specialty here

Gary Farrell—Rich, flamboyant Chardonnay; Pinot Noirs of intense structure and ageworthiness

Iron Horse—Estate Pinot Noir and Chardonnay from Green Valley intense and pure; sparkling wines among California's best

Joseph Swan—Dense, ageworthy Pinot Noir; rich, complex Zinfandel; Cabernets full and cellarworthy

J Vineyards & Winery—Rich French-style bubbly; smooth, delicious Pinot Noir; Zinfandel with plenty of stuffing; spicy Pinot Gris; fruity Viognier

Korbel—Great assortment of value wines across the board; Pinot Noir especially nice; a source of complex, affordable sparkling wines of various styles

Longboard—Dense, complex Syrah; elegant Cabernet

Lynmar—Among the best Chardonnays from the appellation; Pinot Noir of intensity, especially reserve

Marimar Torres—Pinot Noirs of great integrity and intensity; Chardonnays firm, with acidity

Martinelli—Good Zinfandel, especially Jackass; single-vineyard Pinot Noirs are cult wines

Merry Edwards—Pinot Noirs of power and charm from across the appellation highlight sectional differences

Patz & Hall—Rich, terroir-driven Pinot Noir and Chardonnay, especially vineyard designations

Philip Staley—On the border of the AVA; red and white Rhônes of style and elegance, varietally true

Rochioli—Fabulous estate Pinot Noirs; Sauvignon Blanc among California's best; delicious, appley Chardonnay

Rodney Strong—Pinot Noir classic varietal, especially reserve

Russian Hill—Amazing Syrahs, especially Top Block

Rutz—Delicious, complex, but easy-to-drink single-vineyard Pinot Noir and Chardonnay

Saxon Brown—Pinot Noirs are complex, layered, Burgundian

Tandem—Classic single-vineyard Pinot Noir and Chardonnay

Williams Selyem—Complex Pinot Noirs, especially single-vineyard examples, of early charm but cellarworthy; rich, ripe Chardonnay; Zinfandels of great power

SONOMA COAST

Failla—As estate vineyards mature, increasingly intense Pinot Noirs and Chardonnays display true Coastal character

Flowers—Estate Pinot Noirs and Chardonnays display immense power in youth and age well

Hirsch—Long the source of bottlings for others; now its own winery

W. H. Smith—Classic Pinot Noir built along Sonoma Coast lines; Maritime Ridge bottling especially complex, ageworthy

Look also for single-vineyard bottlings from Precious Mountain, Coastlands, Hellenthal, Nobels, and Hirsch.

REFERENCES

AND SUGGESTED READING

Adams, Leon D. *The Wines of America.* Boston: Houghton Mifflin, 1973. Sets the standard for intelligent, thorough historical narrative and is still one of the best sources around.

Alexander, Charles. *The Life and Times of Cyrus Alexander.* 1876. Reprint, Los Angeles: Dawson's Bookshop, 1967.

Amerine, Maynard A., and Vernon L. Singleton. *Wine: An Introduction.* Rev. ed. Berkeley: University of California Press, 1977. Originally published 1965.

Benson, Robert. *Great Winemakers of California.* Santa Barbara, CA: Capra Press, 1977. A perennial favorite. Lively and provocative, these Q&As with the first wave of boutique winery owners and winemakers capture the spirit of the times and each vintner's distinct, sometimes eccentric, personality.

Cass, Bruce. *The Winewright's Register.* Santa Rosa, CA: Winewright's Register, 1985. Winewrights are small artisan wineries; Cass's compendium of winewrights in California offers a valuable snapshot of the scene in the mid-1980s.

Darlington, David. *Angels' Visits: An Inquiry into the Mystery of Zinfandel.* New York: Henry Holt, 1991.

Durham, David L. *Durham's Place-Names of California's Old Wine Country.* Clovis, CA: Word Dancer Press, 2000. A fun, lively little book, available in many Sonoma County bookstores. Chockful of useful information.

Latimer, Patricia. *Sonoma & Mendocino Wine Book.* St. Helena, CA: A Vintage Image Book, 1979. Although much of the material is outdated, this frozen-in-time glimpse of a bygone era offers much that is fun and rewarding. Latimer's historical research was first rate.

Mabon, Mary Frost. *ABC of America's Wines.* New York: Alfred A. Knopf, 1942. Long out of print but still available in used bookstores. Tells it as it was long ago, when the U.S. wine industry was still reeling, but recovering fast, from the debacle of Prohibition.

Miller, Vernon C., et al. *Soil Survey, Sonoma County, California.* U.S. Department of Agriculture, in cooperation with the University of California Agricultural Experiment Station, 1972. For geeks only; heavy-duty but compellingly interesting and informative analysis of every square inch of dirt in the county.

Munro-Fraser, J. P. *History of Sonoma County.* San Francisco: Alley, Bowen, 1880. Available, so far as I know, only in the reference section of the Sonoma County Wine Library in Healdsburg. Beautifully bound; a treasure trove of facts, history, and reminiscences. Fans of old books, not just wine lovers, will go delirious.

Muscatine, Doris, Maynard A. Amerine, and Bob Thompson, eds. *The University of California / Sotheby Book of California Wine.* Berkeley: University of California Press / Sotheby Publications, 1984. This colossus was hugely influential a generation ago and is still one of the best. A superb source of information, analysis, and historical reminiscence from some of the best wine writers in America.

Northern California's Sonoma Coast: The Emergence of a Diverse Viticultural Region. Santa Rosa, CA: Artisans & Estates, 1997. Funded by a branch of Kendall-Jackson, this book contains useful technical and historical information.

Olney, Richard. *Romanée-Conti.* New York: Rizzoli, 1995. Originally published 1991.

Saintsbury, George. *Notes on a Cellar-Book.* New York: Macmillan, 1933. Perhaps the best wine book ever; certainly a classic. Knowledgeable, regal, and classically Victorian, Saintsbury had one foot in the mid-nineteenth century even as he handed down tradition to the twentieth. The professor epitomized gastronomy and oenophilia as only the Brits used to.

Schoenherr, Allan A. *A Natural History of California.* Berkeley: University of California Press, 1992. From alpine zones to the zebra-tailed lizard, Yosemite Valley to the biomass pyramid, this is a comprehensive look at California's astonishingly rich natural diversity.

Schoenman, Theodore, ed. *The Father of California Wine: Agoston Haraszthy.* Santa Barbara, CA: Capra Press, 1979. The standard work on one of the most colorful and influential figures in California wine history. Includes a reprint in full of Haraszthy's 1862 classic, "Grape Culture, Wines, and Wine-Making."

Schoonmaker, Frank, and Tom Marvel. *American Wines.* New York: Duell, Sloan and Pearce, 1941. Schoonmaker was a path-blazing visionary who pushed for wine quality and truth in labeling in the years following the repeal of Prohibition.

Shabram, Patrick L. *Petition to Bureau of Alcohol, Tobacco, and Firearms for Establishment of an American Viticultural Area to Be Named Fort Ross Seaview.* 2001. The official petition for this important winegrowing region. Courtesy of the author.

Sommelier Summit 2001—Alexander Valley: An Appellation Coming of Age. St. Helena, CA: Franciscan Estates, 2001. A rich and in-depth study of the appellation's history, climate, geography, geology, wines, and vines. The part by historian William F. Heintz contains much that is useful and rare.

Sorrells, Jim. *Welcome to the Lower Russian River.* Sebastopol, 1999. Quirky and personal, this is an insider's take on life among the Russian River denizens. Self-published by the author, it is available at local bookstores.

Street, Julian. *Wines.* New York: Alfred A. Knopf, 1948. Another frozen-in-time book from way back when. Street, a successful Broadway playwright, eloquently reviews the worldwide wine scene. The chapter on California is prescient.

Sullivan, Charles L. "A Miraculous Intervention: A Short History of Viticulture and Winegrowing in Western Sonoma County." Manuscript. Los Gatos, CA, 2001. Historian Sullivan dug deep, found isolated scraps of history, and pieced them together to produce the most in-depth story yet told of the coastal regions. Manuscript courtesy of the Russian River Valley Winegrowers.

———. *Zinfandel: A History of a Grape and Its Wine.* Berkeley: University of California Press, 2003.

Thompson, Bob. *The Wine Atlas of California and the Pacific Northwest.* New York: Simon & Schuster, 1993. From the dean of California wine writers. Authoritative and beautifully written, and the maps still set the standard.

INDEX

Page numbers in italics indicate illustrations.

Text: 11/15 Centaur
Display: Centaur
Designer: Sandy Drooker
Compositor: Integrated Composition Systems
Printer and Binder: Thomson-Shore, Inc.